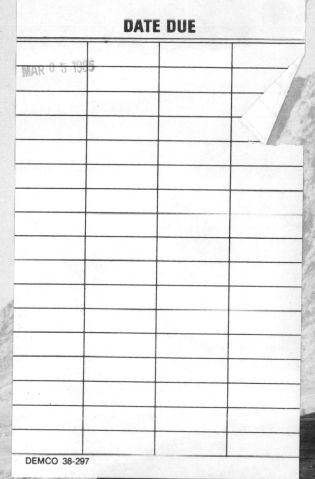

LIVING WITH THE BIBLE

MOSHE DAYAN

LIVING WITH THE BIBLE

WILLIAM MORROW & COMPANY, INC.
NEW YORK 1978

4269376
DLC

1-21-85 JH

To my wife, Rahel

The majority of the photographs for
this book were taken by Gemma Levine, who
also painted the water-colours.

Designed by Sheila Sherwen and Anthea Pender
for George Weidenfeld and Nicolson
11 St John's Hill London SW11

ISBN 0-688-03361-x

Library of Congress Catalog Card Number 78-52478

Colour separations by Newsele Litho
Printed in Great Britain

Contents

List of maps

Prologue

THE PEOPLE OF ISRAEL were exiled from their land, but their land was never exiled from their hearts. In whatever country they dwelt throughout the nineteen Diaspora centuries, they yearned for their homeland, Israel. The Jordan and the Kishon were their rivers, Sharon and Jezreel their valleys, Tabor and Carmel their mountains, and the cities of their fathers were Jerusalem, Hebron, Bethel, and Samaria.

In 1937 the British government, which was then the mandatory power in Palestine, recommended the partition of the land of Israel into two states, Jewish and Arab. Under this proposal, the Jewish State was to include Galilee, the valleys and the coastal plain, but not the remaining territory which had been part of biblical Israel. Jerusalem and Mount Hebron were to be excluded.

This British partition proposal was hotly debated by the Jewish community, and I followed the discussion between our leaders with keen interest. David Ben-Gurion favoured its acceptance. His friend Berl Katznelson, the leading Zionist theoretician in the country, urged its rejection. He argued that the nation of Israel cherished not only the parts of its land which it had settled by then, but also its age-old yearnings, not only 'its today but also its tomorrow', and it should never agree to its division and abandon the hope of returning to its ancient homeland.

My own feelings were with Berl Katznelson. My heart responded particularly to his words on love of homeland:

What is its source? [he asked]. Is it the physical link with the soil our feet have trodden since childhood? Is it the flowers which have delighted our eyes, the purity of the air we breathed, the dramatic landscape, the sunsets we have known? No, no. Our love of homeland springs from the timeless verses of the Book of Books, from the very sound of the biblical names. We loved an abstract homeland, and we planted this love in our soul and carried it with us wherever we went throughout the generations.

To one who was born in Israel, love of homeland was not an abstraction. The Rose of Sharon and Mount Carmel were very real to me, as were the sweet-scented blossom and the hills whose paths I climbed. Yet this was not enough. I was not content only with the Israel I could see and touch. I also longed for the Israel of antiquity, the Israel of the 'timeless verses' and the 'biblical names', and I wanted to give tangibility to that too. I wished to see not only the River Kishon marking off the fields of Nahalal from those of neighbouring Kfar Yehoshua;

The 'Rose of Sharon'.

I wished also to visualize the biblical Kishon sweeping away the Canaanite chariot forces of Sisera.

My parents who came from another country sought to make the Israel of their imagination, drawn from descriptions in the Bible, their physical homeland. In somewhat the reverse way, I sought to give my real and tangible homeland the added dimension of historical depth, to bring to life the strata of the past which now lay beneath the desolate ruins and archaeological mounds – the Israel of our patriarchs, our judges, our kings, our prophets.

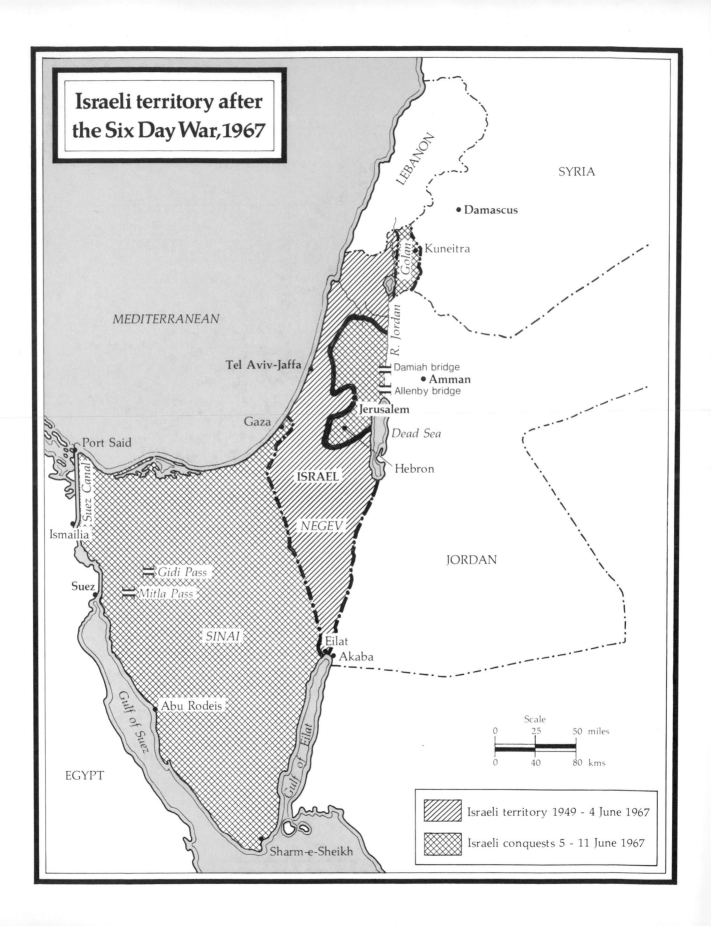

Israeli territory after the Six Day War, 1967

MEDITERRANEAN

LEBANON

SYRIA

• **Damascus**

Kuneitra

Golan

R. Jordan

Tel Aviv-Jaffa

Damiah bridge

• **Amman**

Allenby bridge

Gaza

Jerusalem

Dead Sea

Port Said

Hebron

Suez Canal

ISRAEL

Ismailia

NEGEV

JORDAN

Suez

Gidi Pass

Mitla Pass

SINAI

Eilat

• Akaba

Gulf of Suez

Gulf of Eilat

Abu Rodeis

EGYPT

Sharm-e-Sheikh

Scale

0   25   50 miles

0   40   80 kms

Israeli territory 1949 - 4 June 1967

Israeli conquests 5 - 11 June 1967

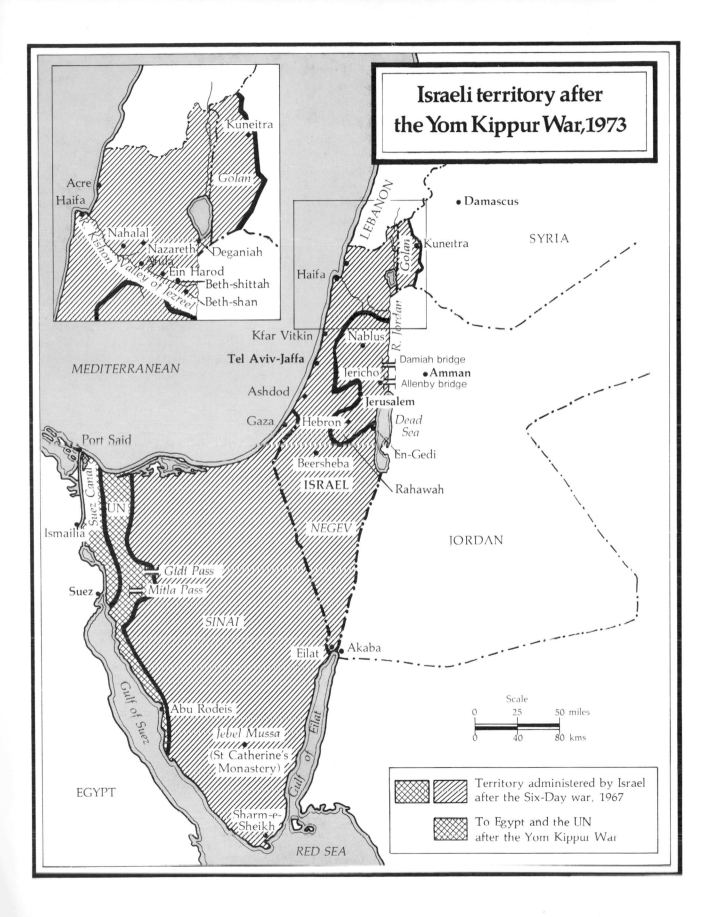

Israeli territory after the Yom Kippur War, 1973

Inset map:

Kuneitra
Golan
Acre
Haifa
Nahalal
Nazareth
Deganiah
Afula
Ein Harod
Beth-shittah
Beth-shan
R. Kishon
Valley of Jezreel

Main map:

LEBANON
Damascus
Golan
Kuneitra
SYRIA
Haifa
R. Jordan
Kfar Vitkin
Nablus
Damiah bridge
Tel Aviv-Jaffa
Jericho
Amman
Allenby bridge
Ashdod
Jerusalem
Gaza
Hebron
Dead Sea
Port Said
Beersheba
En-Gedi
ISRAEL
Rahawah
UN
NEGEV
Ismailia
Suez Canal
JORDAN
Suez
Gidi Pass
Mitla Pass
SINAI
Eilat
Akaba
MEDITERRANEAN
Gulf of Suez
Abu Rodeis
Jebel Mussa
(St Catherine's Monastery)
Gulf of Eilat
EGYPT
Sharm-e-Sheikh
RED SEA

Scale
0   25   50 miles
0   40   80 kms

Territory administered by Israel
after the Six-Day war, 1967

To Egypt and the UN
after the Yom Kippur War

PART ONE
THE PATRIARCHS

left 'Abraham planted a tamarisk tree in Beersheba.'

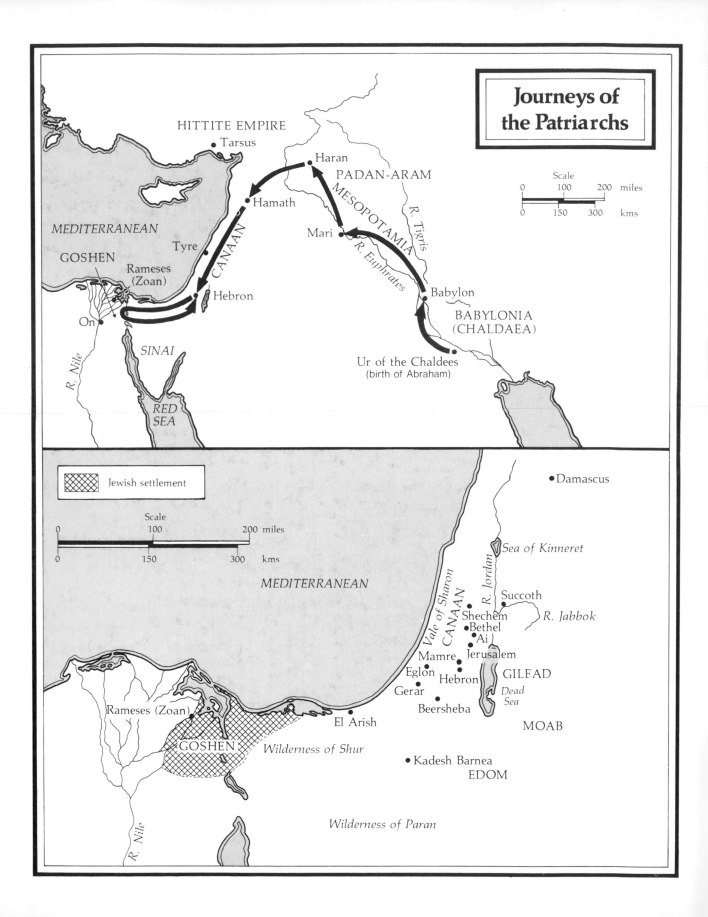

Journeys of the Patriarchs

Scale
0   100   200 miles
0   150   300 kms

HITTITE EMPIRE

Tarsus

Haran

PADAN-ARAM

MESOPOTAMIA

R. Tigris

Hamath

MEDITERRANEAN

CANAAN

Mari

R. Euphrates

GOSHEN

Tyre

Rameses
(Zoan)

Hebron

Babylon

BABYLONIA
(CHALDAEA)

On

R. Nile

SINAI

Ur of the Chaldees
(birth of Abraham)

RED
SEA

Jewish settlement

Scale
0   100   200 miles
0   150   300 kms

•Damascus

Sea of Kinneret

MEDITERRANEAN

R. Jordan

Succoth

Vale of Sharon

CANAAN

Shechem

R. Jabbok

Bethel

Ai

Mamre

Jerusalem

Eglon

Hebron

GILEAD

Gerar

Dead
Sea

Rameses (Zoan)

Beersheba

MOAB

GOSHEN

El Arish

Wilderness of Shur

Kadesh Barnea

EDOM

R. Nile

Wilderness of Paran

1
They walked alone

I WAS INTRODUCED to the stories of the Bible as a boy, like all Jewish children born in the Land of the Book. My teacher at Nahalal in the Valley of Jezreel, Meshulam Halevi, not only taught us about the early days of our people; he also invested them with a sense of present reality. It was as though events that had occurred three and four thousand years ago were happening now. Our actual surroundings served further to bridge the distance in time, returning us to the days of antiquity, to our patriarchs and to the heroes of our nation.

The language we spoke – the only language we knew – was Hebrew, the language of the Bible. The valley in which we lived, the nearby hills and streams were the valley, hills and streams of the Bible: Jezreel, Carmel, Mount Gilboa, the River Jordan. Our Arab neighbours, too, followed a pattern of life and work which recalled descriptions in the biblical books. They ploughed with oxen in tandem, using an ox-goad; assembled their sheaves at the village threshing floor; freed the grain with a threshing-sledge; winnowed the chaff with a pitchfork. (The biblical mood was heightened for us since we thought and spoke of these farming activities and implements in the very Hebrew phraseology used in the Bible.) After their labours they rested 'under their vine and under their fig tree'. They mourned their dead with a primitive wailing that could be heard from afar, an ancient stylized keening that broke the heart.

The people closest to me were the founders of our nation, the patriarchs Abraham, Isaac and Jacob. They wandered over the length and breadth of the land with a staff in their hand, a knotted stick fashioned from the branch of an oak, the strongest and stoutest of trees.

The patriarchs were independent beings who walked alone. They left the homes of their parents, parted from their brethren, and embarked on their lonesome path. They carried a weighty burden – a new faith, a new nation, a new land. Deganiah, the kibbutz on the Sea of Galilee where I was born, and Nahalal, the moshav where I grew up, were to me a continuation of their path. This was not only because the members of these pioneer farm settlements also came to a country they had not known and made it their homeland; it was above all because their aim, too, was not how to live but to what purpose. Their main concern was not the present but the future, not themselves but the generations of their nation who would come after them.

THE BIBLE records that Abraham, first of the patriarchs, came to the land of Canaan when he was seventy-five years old. His sons and their sons and those

Primitive methods of ploughing are still used, though animals have largely been replaced by the tractor.

who followed appear on the biblical stage as children; but he himself enters the historic chronicles with his infancy and youth behind him. He is already a mature adult, tried and experienced, familiar with the vagaries of life. The Lord directs him, and he obeys. He sets out on his wanderings, and goes south.

In his northern birthplace, Ur of the Chaldees in Mesopotamia, springs gush forth in abundance, rains pour from the heavens, green pastures and golden corn-fields flourish, and the land is alive with sheep and cattle, with men, women and children.

In the south, whither Abraham turned his face, all was desert. In the Negev, in Beersheba, and beyond Mount Hebron, rainfall is slight, pasture-land is poor, springs are meagre, and the population is sparse. Yet here, alone with his tents, Abraham would build his home, remote from tribe and nation, far from the pagan gods Moloch and Astarte. Abraham's caravan moved slowly and steadily south-wards. The northern-born sheep and cattle had grown up in a cool climate, with an abundance of water and soft grass, and found it hard to adapt to the parched and arid south.

In the beginning years of Deganiah and Nahalal, my father and his friends would travel in the reverse direction – to the north, to Syria, to buy the superior milch cows, the Damascus cow. These were sleek animals, tall, dark brown, with soft, smooth hide, and full udders. By contrast, the local cows seemed like wild animals which had not yet been domesticated, ugly, short-limbed, with tiny dugs, and their bodies covered with long, tough hair. Yet though the Damascus cows were larger, the local ones shoved and butted and pushed and chased them away whenever they stood in their path in the meadow or *en route* to the watering-place. These local cows would never have won a 'Queen of the Milk' contest. But they knew how to find sustenance in the warm fields of Canaan. Even at summer's end, when all that remained was the sharp and wild mesquite thorn in the wadis, they would return from pasture with full bellies.

Abraham remained in the Negev. Beersheba was his base, and from there he wandered north-eastwards to Mount Hebron and the Judean desert, and west-wards as far as Wadi El Arish. His pattern of living was like that of the Bedouin. He did not work the land, he fashioned no bricks, built no houses. His wives, his sons, his manservants and his maidservants dwelt in tents.

The sides of the tent – like the tents of the Bedouin I saw as a boy – were made of materials easy to fold and move: reeds and woollen cloth. The roof was always of goat's hair, tightly woven into heavy strips, with each strand firmly attached to its neighbours. They were proof against the penetration of dew in summer and rain in winter. When moist, the goat's hair swells, sealing any gap.

Abraham lived off his flocks and herds – sheep, goats, cattle, camels and asses. The goats, fleet of foot, pastured on the lower slopes of Mount Hebron, clambering over boulders and beating a path between the rocks. In summer they cut into the dry earth with their sharp hooves to expose moist roots which provided them with tasty food. In the spring they rose on their hind legs to reach and nibble away at the buds and soft branches of the forest trees.

above Morning dew in the Negev.

right Bedouin tents in the desert: the life-style has changed little throughout the ages.

The other animals were brought down to the plains, to the foot of Tel Arad and to the area of Beersheba and the Negev. The cattle and the asses, strong and robust, covered great distances, grazing and moving by day and by night. The sheep, cumbersome and less sinewy, went at a slower pace. At dusk they were corralled, and were not released till the sun was up. If a shepherd was slack and they got out in the early hours of the morning when the grass was still cold and wet, they would get stomach cramp. They also had to be sheltered from the burning rays during the midday hours. If they happened to be far from trees, the flock would huddle close and each sheep would thrust his head in the protective shade of the belly of another.

As though to emphasize the fact that Abraham was not a settled farmer who worked the land, the Bible makes special mention of the one tree he planted: 'Abraham planted a tamarisk tree in Beersheba.' (*Genesis* 21 :33.) This is an evergreen desert shrub which bears no fruit. Its blessing lies in the shade cast by its spreading branches which the animals could enjoy. There is also a specific reference to trees in the biblical account of the field which Abraham bought from Ephron the Hittite in Hebron. He acquired not only the Cave of Machpelah but also the grounds, 'and all the trees that were in the field, [and] that were in all the borders round about.' However, Abraham bought the field not to sow and reap but to bury his wife Sarah and to secure 'possession of a sepulchre' for his family.

Abraham erected altars on the summit of several mountains – at Moreh near Shechem, at Bethel, and at Mount Moriah in Jerusalem – where he offered sacrifices and served his God. From earliest times, thousands of years before Abraham migrated to Canaan, this mountain range, running southwards from Shechem (today's Nablus), through Jerusalem to Hebron, drew people to ritual worship. Here they established shrines and uttered prayer and supplication to the mysterious forces on high, creators of the world and its masters.

This lofty range soars above its surroundings, the rift of the Dead Sea and the Jordan Valley on one side, the foothills and the Vale of Sharon on the other. From its peaks on a clear day one can even see as far as the mountains of Moab and Gilead in the east, and in the west the Great Sea, the Mediterranean, the vast stretch of blue merging with the sky in the distance.

I was fortunate enough to acquire a ritual article from this region, a magnificent mask which French archaeologist Jean Perrot judged to be nine thousand years old. Made of stone, it has holes along its edges so that it can be tied to the head. The marvel, apart from its age, lies in its facial expression. It has circles for eyes, a small nose, and prominent grinning teeth. It is a human face, but one that strikes terror in its beholder. If there be any power in the world able to banish evil spirits, it must assuredly dwell in this mask.

This rare antiquity was discovered by chance. It had been turned up by an Arab day-labourer while ploughing by tractor. He sold it to an antique dealer, Ibrahim al-Maslam from the Arab village of Kfar Idna, and he sold it to me.

Before handing it to experts at the government department of antiquities for

right In this land of antiquity
the ploughman occasionally
turns up a treasure
of the past.
below The stone mask,
judged to be about nine thousand
years old, found by
chance near Hebron.

their study and confirmation of the dating, I was anxious to inspect the site where
it was found. I drove to the tractor-driver's home in the village of Dahariah, south
of Hebron, and he took me to the field he had ploughed. It was a bare, im-
poverished mound, its principal asset being the magnificent view it commanded.
Miles away to the west, one could see the golden stretch of the coastal plain, its
villages, groves and wadis laid out like modelled miniatures.

I examined the ploughed soil and spotted bits of bone and fragments of stone
vessels between the clods of earth in the furrows. Buildings may once have stood
upon this site, but there was now no sign of them. There were a few uncommon
stones partly embedded in the ground with man-made depressions scooped out
of the upper surface. They must have served some purpose, but what it was I
could not fathom.

On sites which have held a settled population over the centuries, there arises
what is known as a *tel*, an archaeological mound. It consists of layer upon layer
of the ruins of structures and the material remains of successive settlements, each
community building upon the layer of dirt and rubble that held the remains of its
predecessor. The older the site, the more numerous the period levels and the
higher the mound, the final settlement towering above its surroundings.

This, however, was not what had happened on the site where my mask was
found, for it had been used not for settlement but solely as a place of worship.
Here the process was reversed. The rains in winter and the winds in summer
sweep away the upper levels of earth and all that they hold. Thus, articles buried

19

thousands of years ago in caves and burrows eventually end up near the surface of the ground at the foot of the mound, within easy reach of a ploughshare.

While running my hands through the upturned earth in this field, I was approached by an elderly Arab from the nearby village of Yatta who introduced himself as the owner of the plot. After the customary exchange of greetings, he spread his cloak on the ground, sat cross-legged upon it, tucked his feet beneath him, and uttered a deep sigh. When I failed to respond, he emitted a more pitiful groan, and punctuated it with the cry 'Ya, Allah the merciful'. There was now no escape, and so I asked whether anything ailed him, and if I could help. No, nothing, he assured me; he wanted nothing. All he wished was to pour his heart out.

All his life, he said, he had ploughed and sowed this stony, rugged ground, raising poor harvests which barely covered the cost of the seed. And now, when a treasure of antiquity was discovered on this ground, the money it commanded was given to the day-labourer he had hired, an outsider. And why? 'Because he had asked me, as was the custom, to bring him food to break his hunger. So I went to my house and I brought him a basket of pitta [flat Arab bread], olives, and a little cheese, and behold, precisely during the hour that I was away from the field, the plough turned up the mask. Where is justice? Where is the Lord?'

The Lord and justice were not in my gift, but a 50-pound note was, and I gave it to him 'to buy sweets for the children', a formula that could not be refused.

The hired labourer who had found the mask also had a request, but only with diffidence did he give it voice. He was a tractor-driver of long experience, yet he had no licence. It had been refused. He had no doubt, however, that I, General Dayan, could arrange for him to get one. I asked him why it had been denied, but he was reluctant to state the reason. All he could do was stammer unintelligibly and shake his head. He finally thrust his face close to mine, and only then did I see why he was too embarrassed to put it into words: he had only one eye. The left, like mine, was missing.

I pulled a pad from my pocket and gave him a note to the licensing bureau in Beersheba telling them not to underrate the power of vision of the one-eyed!

2
The pledge

THE PATRIARCHAL DYNASTY passes from father to one son alone for three generations. Only in the fourth generation does the singular give way to the plural and we begin to read of 'the children of Israel' when all the sons of Jacob are privileged to belong to a new nation, the nation of Hebrews.

When Abraham hearkened to the voice of the Lord and left his country, his kindred, and his father's house in Haran for the land to which he would be directed, he was accompanied by Lot, his brother's son. Together they journeyed forth into the land of Canaan, and pitched their tents in the hill country north of Jerusalem, between Bethel and Ai. But Abraham preferred to be alone, and told Lot to 'separate thyself, I pray thee, from me'. (*Gen.* 13:9.) Lot turned to the south-east, to the plain of the Jordan, and Abraham 'dwelled in the land of Canaan'. Abraham behaved in the same way towards his sons. He sent the elder, Ishmael, to the wilderness of Paran. His younger son, Isaac, dwelt in Beersheba, the sole heir to carry on the development of the nation that had come into being.

The same thing happened in the third generation. Isaac also had two sons, and they too went their separate ways. Esau, the first born, chose to dwell in the mountain region of Seir, south-east of the Dead Sea, in the land of Edom. His brother Jacob, returning from Padan-aram and meeting him *en route*, promised to join him, but did not do so. When Esau left for his southern home, Jacob turned north to Succoth. He later crossed the Jordan and settled near Shechem in Canaan.

Abraham, Isaac and Jacob parted from their brothers and led a nomadic existence, pasturing their flocks in the hill country between Shechem and Hebron, and in the plains of the Negev, in the areas of Beersheba, Gerar and Kadesh-Barnea. In their journeyings they experienced and withstood much tribulation. They went hungry, fell sick, and suffered other hardships. They scuffled with the Canaanite herdsmen over grazing grounds and water sources, but then made peace pacts with the local rulers. They lived as neighbours with the Canaanites but never intermingled with them. They remained strangers, separate, pursuing their special ways, a people apart, solitary but not lonely. The Lord was with them. In the darkness of night he called them by name. His angels came to their tents, and 'a flaming torch passed between the divided pieces' of the sacrificial offerings to mark the covenant between them and the Lord.

Suffusing their day-to-day life was their spiritual life, the vision of the future. In their practical life the patriarchs made their way with their own resources. When Abraham went off to battle the four kings of the north who had taken his

Abraham, Isaac and Jacob pastured
their flocks in Gerar, north-west
of Beersheba, as do the Bedouin
today.

nephew Lot captive, he did not turn to the Lord for help. He set off at the head of his household servants and pursued the marauders from the south of the country to the north, from Mamre near Mount Hebron to 'Hobah, north of Damascus'. He himself, together with his followers, did the fighting. When famine struck the land of Canaan, Abraham did not beseech the Lord for dew and rain. He took his herds and flocks, crossed the Desert of Shur and went into Egypt to sate their hunger. In the summer they dug wells in the dried-up wadis, and when the rains came they sowed barley.

The revelation of the Lord to the patriarchs and his talks with them were concerned exclusively with the future, with the divine mission with which they were entrusted. On every occasion that the word of the Lord entered their souls, it was the repetition of a single theme: the promise to multiply their seed, their descendants to become a great nation, and the land of Canaan to be their land. These were the first words which the Lord spoke to Abraham: 'Get thee ... unto a land that I shall shew thee. And I will make of thee a great nation.' (*Gen.* 12:1, 2.) These were also the words he said to Isaac. And this was the blessing he gave to Jacob: 'Israel shall be thy name ... be fruitful and multiply; a nation and a company of nations shall be of thee.... And the land which I gave Abraham and Isaac, to thee I will give it, and to thy seed after thee I give the land.' (*Gen.* 35:10–12.)

THE PATRIARCHS trekked from place to place, at times alone, at times with their household and their wealth of livestock, covering considerable distances, from Padan-aram in Mesopotamia in the north-east as far to the south-east as Zoan in Egypt. As they trudged through the open stretches of the Negev, as they gazed at the star-strewn skies, and when they slept with a stone for their pillow, the Lord and his angels appeared to them in vision and dream. And their hearts were strengthened against fear of the peoples who surrounded them, the Kenites and the Kadmonites, the Hittites, Perizzites, Rephaims, the Amorites and the Canaanites, the Girgashites and the Jebusites. When they were childless, they were promised that their wives would be blessed and give birth. And when their spirits lagged, they were uplifted by faith.

KIBBUTZ DEGANIAH and its members were to me part of the 'patriarchal period' of our own times. People like Tanhum, Yitzhak Ben-Yaacov, Jacob Lichtenstein and Miriam Baratz are engraved on my memory as wonderful beings, distinctive, different from all who came after them.

The poetess Rachel belonged to this group, and the sight of her countenance, noble, pallid, remains fresh in my mind to this day. She looked after me in the kibbutz when I was about five. A little later, however, she showed symptoms of tuberculosis and had to be kept away from infants. She was given other employment while undergoing treatment. But she did not respond to the medicine of that day, grew steadily worse, and was finally advised by the doctor to leave Deganiah for a more salubrious part of the country. She died in 1931 at the age of forty-one.

The archaeological site of ancient Ashdod.

25

The grave of Rachel the poetess at kibbutz Deganiah. Her poems are kept in a box at the side for visitors to read.

There was a depth of meaning to Rachel's poetry which I could grasp only in later years, when I had come to know something of life's struggles. But even as a child I was much moved by the poem entitled, after her matriarchal namesake, 'Rachel'. To me it read like a Bible story. I loved its content, its rhythm, its short lyrical lines, its fantasy and its longings. I took in the words at their face value, and I believed them. I knew that they were the truth. I knew that the gentle Rachel Bloustein with the limpid eyes and golden hair, who had come to Deganiah from Russia, carried in her veins the blood of Rachel, daughter of Laban. I knew that this Jewish girl who was born on the banks of the Volga and had grown up in the Ukraine now paced the banks of the Sea of Galilee with the absolute conviction that her feet were treading familiar soil that held memories of long long ago. In the same way, I knew that the words of command to Abraham, 'Get thee out of thy country and from thy kindred, and from thy father's house, unto a land I will shew thee,' were also heard by my father and mother, by Rachel and Tanhum and the others; and it was these words that had brought them to Deganiah.

Rachel was the voice of her comrades not only in her poetry but also in her

Children at Nahalal in the valley of Jezreel, where Dayan lived in his youth.

prose writings. In 1919 she expressed what was felt by the first pioneer settlers in the Jordan valley: 'We trod ground which preserves the footsteps of our father Abraham; we heard the echo of the ancient word of the Lord "and I will make thy name great".' She loved Kinneret (Hebrew for the Sea of Galilee): 'Its waters are said to be blessed with wondrous properties: whosoever drinks therefrom albeit only once will return again and again. Is it not that our sons in strange lands yearn for the quiet shores of the Sea of Galilee for here their forefathers broke their thirst?'

Of those early days near the River Jordan, Rachel wrote: 'The more meagre the meal, the more joyous were our youthful voices. We shunned material comfort as an abhorrence, and welcomed hardship, sacrifice, privation. Through them we would sanctify the name of the homeland. The Sea of Galilee is not merely a scenic gem, a fragment of geography. It is interlocked with the destiny of a nation. From its depths our past gazes upon us with innumerable eyes, and with innumerable lips speaks to our hearts.'

Not only Rachel but all who have lived near the Sea of Galilee retain an undying

27

love for it. I was born on its western shore, and at the age of six I moved with my parents to Nahalal in the Valley of Jezreel. In my heart I have never been cut off from Kinneret. Its voice of the biblical past and of our national destiny, which was heard by Rachel, rings even more powerfully in my ears; for to it are added the voices of the first settlers of Um Juni and Kinneret Farm – precursors of Deganiah – and of A. D. Gordon and Rachel herself, notably in her poem 'Kinneret Sheli' ('My Sea of Galilee').

As to the waters of the sea, it is indeed true that they have a special taste, as though flavoured with sharp and pungent spices. I have been told that this is due to its sulphurous springs. Perhaps. I have never seen these springs. But I have tasted the waters of Kinneret: delicious.

THE 'FOOTSTEPS OF ABRAHAM', of which Rachel wrote, doubtless echoed in the hearts of the poetess and her friends in Deganiah. In fact, however, it is unlikely that Abraham would have passed close to the Sea of Galilee in his journey from Haran to Canaan. The patriarchs chose routes which kept them away from populated areas. The Vale of Sharon, the coastal plain and the Valleys of Jordan and Jezreel were regions of Canaanite settlement. Only the forested, boulder-strewn mountain slopes and the arid Negev were uninhabited, and those were the regions selected by Abraham, Isaac and Jacob for their journeyings.

The patriarchs were not men of war, and they made their way through Canaan without the use of sword and bow. The only combat in which any of them took part was Abraham's battle with the four northern kings – 'Chedorlaomer king of Elam, Tidal king of Goyim, Amraphel king of Shinar, and Arioch king of Ellasar.' (*Gen.* 14:9.) The biblical report of this battle makes detailed mention of the names of the rulers and the places where the fighting took place, but no mention of killing or of weapons. There is no word of blood, casualties, or sword. War without bloodshed! These kings defeated but did not capture the rulers of Sodom and Gomorrah, who managed to hide in the bitumen pits of the Vale of Siddim near the Dead Sea, while most of their men 'escaped to the hill country'. Abraham's nephew Lot, however, was among those taken captive, together with his household and animals; but Abraham managed to rescue them all, and retrieve their property.

After winning the battle, Abraham did not seize and settle in the territory of the vanquished kings. Nor did he take any booty for himself. 'Not a thread nor a shoe-string will I accept,' he said to the king of Sodom who offered Abraham the wealth he had recovered. 'I will not take any thing that is thine, lest thou shouldest say, I have made Abram rich.' (*Gen.* 14:23.) The patriarchs secured their property – camels, sheep, cattle, tents, silver and gold – by their own labours and with the blessing of the Lord, not through wars.

In critical situations they usually sought to extricate themselves by peaceful means. When 'famine was grievous' in the land of Canaan and Abraham and his household went down to Egypt, he told his wife Sarah that since she was 'a fair woman to look upon', her beauty would captivate the Egyptians and they would say, '... this is his wife: and they will kill me.... Say, I pray thee, thou art my

The southern end of the Sea of Galilee.

sister: that it may be well with me for thy sake.' (*Gen.* 12:11–13.) He did the same when he came to Gerar, and King Abimelech behaved as had the pharaoh in Egypt. He took Sarah into his house and Abraham went unharmed. Abraham also took the peaceful way out when there was trouble 'between the herdmen of Abram's cattle and the herdmen of Lot's cattle'. He told his nephew: 'Let there be no strife, I pray thee, between me and thee', and he allowed him to choose the best grazing lands.

Isaac, like his father, was also driven by famine to Gerar, and he too passed off his wife as his sister, lest 'the men of the place should kill me for Rebekah, because she was fair to look upon'. (*Gen.* 26:7.) Later, when there was conflict over water rights between his herdsmen and those of Gerar, he was the one who ended the quarrel by leaving and digging other wells.

Jacob also chose the pacific path when he found himself in jeopardy. The threat to his life when he was a young man came from his brother Esau, because of the birthright Jacob had secured by deceit. Jacob hearkened to the voice of his mother Rebekah and fled to the home of his maternal uncle, Laban, in Haran. When he returned to Canaan twenty years later and met his brother *en route*, he appeased Esau with a munificent gift and there was no violence.

It was some time after parting from his brother that trouble befell Jacob, and the episode that followed was violent indeed. But the aggression did not come from Jacob but from two of his eleven sons, who were now grown men though still under the patriarchal roof. It occurred when Jacob, having gone first to Succoth and later turned to the hill country of Canaan, pitched his tents on land near Shechem. He had bought it from the family of Hamor. The son of Hamor encountered Jacob's daughter, Dinah, one day, 'took her, and lay with her'. (*Gen.* 34:2.) He then expressed his wish to marry her and sought Jacob's consent.

The sons of Jacob were furious when they heard the news and took matters into their own hands. They were determined to avenge the dishonour done to their sister. Unbeknown to their father, they duped Hamor and the men of Shechem by persuading them to undergo circumcision, and when they were disabled, two of the sons, Simeon and Levi, went into the city, slew all the males, and brought Dinah home. Although his daughter had been violated, Jacob found the action of his sons repugnant. This was not his way. 'Ye have troubled me to make me to stink among the inhabitants of the land,' he told them; and he took his household and went to live in Bethel.

3
The wise Bedouin

THE PATRIARCHS kept their distance from the other peoples, and avoided involvement in the wars of the local kingdoms. Abraham journeyed to the edge of the desert and made his home in Beersheba. Beyond Beersheba the deserts begin – the Judean desert to the north, the wilderness of Paran to the south, and the Desert of Shur to the west. Yet even Beersheba is not entirely free from attempted encroachments of the desert, exposed as it is to drought, sandstorms, and the hot *sharav* wind. But it manages to escape its grip. It averages an annual rainfall of 100 to 150 millimetres, which makes possible the raising of barley (one of the most ancient of the cultivated grains). In a year of meagre rains, the stalks are stunted and the crop is poor and shrivelled.

Beersheba has no gushing springs. To get water one has to dig wells in the wadis. These dry river beds are now shallow, but hundreds of thousands of years ago they were deep gorges. Over the ages, flash floods and sandstorms have swept into them stones and sand, pebbles, dust and ashes, and turned them into reservoirs for the rainwater flowing into them in winter. With a perceptive eye, experience, and luck, one can detect a spot in these wadis beneath which – perhaps twenty or thirty metres below the surface – lies a storage of water. Such a well continues to be replenished by water held within the porous layers of sand and stone that encompass it. The water seeps through into the well in slow but steady drops and has done so throughout the millennia.

However, at times the desert is victor, and even the small quantities of rain fail to arrive. The wells run dry, fields are parched, and pastures vanish. The only course is to move. The people go forth with their livestock to seek out other grazing grounds until the famine breaks with the next winter rains.

In Israel today, in years of drought, the Bedouin of the Negev send their shepherds north with their flocks, while the rest of the families remain in their homes, and the sheikhs go up to Jerusalem to receive drought compensation from the government.

Some years ago, when I was Minister of Agriculture, I spent a Sabbath wandering round Wadi Shikma and the archaeological mound of Tel el-Hesi, which stands on its southern bank. This mound, some fifteen miles north east of Gaza, is considered by modern scholars to be the site of biblical Eglon. On its slope I suddenly came across the subterranean home of a family of hedgehogs. There were three entrances to their burrow, and outside each lay a small heap of earth and potsherds, the product of their excavations. I looked at the shards and

identified several as parts of what is known as a Cypriot 'milk bowl', with characteristic striped decorations, belonging to the second millennium BC. So I went on
searching, hoping to find some artefact of interest.

Not far from where I was scrabbling about in the dirt stood an old Bedouin
shepherd with his flock. He watched me for a few moments, recognized my black
eye-patch and came over. At first he helped me examine the potsherds, assuring
me that they were 'very old, from long, long ago'. He then turned to the subject
for which he had approached me. His opening was impressive, pure philosophy:
all the evils of the world, he said, come from heaven; all the blessings – from
the government.

At pasture in the desert.

I could not remain impassive to such a declaration, and asked for the evidence. 'Look, O *Wazir*, sickness comes from the Lord, and the doctors are provided by the government. Not so? Wars are arranged in heaven [it was shortly after the 1956 Sinai Campaign], and peace is made by the government. Not so? Now, this year, drought has come from heaven, but we shall receive compensation from the government, shan't we?' My heart naturally swelled with pride in my government which corrects on earth the injustices committed by heaven. I of course agreed with every word he uttered, and a beatific expression lit his face. That evening he would tell his companions in his tent that the Minister of Agriculture had confirmed the grant of drought-compensation to their tribe.

OF THE THREE PATRIARCHS, Isaac travelled the least. Abraham journeyed all the way from Haran (Mesopotamia), and in the years of drought moved on to Egypt. Jacob fled to Haran as a young man, and towards the end of his life went down to Egypt. Isaac, however, never left the country. He married a girl from Mesopotamia, as did his father and his son; but he himself did not go there. He stayed at home, while Abraham's steward, Eliezer, went to the city of Nahor and brought him back a bride, Rebekah, grand-niece of Abraham. Isaac, too, experienced famine and had to move; but he remained within the confines of the northern Negev, taking his flocks to Gerar, north-west of Beersheba and nearer to the coast, which gets rain every winter.

Isaac was born in the Negev and knew its ways and its secrets. Of his two sons, the younger, Jacob, 'a quiet man, dwelling in tents' (*Gen.* 25:27), was the favourite of his mother, Rebekah. But Isaac loved his first-born, the tough, coarse and hairy Esau, 'a cunning hunter, a man of the field', who went after game in the beds of the wadis. In the evenings, he would return with his prize and fill the tent with the aroma of the countryside – not the sweet scent of the lily of Sharon, but the sharp, pungent smell emitted by the downy bush of the desert foxglove.

Isaac grew old. But his soul still thirsted for the wide spaces, the hot breath of the *sharav* wind, the hunting forays for ibex, rock-pigeon and partridge. Flights of partridges strut about in the open fields, and at the approach of man take off in all directions. But the hare and gazelle forage in the dry river beds and can be ambushed with ease and brought down with the bow. They emerge in the early-morning hours to nibble the moist grass and lick the dewdrops from the leaves of bushes. They never get to the wells, but adapt themselves to the conditions of the Negev and quench their thirst with dew.

Isaac blesses Jacob. A 17th-century painting by the Spanish artist Jusepe de Ribera.

Isaac's field days were over. His legs were weak and his eyes dim. The time had come to bless his first-born. Summoning Esau, he told him to take 'thy weapons, thy quiver and thy bow, and go out to the field, and take me some venison; and make me savoury meat, such as I love, and bring it to me, that I may eat; that my soul may bless thee before I die'.

Rebekah had been listening to Isaac's words, and when Esau left – he would not be back before sundown – she commanded her beloved son Jacob to go out to the flocks and bring home two kid-goats, 'and I will make them savoury meat for thy father, such as he loveth'.

Rebekah knew what she was about when she asked him to bring young goats. The meat of a calf is sweet. The meat of a sheep has a fatty smell. But a kid-goat is as lean and sinewy as a game animal, and even Isaac the experienced hunter would be unable to tell the difference in taste and texture between the flesh of the kid that Jacob slaughtered and that of the young hart which Esau hunted. The blessing of the first-born would be given to Jacob, albeit by deceit.

When Isaac later blessed his sons, Jacob first and then Esau, he entreated the Lord 'to give thee of the dew of heaven'. (*Gen.* 27:28.) He made no mention of rain or shower. In my own village of Nahalal, all blessings would include a plea for rain. The blessing of dew was intended for the Negev, for the plants that flourish in arid zones, for the beasts and birds who can exist in rainless regions – and for the humans who live with them.

4
An unpardonable sin

THE PATH OF JACOB'S LIFE was marked by dramatic twists and turns. At some points its direction contrasted strangely with that taken by his grandfather. Abraham, first of the patriarchs, had gone to Canaan to make it his home and his country; there he would father his sons and found a nation. Jacob, last of the patriarchs, left Canaan in his declining years and followed his sons to a foreign land, Egypt.

Jacob's mother Rebekah had been brought from Mesopotamia to Canaan by Abraham's steward, Eliezer, as a wife for Isaac, and Eliezer had arrived at her home with 'camels of his master' laden with costly gifts which Abraham had sent for her and members of her family. Among them were gold earrings and bracelets and other 'jewels of silver, and jewels of gold, and raiment . . .' (*Gen.* 24 : 10, 22, 53.)

When Jacob in his time went to Mesopotamia to the home of Rebekah's brother Laban, he arrived with nothing. He rode on no camel, as his grandfather's steward had ridden, and he brought no precious gifts, though he was the son and grandson of wealthy men. He went on foot, and all he carried was a staff.

Eliezer, on arrival in Mesopotamia, had met Rebekah at a well. The girl hastened to offer him water from her jug and had drawn water from the well for his camels. Jacob, in his turn, when he reached this northern country, met Rachel at a well. But she gave him no water. It was Jacob who rolled the stone from the mouth of the well and watered her sheep, the flocks of her father Laban. Then 'Jacob told Rachel . . . that he was Rebekah's son' and he 'kissed Rachel, and lifted up his voice, and wept'.

Jacob had worked hard to build up his household and his possessions. He served Laban for twenty years, seven for Rachel, seven for Leah, and another six to acquire the flocks which made him independent. He received nothing from his father Isaac and nothing *gratis* from his father-in-law Laban. All his possessions were the product of his own labours, and they had been harsh. He had worked through hot day and cold night, year after year. But there was blessing in his toil and he had prospered greatly.

He then heard the voice of the Lord: 'Return unto the land of thy fathers, and to thy kindred; and I will be with thee.' (*Gen.* 31 :3.) This was the first time since he had left Canaan that the Lord had spoken to him. On the night of his departure from Canaan as a young man, when he had lain down to sleep at Bethel with a stone for his pillow, he had dreamed of the ladder going up to

Bedouin women fetch water from the well in jars they carry on their heads, as the women may have done in patriarchal times.

36

Desert transport, today as in ancient times.

heaven with angels ascending and descending, and 'the Lord stood above it' and promised Jacob that 'the land whereon thou liest, to thee will I give it, and to thy seed'. (*Gen.* 28 : 13.) Now, in Mesopotamia, the Lord had again revealed himself to Jacob and called on him to return to his homeland.

Jacob left Padan-aram stealthily, while his father-in-law Laban was away helping his sons with the sheep-shearing. With the arrival of spring and the easing of winter's frost, the sheep no longer need their woolly cloaks to guard the heat of their bodies. Jacob set his wives and sons on camels and started on his way south, together with all the livestock which he had gained.

They travelled slowly. Young lambs, kids and calves, born in the spring, are still frail and tender, and must not be over-driven. They must be returned from pasture before nightfall, to allow the new-born to suckle, and the herdsmen and maid-servants to do their work – to milk the cows and sheep and churn the milk into butter and cheese.

It was the beginning of summer when Jacob reached the ford of the Jabbok. He was now riven by anxiety: his brother Esau was coming to meet him at the head of four hundred men. Did this mean there was still enmity in his heart? Was it his purpose to 'slay us all, the mothers with the children'? Jacob had with him his eleven sons and one daughter, Dinah. All had been born in Padan-aram, seven to Leah, two to Bilhah, two to Zilpah, and one to Rachel. The eldest, Reuben, was not quite thirteen years old, and the youngest, Joseph, seven. It was for them that he had toiled and sweated in the service of Laban. They, his children, were his great hope. It was of them that the Lord had told him, 'I will surely do thee good, and make thy seed as the sand of the sea, which cannot be numbered for multitude'. (*Gen.* 32:12.) And Isaac had given him the blessing 'to thee, and to thy seed with thee; that thou mayest inherit the land wherein thou art a stranger, which God gave unto Abraham'. (*Gen.* 28:4.) Now, as he stood on the threshold of this land, would the words of the Lord and the blessing of his father be fulfilled if he were confronted with the sword of Esau?

They met. Esau was reconciled, and he accepted Jacob's gift: sheep and goats and cattle, asses and camels, superior herds, streaked, speckled, spotted and dappled, the result of cross-breeding from varied stocks. With one exception, each herd and flock contained both male and female: 'two hundred she-goats, and twenty he-goats, two hundred ewes, and twenty rams ... forty kine, and ten bulls, twenty she-asses, and ten foals.' (*Gen.* 32:14, 15.) Only the herd of camels was exclusively female: 'thirty milch camels with their colts.' Male camels harry the females and their young, and so they are pastured separately. Only in the autumn, when the she-camel is on heat, are they brought together, but once the females are pregnant they are again separated.

[Some modern scholars hold that the domestication of the camel was fully developed only in the twelfth century BC, some five or six centuries after the patriarchal period, and that its mention in the biblical stories of Abraham, Isaac and Jacob is therefore anachronistic. However, while the use of the camel as a beast of burden became widespread only by the twelfth century BC, it certainly served as a means of transport much earlier. The camel is mentioned in an eighteenth-century BC cuneiform tablet discovered in Alalakh in northern Syria. Camel bones were found in Mari (Tel el-Hariri) on the Euphrates in a building belonging to about 2400 BC. An eighteenth-century BC relief found at Byblos in Phoenicia depicts a kneeling camel. And camel riders appear on cylinder seals recently discovered in Mesopotamia belonging to the patriarchal period.]

Esau parted from his brother, his men took charge of the gift animals, and they wended their way southwards, back to their country, the region of Mount Seir.

Jacob, watching their departing backs, felt a deep sense of relief. The blessing had come to pass. His offspring were with him, unharmed, the children with whom he had been favoured by the Lord. They would settle in Canaan, would grow and prosper and become a nation, and the land they worked they would make their country.

After he had organized the crossing of the Jabbok by his entire caravan, Jacob, alone at night near the river bank, was seized by a man who wrestled with him until the break of day. When the man 'saw that he prevailed not' against Jacob, 'he touched the hollow of his thigh; and the hollow of Jacob's thigh was [put] out of joint'. The man, an angel, sought release from Jacob's grip, but Jacob said, 'I will not let thee go, except thou bless me'. The angel then blessed him: 'Thy name shall be called no more Jacob, but Israel' (Hebrew for 'he who strives with the Lord', or 'the Lord strives'); for Jacob had striven 'with God and with men, and hast prevailed'. So Jacob called the name of the place Penuel (the face of God), 'for I have seen God face to face, and my life is preserved'. (*Gen.* 32:24–30.)

The sun rose upon him and, limping from the injury to his thigh, he passed through Penuel, joined his caravan and led it onwards. Behind him came the string of camels carrying the womenfolk and his twelve children, the Children of Israel.

After parting from Esau, Jacob journeyed to Succoth on the east bank of the River Jordan, and there he 'made booths for his cattle'. (Succoth is Hebrew for booths.) With rainfall sparse in the Jordan valley, one need only cover the reed roofing with loam to make the booths waterproof.

At Succoth Jacob also 'built him an house'. Here he would stay until his sons grew up. He would cross the river Jordan and enter Canaan, but not as he had left it, alone, with only a staff for his worldly goods. Now he would return in style, with his wealth of livestock and his man-servants and his maid-servants and his great household.

That indeed is how he eventually returned to Canaan. By then, however, though he was still head of the family, it was his eleven grown sons who set the tone for its conduct. Simeon and Levi slew the men of Shechem; Reuben lay with Bilhah, his father's concubine; and Joseph's brothers conspired to sell him to the Ishmaelites.

When there was famine in the land, as in Abraham's time, Jacob too went down to Egypt after sending his sons to buy food from the granaries of the pharaoh. But they, unlike Abraham, left Canaan and did not return. They joined brother Joseph, and remained to settle in the region of Goshen. At first they lived well; but later they were struck by misfortune and became slaves.

THE ATTEMPTS by our Bible teacher in the village school to explain that circumstances were different in the patriarchal period from what they are now proved of no avail. For us, the children of Nahalal, to leave our country in any epoch was an unpardonable sin. How could the children of Israel forsake their land? Had Abraham journeyed from Haran to Canaan so that his grandson Jacob and Jacob's children should abandon it?

The act of leaving Israel was not strange to us, for it happened to one of our members. He was Avraham Mahlin, one of Nahalal's first settlers. Five years later, in 1926, he emigrated. Mahlin was a superb farmer. He came of farming stock, and he ploughed his land with a pair of oxen, as he had been brought up to do at his home in Beer Tuviah. His wife Esther, a pleasant woman who sang a sweet soprano in our village choir, was also Israeli-born. She came from Ekron.

One day the Mahlin family announced that they were leaving for Australia to join their friends, who had been born and brought up in the private farm settlements of the 'Biluim'. (These were a group of young Russian Jews who pioneered the modern return to Israel in the early 1880s and established the first Zionist villages. The name derives from 'Bilu', the Hebrew acronym for 'O House of Jacob, come ye and let us go'. Unlike the kibbutz collective, or the moshav co-operative, the Biluim villages were settled by private farmers.) In Australia, said the Mahlins, there were wide empty spaces blessed by an abundance of water and sun, and expert farmers like themselves could own huge estates covering thou-

An early photograph of Nahalal, where Dayan grew up. Established in 1921 as the first cooperative farming village in the country, it was given a spectacular wheel-shaped design by the architect Richard Kaufmann, with the community and service buildings as the hub, and the individual farmsteads radiating out like spokes.

sands of acres. A single Australian farm, they said, had as much land as the whole of Nahalal. And these were the children of Biluim!

In stark contrast, symbol of the very reverse of Mahlin and his action, was the unforgettable Russian-born Eliezer Bron. Like Esther Mahlin, he too sang in our choir – and not only in the choir. On clear winter mornings during the sowing season, his singing could be heard from afar in a powerful voice, exuding faith: 'Scorn, yea, scorn the dream I dream, but ...' with the accent on the harsh opening word. At festive celebrations in Nahalal when we all gathered in the village hall, or when we had a musical recital with a visiting artist from Tel Aviv, my eyes would always be on Eliezer Bron. He was short and thin, yet very impressive, with his fiery eyes and his hair curling heavenwards. Even when the stage of the hall was filled with players, or the lectern commanded by a declamatory orator, Eliezer would sit sunk in his inner thoughts, quietly humming his own tunes. The orchestra or the visiting singer on the stage would play or sing their music, while he, with barely a sound but with extreme devotion, hummed to himself the songs of Zion, the songs most dear to his heart, which never left his lips.

Mahlin's departure left a bitter taste in Nahalal, but no void. The village assembly soon approved the membership of a newcomer who took over the farm that had been forsaken. Continuity was maintained.

Our Bible teacher, Meshulam, was already preparing us for the next chapters, the Exodus from Egypt. But my troubled mind still lingered over Jacob and his sons. 'Leaving the country? The House of Jacob, born in the land? No wonder they eventually became slaves. They deserved it!'

THE BIBLE TELLS US that Jacob lived to the age of 147, the last seventeen years spent in Egypt, in the land of Goshen. Isaac was 180 when he died, and Abraham 175. Jacob's life had been hard, and he said so when he arrived in Egypt and was presented by his son Joseph to the pharaoh. Asked how old he was, Jacob told the king, and added, 'Few and evil have the days of the years of my life been, and have not attained unto the days of the years of the life of my fathers' (*Gen.* 47:9), who had pursued their tranquil existence in their own land and had not been subject to his travails and his migrations.

When he felt death was near, Jacob pleaded not to be buried in a strange land. 'If now I have found grace in thy sight', he said to Joseph, 'put, I pray thee, thy hand under my thigh, and deal kindly and truly with me; bury me not, I pray thee, in Egypt: but I will lie with my fathers.' (*Gen.* 47:29, 30.) His grandfather Abraham had gone through a similar oath ritual with his steward Eliezer when he wanted his promise that he would not take Isaac out of Canaan to Mesopotamia: 'Put ... thy hand under my thigh: and I will make thee swear by the Lord, the God of heaven, and the God of the earth, that ... thou bring not my son thither again.'

Joseph then took his two sons, Manasseh and Ephraim, to Jacob's bedside to be blessed. Jacob's eyes were dim with age and he could barely see the visitors. Sick and weak, he had to summon all his strength to sit up in bed. The sons were brought closer, and Jacob kissed them and embraced them. He then placed his right hand upon the head of Ephraim and his left upon the head of Manasseh, thus favouring the younger son over the elder – as his father and grandfather had done in their day. Joseph, seeking to correct what he thought was his weak-eyed father's mistake, removed Jacob's right hand in order to guide it to the head of Manasseh, saying, 'Not so, my father: for this is the firstborn; put thy right hand upon his head.' (*Gen.* 48:18.) But Jacob refused. 'I know it, my son, I know it,' he said, and he continued to keep his hands crossed, with the right upon the head of Ephraim, and to him he gave the first-born's blessing. Thus had he, Jacob, received the major blessing that should have gone to his brother Esau; and thus had his father Isaac received the blessing from Abraham, who had favoured him, the younger son, over Ishmael.

Jacob then called all his sons to gather at his bedside, and to each he gave the blessing appropriate to his character. He told them 'that which shall befall you in the last days' (*Gen.* 49:1), and ended by charging them to bury him with his

above This 6000-year-old Chalcolithic ossuary was assembled by Dayan from the potsherds he found at Azor, near Tel-Aviv and *below right* a pottery figure of a woman in mourning, about 10th century BC; also found at Azor.

fathers 'in the cave that is in the field of Machpelah ... which Abraham bought ... for a possession of a buryingplace'. (*Gen.* 49 :30.) Abraham and his wife Sarah were buried there, as were Isaac and his wife Rebekah, and there Jacob had buried Leah. Rachel alone was buried elsewhere. As Jacob told Joseph, 'When I came from Padan, Rachel died by me in the land of Canaan in the way, when yet there was but a little way to come unto Ephrath; and I buried her there in the way of Ephrath; the same is Bethlehem.' (*Gen.* 48 :7.)

Rachel, youngest of the matriarchs, had died after giving birth to Benjamin, the only one of Jacob's sons who was born in Canaan. That perhaps was the reason why Jacob called him Benjamin, Hebrew for 'son of the south', as against all his other sons who were born in the north, in Mesopotamia. Rachel, with her dying breath had called him Ben-oni, Hebrew for 'son of my sorrow', for her travail had been hard and painful, and her end tragic.

WHEN WE WERE STUDYING this Bible chapter at the village school, I could not help linking Rachel's sufferings with the idea of the 'household gods' (*terafim* in Hebrew). She had taken them from the house of her father Laban when she left Mesopotamia with Jacob, and put them in the camel's saddle 'and sat upon them'. (*Gen.* 31 :34.) The household gods were worthless idols, but Rachel clung to them, believed in them, wanted them with her. She lied to her father when he came searching for them in her tent; nor did she tell her husband Jacob that she had them. She kept them throughout the long journey from Padan-aram to Canaan. She believed that they watched over her, gave her protection.

Then before her great day, the day she was to give birth, her 'guardians' were taken from her. Jacob commanded his household and all who were with him to 'put away the strange gods that are among you, and be clean'. So they gave them to Jacob, together with 'their earrings which were in their ears: and Jacob hid them under the oak which was by Shechem'. (*Gen.* 35 :3, 4.) The caravan then pressed on to Bethel where Jacob built an altar and called on the name of the Lord. The Lord responded and wrought terror among the surrounding Canaanite cities so that they did not molest the House of Jacob.

Jacob and his family continued on their way. But it was a sorrowful journey. The aged Deborah, who had been wet-nurse to Rebekah, died when they were at Bethel. After her burial, they pressed on towards Ephrath; and while they were *en route* Rachel was stricken by labour pains, gave birth and died. Jacob set up a pillar upon her grave. It 'is the pillar of Rachel's grave unto this day'. (*Gen.* 35 :20.)

I do not, of course, believe in pagan images; but I do believe in the power of belief, in the comfort that faith can bring. You have only to observe the serenity in the face of a child who falls asleep with a tattered teddy-bear clasped in its arms. Rachel believed in her household gods. They were paltry toys. But she assuredly missed them and was pitifully forlorn without them during the wretched moments of her fatal childbirth.

We cannot know with certainty the shape and form of the particular *terafim* that Rachel took with her from her father's house. We know only their purpose: they were believed to be the guardians of the home and to ensure that the family would prosper and be fruitful. For years I had been looking out for such deities of ages past, and dealers would occasionally show me fertility figurines which had been unearthed in Syria and Iraq. But none matched the model of the *terafim* I had conceived in my imagination.

Now, however, I have in my possession an earthenware figurine which I feel must be similar to one which Rachel had taken with her. I came across it in a New York Madison Avenue antique store run by an Iranian Jew. It is from Sumer, in Mesopotamia, and is four thousand years old. A female form, she has narrow elongated eyes, wears a necklace and bracelets, and carries an infant in the crook of her left arm. Neither mother nor child has the slightest claim to classical beauty, but not for aesthetic delight were they designed. The function of such household gods was to persuade the powers in the heavens on high and in the nether world below to bestow their blessings upon – or withhold their curses from – the home. And this function they performed, despite their grotesque appearance, when the household believed in them.

Dayan holding the four-thousand-year-old earthenware figurine from Sumer in Mesopotamia, which may well resemble the 'household gods' taken by Rachel from her father's home when she left with Jacob for Canaan.

5

The girl in the Hebron cave

AND WHEN JACOB had made an end of commanding his sons, he gathered up his feet into the bed' (*Gen.* 49 :33), and breathed his last. The Egyptian beds in those days were made of wood and were upholstered. When Jacob talked to his sons, he would use the bed as a sofa, sitting on it with his feet touching the floor. When he wished to lie back, he would 'draw up his feet' and tuck them under him. Abraham and Isaac did not possess beds, and nor did Jacob in the years that he lived in Canaan. When they slept under cover, their 'couch' would be a rug spread on the floor of the tent. Out in the field, they would stretch out on the ground wrapped in a sheepskin cloak and rest their head on a stone.

Nor did they have horses or wagons. They rode on camels in the plains and in the desert, and mounted asses to negotiate the tortuous mountain paths that wound between boulders and trees.

When Jacob and his household went down to Egypt during the famine, they took with them choice produce from the land as gifts for the pharaoh's officials: 'a little balm, and a little honey, spices and myrrh, nuts, and almonds' (*Gen.* 43 :11), aromatic herbs and dried fruits from Gilead and from Mount Hebron.

When Jacob died, Joseph arranged for 'the physicians to embalm his father'. Forty days were required for it, and local Egyptian custom called for seventy days of mourning. Joseph then received permission from the pharaoh to leave Canaan in order to bury Jacob in the Cave of Machpelah, and he set out with his brothers. This time, however, the amenities of the journey were far more elaborate than on the original trek from Canaan to Egypt. There was an escort of 'chariots and horsemen . . . a very great company'. (*Gen.* 50:9.)

The period of the patriarchs had ended. It had begun with their departure from Mesopotamia, continued with their freedom in Canaan, and closed with their descent into Egypt and eventually into bondage. Jacob, last of the patriarchs, returned, embalmed, to his fatherland, borne from the estate granted him by the pharaoh of Egypt in the land of Goshen to the burial estate in the field of Machpelah, purchased by Abraham from Ephron the Hittite, with the family tombs scooped out of the rock. He had prepared his own burial niche when he lived in Hebron. He had followed his sons to Egypt so that before he died he could once again see his beloved Joseph, the lad who had been sold into slavery and had become Egypt's governor. After burying him, his sons returned to Egypt. Thus Jacob alone remained in Canaan, to rest with his fathers in the Cave of Machpelah.

FOR EXACTLY seven hundred years, from the thirteenth century (1267 AD) until 8 June 1967, the structure above the traditional Cave of Machpelah, and of course the cave itself, had been barred to Jews. The closest they were allowed to get to the cave area throughout those centuries was the steps on the outside of the eastern wall, and even then they were permitted to ascend only to the seventh step. From there they could insert a note of petition and supplication into a small hole in the wall and it would flutter into the cave below.

On the fourth day of the Six Day War, when the Israeli army captured Hebron, the seven-hundred-year anti-Jewish ban was broken. Jews ascended beyond the seventh step and entered the building which marks the tombs of the patriarchs.

The building had been erected as a Jewish shrine by King Herod towards the end of the first century BC. After the Moslem conquest in the seventh century AD, it was turned into a mosque. It was converted into a church by the Crusaders in the twelfth century, and reconverted into a mosque after the Mameluke conquest a century and a half later. Its east wing served as a Moslem house of prayer. The west wing holds the tombs which represent the sepulchres of the patriarchs.

If indeed this is the authentic site of historic Machpelah, the cave lies somewhere beneath the floor of the structure. The representational tombs seen in the halls belong to a much later period. They were built above a large subterranean chamber containing sepulchral niches, to which entry is forbidden.

Jewish visitors came to Hebron in their tens of thousands after the Six Day War to pay homage at the tombs of the patriarchs, after being denied access for so long. Some brought with them *Torah* scrolls and a holy ark to house them, and turned the west wing into a synagogue. This created the uneasy situation of a mosque and a synagogue housed cheek by jowl in one building, with Jews and Moslems under the same roof offering their different prayers within sound of one another.

We had to devise an arrangement which would enable both communities to worship at the shrine without interference, disturbance and clash. This would best be done by separating the two prayer halls even further, and providing each with its own entrance. During our study of the problem, a proposal was put forward to erect a special synagogue hall just outside the building, and to link it to the underground storey, namely, the very underground chamber which, by tradition, holds the patriarchal tombs. The proposal was thought feasible because it was said that this chamber had once had an opening, now sealed, to the outside. If this proved true, it could now be reopened, and the sealing bricks replaced by a door. This would make the synagogue a symbolic part of the building housing the shrine, and it would also serve as an entrance for Jewish visitors who could proceed to the tombs without having to go through the mosque.

However, to discover whether there was indeed a sealed opening required a close inspection. This was not easy, for the chamber had no doors and in any case entry was barred. It – or rather its darkness – could only be glimpsed through a grilled aperture in the floor of the mosque, which told us nothing. If entry were to be effected at all, it could be only through the aperture.

The building on the traditional site of the Cave of Machpelah in Hebron, burial place of the patriarchs.

The first of such entries was undertaken by Michal, the daughter of one of our people. She was then a slender twelve-year-old, able to wriggle through the eleven-inch-diameter aperture above the chamber. But more than that, she was a bright and courageous little girl who was unafraid not only of ghosts and spirits – their existence was not proven, she said – but also of snakes and scorpions, which were a very real danger.

In the classic opening manner of suspense stories, on one dark and gloomy night she was lowered by rope to the floor of the subterranean area, holding a torch in one hand and a camera in the other. She took a number of photographs and also made notes and sketches.

It appeared that there were several later tombstones, burial niches, and a flight of steps that did indeed lead to, and end at, a sealed opening. But it had given entry only to the upper storey. There was no sign in the photographs of a sealed exit that had once led directly to the outside.

Twelve-year-old Michal is lowered through the narrow aperture into the Cave of Machpelah.

I asked Michal for her photograph as a memento, together with a report of her survey adventure. This is what she wrote:

Visit to the Cave of Machpelah. On Wednesday, 9 October 1968, my mother asked me if I would agree to go through a small hole leading into a cave. After I agreed, she told me that it was to be the underground Cave of Machpelah.

A few hours later, my father woke me. I dressed and went into the car. In the car I wrapped myself in a blanket. I must have looked like a bundle dumped on the back seat. We set off and reached Hebron. We stopped for a while at the police station, and we then went on to the building of the Cave of Machpelah. I got out of the car, still covered in a blanket, and went into the mosque.

I then saw the opening through which I was to enter. It was measured and found to be exactly eleven inches in diameter. Ropes were tied round me, I was given a torch and matches (to test the air below) and I was lowered. I landed on a heap of papers and money-bills.

I found myself in a square room. Opposite me were three tombstones, the middle one higher and more decorated than the other two. There was a small square opening in the wall opposite me. They released more rope and I went through the opening, and found myself walking through a low, narrow corridor whose walls were cut out of the rock. The corridor had the shape of a box; its corners were right-angled. At the end of the corridor was a stairwell and the steps ended in a built wall.

I left, was drawn through the aperture, recounted all I had seen, and went down again. I measured the narrow corridor – it was thirty-four paces long.

When I counted the stairs, there were fifteen when I went up but sixteen when I went down. I counted them again, going up and down five times, but the results were the same. ... The riser of each step was ten inches.

I went up the stairs the sixth time and knocked on the ceiling. I received answering knocks in return, and they pulled me back. They gave me a camera and I went down again and photographed the square room, the tombstones, the corridor and the staircase. I went up again, got a pencil and paper, returned below and made sketches. I measured the room. It was six paces by five. The width of each tombstone was one pace, and the space between the tombstones was also one pace. The width of the corridor was one pace, and its height was about a metre.

I was pulled back up. On the way I dropped the torch, and so I went down for it and was drawn up again. Michal.

Although we did not find the opening we were looking for, I am sure that the chronicles of Israel will record with pride this visit of Michal, the first visit by a Jew to this site in seven hundred years.

PART TWO
FROM SLAVERY TO FREEDOM

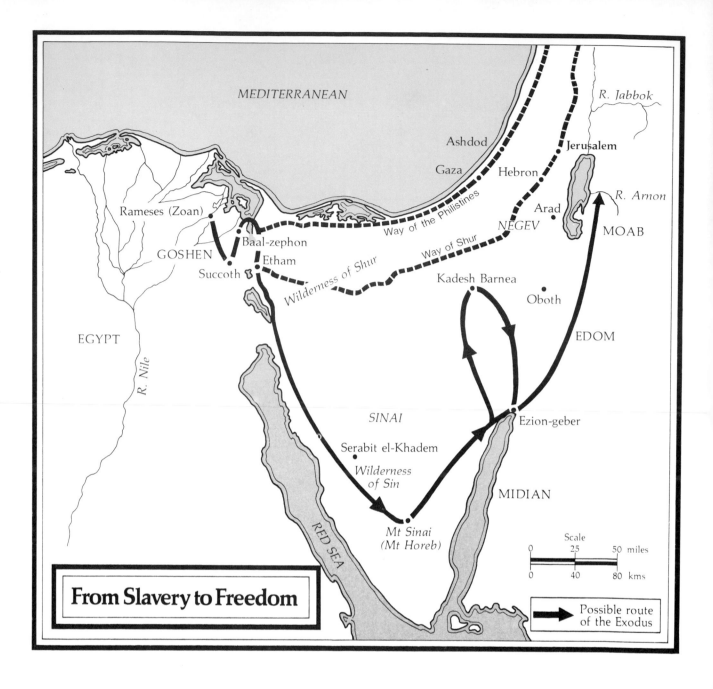

MEDITERRANEAN

R. Jabbok

Ashdod

Jerusalem

Gaza   Hebron

Way of the Philistines

R. Arnon

Rameses (Zoan)

Arad   MOAB

NEGEV

Baal-zephon

Way of Shur

GOSHEN

Etham   Wilderness of Shur

Succoth

Kadesh Barnea

Oboth

EDOM

EGYPT

R. Nile

SINAI

Ezion-geber

Serabit el-Khadem

Wilderness
of Sin

MIDIAN

Mt Sinai
(Mt Horeb)

RED SEA

Scale
0   25   50 miles
0   40   80 kms

From Slavery to Freedom

Possible route
of the Exodus

6
A prince of Egypt

OUR GENERATIONS after the sons of Jacob left Canaan for Egypt and ended up as slaves, the renewed redemption of Israel began. This time it was not a single family but an entire nation who had to free themselves from bondage, embark on a long journey, return to their homeland, and capture it from those who had settled in it – the Canaanites and the Hittites, the Amorites and the Perizzites, the Hivites and the Jebusites.

The man who led the Exodus and took the Hebrews out of slavery and into freedom was Moses, the son of Amram. Though he was a Hebrew, he was not numbered among the community of his enslaved brothers. He was brought up by the pharaoh's daughter as an Egyptian, unfettered, free. A young man, upright, fearless in spirit and strong in body, he went out to his people and witnessed their suffering. At first he sought to protect them with the power of his right arm, but he was unsuccessful. He realized that this was not the way. They had to be taken out of Egypt and brought back to their own country.

The objective of Moses was not personal, as it had been for Abraham, Isaac and Jacob. Moses was not concerned simply with leaving land and kin in Egypt and moving with his family to Canaan. His mission was to lead the nation, the entire House of Israel.

His primary task, therefore, was to gain the trust of his brethren, and to be recognized by the Hebrews as their leader, as a man whose words should be heard and heeded. In my mind I associated Moses with Herzl, Weizmann and Ben-Gurion in our own day. They were the leaders who arose before the Jewish nation in the Diaspora and called upon her sons to leave the lands in which they dwelt and 'ascend' to the land of Israel, to work it, settle it, revive it, and re-establish their independent statehood.

At first sight it would seem that Moses was launched on his path by chance. He got caught up in two quarrels. In one, he saw an Egyptian overseer striking a Hebrew slave. He rushed to the help of the Hebrew, killed the Egyptian and buried his body in the sand. The second was between two Hebrews. Moses tried to separate them, but when he asked the aggressor, 'Wherefore smitest thou thy fellow?', the response was, 'Who made thee a prince and a judge over us? Intendest thou to kill me, as thou killedst the Egyptian?' (*Exodus* 2:13, 14.)

Surprised that the deed was known and would assuredly reach the ears of the pharaoh, Moses fled to save his life and went to a strange land – as had the patriarch Jacob in his time. Like him, Moses crossed the desert, rested near a well, met

previous pages The mountains of Southern Sinai, and at their heart the 'Mount of the Lord'.

53

shepherdess maidens (daughters of Jethro), helped them water their father's flocks, eventually married one of them (Zipporah), and remained, spending the next few years tending his father-in-law's sheep.

It had been Midianite merchants who had brought Jacob's son Joseph from Canaan to Egypt. Now it was a Midianite priest, Jethro, who gave shelter to the man who was to bring the Israelites from Egypt to Canaan.

The Midianites were a desert people. They raised sheep and camels and wandered and traded between the Euphrates in the north-east and the Nile in the south-west. Their routes ran from Gilead in trans-Jordan to Zoan, the

top The Egyptian smites the Hebrew: *bottom* Moses slays the Egyptian, from the Winchester Bible, 12th century.

Egyptian capital, and from Ezion-geber in southern Israel to Upper Egypt.

Jethro dwelt in the Sinai Desert in the oasis of Paran close to the mountain route which links the Red Sea with Egypt. This track runs along a narrow winding valley which cuts through the block of tall mountains in southern Sinai. The waters from the melting snow and driving winter rains rush down the mountain slopes and sweep with them reddish sand from the granite rock. This pads the stony path, so that not only asses but also camels can tread it without slipping.

The mountain route was not the only one which ran from Arabia and Edom westwards to Egypt. Indeed, it was the least-used. The two main highways were the 'Way of Shur' and the 'Way of the Philistines'. Both ran through the flat terrain of northern Sinai; but in Moses' day they were controlled by the Egyptian army. The mountain path, however, was impassable to vehicles, and this was under the control of the camel-riding Midianites. Their dwelling places were concealed in the deep ravines and were beyond the reach of the pharaoh's troops.

In winter the Midianites pastured their flocks in the coastal belt and the valleys, lush with grass from the mountain rains. With the onset of the hot season when the sun's burning rays wither the vegetation, the Midianites would move their animals to the upper slopes. Here the high granite mountains are constantly wind-swept, and the moisture in the clefts is retained throughout the year. The acacia trees and broom shrubs that grow in the ravines and fissures of the mountainside never lose their green freshness, even in the scorching summer.

Moses, too, during his years with Jethro, moved his flocks in the search for pasture from the desert up into the mountains, and so reached the foot of Mount Horeb, 'the mountain of God'. There, 'in the midst of a bush' that 'burned with fire' yet 'was not consumed' (*Ex.* 3 : 1, 2), an angel appeared. Then came the voice of the Lord calling his name and investing him with the mission to save the children of Israel. 'I will send thee unto Pharaoh, that thou mayest bring forth my people the children of Israel out of Egypt.' Moses was also to inform the elders and the people that he had been entrusted with the divine task of liberating them from their affliction and bringing them to their land, 'a land flowing with milk and honey'. (*Ex.* 3 : 17.)

Moses hearkened to the command of the Lord and set out on his return to Egypt. Leaving his sheep, his cattle and his camels behind, he put his wife and sons on an ass and he walked at their side, taking only a shepherd's crook, 'the rod of God', in his hand.

And thus he walked, departing from the wilderness of Sinai. But Sinai could never depart from his soul – Sinai, its tall mountains soaring above all the heights of Egypt; Sinai, with its copper and its turquoise, and its granite rocks set against the white of snowy peaks; Sinai, its vast expanses spreading in all directions, with no barrier and no ruler; Sinai, the terrain of freedom, and at its heart the Mount of the Lord!

I FIRST GOT TO KNOW Sinai during the 1956 campaign when we captured it from the Egyptians. I was army chief of staff at the time, and I traversed its length

and breadth on land and in the air, discovering a new world, strange and wonderful, from the golden velvet of the sand dunes in the north to the crimson rocks and red coral at its southern tip, the Bay of Ras-Muhammed.

To me, there was no conflict between the various faiths and cultures which had left their imprint on this historic peninsula. I found nothing odd in the presence of St Catherine's Monastery, built by Justinian in the sixth century AD, under the same patch of Sinai sky as the second-millennium BC temple to the Egyptian goddess Hathor at Serabit el-Khadem, or the inscribed pleas of pilgrims and travellers on the rocks and stones of the 'Valley of the Writings' (Wadi Mukhatab). None stood in contradiction to the others. All were an expression of prayer from the human being to his maker, each in his own tongue, his own faith, his own ritual.

It was not given us to remain long in Sinai after the 1956 war. The United States and Soviet Russia joined hands to compel our withdrawal (and the withdrawal of France and Britain from the territory of Egypt proper), and after a few months I bid my adieu. I am not General MacArthur. I did not say, 'I will return.' But the Lord in heaven and some of his perverse mortals on earth brought us

The view from Mount Sinai

Dayan in Sinai at the end of the 1956 campaign.

back. Ten years after the Sinai Campaign, the Egyptians again blockaded the Gulf of Akaba, our vital waterway to Eilat. We again went to war (the 1967 Six Day War), and again captured the whole of the Sinai Peninsula, from the Mediterranean in the north to Ras-Muhammed on the Red Sea in the south; and this time we did not withdraw. More than eleven years have passed – with another war in between, the 1973 Yom Kippur War – and we still hold Sinai.

When I came to Sinai the second time, in 1967 – I was now Minister of Defence – it was without any feeling of surprise. Most of the places and the people were familiar to me. And I, apparently, was familiar to them. Almost every second Bedouin I met reminded me, hand on heart and accompanied by irrevocable oaths, how we had met in the previous war, how he had helped to extricate my vehicle when it got bogged in the sand, and had shown me exactly where the Egyptians had planted mines!

At least one of the Bedouin, however, merited thanks. When the battles were over, I wished once again to see the pharaonic temple erected for the Egyptian overseers who worked in the turquoise quarries at Serabit el-Khadem near the Gulf of Suez. I had managed a brief visit ten years earlier during the Sinai

57

Campaign. I had then gone by command car to the foot of the mount, and made the stiff climb up the steep slope to the peak. It was almost sundown by the time I reached the temple, and I was able to make only a hasty inspection of the open court surrounded by steles (upright stone slabs usually bearing inscriptions), the temple ruins, and the cave.

It was an enchanting sight. The last rays of the sun illumined the hieroglyphs cut in the steles which stood like sentinels arrayed in a semi-circle, the carved portraits of the goddess Hathor adorning the heads of the pillars, and the picturesque reliefs on the stone walls of the temple. The magic of this singular scene of antiquity and the utter stillness transported me to the time of the pharaohs. It was a wrench to leave. But night was falling, and so I picked my way down the mountainside to the vehicles waiting in the valley.

This time, just after the Six Day War, I went by helicopter. It was piloted by Mottie (Major General Mordechai Hod, who was commander of the air force). When we reached the area, we flew round the mountain tops, but could not spot the temple. There were a few other flying officers with us and they came to the help of their commander, drawing lines on maps and checking with compasses; but Serabit el-Khadem remained elusive. No sign of it. Our fuel was running low, and the only thing left to do was fall back on the old device of asking the local Bedouin to show us the way.

We spotted some black tents in one of the valleys and landed near them. An old Bedouin with white hair and wrinkled face came towards us. I offered greetings, and he responded like an old acquaintance: '*Alekum al Salaam*, my lord'.

'Do you know Serabit el-Khadem?'

'Yes, my lord.'

'Can you show us where it is?'

'Yes, my lord.'

Carrying his sandals in his hand, the old man climbed into the helicopter, showed Mottie with a wave of the hand the general direction in which to fly, and sat down.

After take-off we opened a can of bully-beef in his honour. A minute later I felt that we had made an irreparable mistake. The old Bedouin became utterly absorbed in the tin of meat, digging into it with his fingers, piling the chunks into his mouth, munching and crunching and scrabbling in the tin for more, oblivious of anything else. To questions by Mottie for further directions, he answered with quick movements of the hand, as though flicking off bothersome flies. Eventually the tin was empty, and our guide scraped the last remnants of food that still clung to the inside, licked his fingers, sighed (apparently with sorrow that the feast was over), then turned to Mottie and said, 'That's it. Go down here.'

Mottie dropped altitude, circled a few times and landed. We were in the very centre of the temple court of Serabit el-Khadem. I asked the Bedouin the name of his tribe. 'A-Tiaha,' he replied (Arabic for 'The Strayers'). I do not know when his tribe was given this nickname. But if they had ever had problems of navigation, they had assuredly overcome them.

7
Children of the desert

T O WALK from Mount Horeb in southern Sinai to the site of biblical Rameses in north-eastern Egypt takes about six days. First comes the descent from the mountains to the coastal belt, and then the northward trek along the shore of the Red Sea up to the eastern arm of the Nile delta. Here, in Lower Egypt, not far from the Mediterranean coast, stood Rameses, the pharaoh's capital. When Moses returned to Egypt with his family, they on an ass, he on foot, this is almost certainly the route he took. He would have walked by day and spent the night in one of the rest areas for desert travellers, a form of primitive caravanserai.

Such resting places where one could relax, eat and sleep, were established at the side of the main routes close to palm groves and wells. The mountain brooks in southern Sinai carry the rainwater down to the coastal belt where it is absorbed by the porous sand, and wells dug in this area give forth an abundance of sweet water. The sea, too, close to the outflow of the streams, affords excellent fishing; for the bush and scrub from the mountainside carried along in the brooks and swept into the sea attract the fish.

Long ago, ever since people began to journey through the desert, permanent settlements were established at these rest areas. There were enough guests, dates, fishing, trade and smuggling to give the inhabitants a livelihood. The pattern and traditions of centuries in these hostel-settlements have been preserved, and they remain unchanged even in war. The armies of nations may be killing each other in Sinai, but these inhabitants are left unharmed. Their guests arrive in the evening and leave in the morning, each man on his way. No one asks and no one answers. The people in these settlements do not really belong to any of the large states that stretch to their north and to their south. They belong only to the desert; they are its creatures; they are part of it.

The desert is not sand, stone and rock. These are simply strewn across its surface and serve as a covering to conceal its secrets. The true children of the desert are the Bedouin, the Midianites, the camels, ibexes and gazelles, the date palms, tamarisk and acacia trees. It is they who know its mysteries. The legs of man and animal lead them to its hidden sources of water. And the roots of the trees break through its nether depths to reach and find its hidden breast.

MOSES RETURNED to Egypt after an absence of fifty years. He had left as a young man. He was now nearing eighty, his hair white, but his heart full of fire, his

The Dorcas gazelle, indigenous to the Negev.

strength unimpaired. His enslaved brethren had been put to brick-making under the tyrant's whip for the glory of the pharaoh's cities and temples. But no roiling mud had puffed his limbs, and no smoke from fired bricks clung to his body or clogged his lungs. For half a century he had breathed the pure air of the desert. A free man, under no despot or oppressor, he had garnered courage and faith. He would now come to his brethren with the rallying cry of freedom, inspire them with a new spirit, straighten their backs bowed under a cruel bondage, and restore their hopes which had long given way to despair.

Fifty years earlier when he had fled from Egypt, they had not wished to listen to him. 'Who made thee a prince and a judge over us?' he was asked. Now they would hearken to his words, heed his behest, follow in his footsteps. They would hear that the Lord had seen their affliction and would bring them deliverance; and they would be filled with faith.

He would then bring the pharaoh to submission. He would say to him: 'Let my people go.' And if the pharaoh hardened his heart and refused, divine retribu-

60

tion would follow: disaster, plague, death. Moses would go to the king accompanied only by his brother Aaron, without servants and without guards; yet none would dare harm them. Moses was halting of speech, yet all Egypt would hear his voice. The Lord would speak through his lips.

Moses struggled with the Egyptian emperor throughout the winter, pressing his plea that the Israelites be freed. He saw him at the palace and at times he waylaid him 'by the river's brink'. (*Ex.* 7 : 15.) But the pharaoh rejected the plea, and brought down upon himself, his people and his country the curse of Providence. The Lord cursed his waters and his lands, his cattle and his crops; darkened his skies, and slew his first-born. The pharaoh finally gave in, and in the spring, on the fourteenth day of the Hebrew month of Nissan, at midnight, when the moon was full, the children of Israel were liberated from slavery.

The smiting of the first-born, the tenth plague, paralysed the pharaoh, 'and all his servants, and all the Egyptians; and there was a great cry in Egypt'. (*Ex.* 12 : 30.) They were panic-stricken, gripped with fear of the grim hand of the God of Israel. The Israelites did not tarry. They left their homes in haste and set out on their journey. With no time to prepare provisions, they packed 'their dough before it was leavened' and carried it together with their kneading-bowls bound up in their mantles on their shoulders. (*Ex.* 12 : 34.) They roused their cattle and hurried them from their corrals. The Hebrew host, men, women and children, were joined in their departure by a 'mixed multitude' (*Ex.* 12 : 38) from among the other oppressed communities in Egypt. All streamed eastwards, getting as far away as they could from the accursed kingdom, from the hated cities of Pithom and Rameses which they, the erstwhile slaves, had been forced to build.

'And the children of Israel journeyed from Rameses to Succoth' and from there they continued to 'Etham, in the edge of the wilderness'.

The Israelites were out of Egypt, but there would be one more encounter with the pharaoh and his army. The king had had a further change of heart, mobilized his chariot forces and set off in pursuit of his former slaves to return them to bondage.

The Egyptians caught up with the Israelites when they were encamped by the sea, at 'Pihahiroth ... over against Baal-zephon'. (*Ex.* 14 : 2.) Then Moses stretched out his rod over the sea and the waters parted. 'And the children of Israel went into the midst of the sea upon the dry ground; and the waters were a wall unto them on their right hand, and on their left' (*Ex.* 14 : 22), and they reached the other side safely. The Egyptians came after them, but while they were still crossing, Moses again stretched his hand over the sea, and the 'waters returned, and covered the chariots and the horsemen, and all the host of Pharaoh that came into the sea after them; there remained not so much as one of them ... and Israel saw the Egyptians dead upon the sea shore'.

Moses then led his people in song, a song of praise and exaltation to the Lord, 'a man of war' who had cast the pharaoh's chariots and his host into the water. His sister Miriam, taking timbrel in hand, led the women in dance. Miriam may not have known all the words of the song, but she knew the key phrases in the

overleaf
The Ten Plagues. From a Hebrew Haggadah with a Ladino (Judeo-Spanish) translation into Hebrew letters. (from right to left) p. 62: 1 The Nile waters turn to blood; 2 Frogs; 3 Lice; 4 Wild beasts; 5 Pestilence; 6 Boils p. 63: 7 Hail; 8 Locusts; 9 Darkness; 10 Smiting of the first-born.

דָם
סַאנגרי

לאס אגואס די אינ'פטו אין סאנגרי סי טורנארון ·
קי לוס מצריים פור אגואה ריסינטיארון :

צְפַרְדֵעַ
ראנאס

לאס ראנאס קי אין איג'פטו אוביירון · סוכרי
לאס פירסונאס סוביירון :

כִּנִּים
פִּיאוֹגוֹס

פואירון טאנטוס לוס פיאוג'וס קי לה טיירה דייו ·
קי קונפיסארון סיר מאראבילייה די איל רייו :

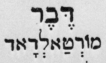

עָרוֹב
מִיסְטוּרָה

אנימאלייאס מאלאס אי סירפיינטים אי מיסטורה
קי אין איג'פטו פואי קונטרה נאטורה :

דֶּבֶר
מוֹרטַאלְדָאד

לאס בהמות די לוס מצריים מוריירון · אי לאס
די לוס ג'ודיוס טודאס ביביירון :

שְׁחִין
סַארְנָה

משה איספארזייו אה לוס סיילום פאביזה · אי
די סארנה סי אינג'יירון קון גראכיזה :

בָּרָד   אַרְבֶּה
פֵידְרִיסְקוֹ   לַאנְגוֹסְטָה

פֵירְרִיסְקוֹ אֲקוֹמְפַּאנְייָארוּ קוֹן פוֹאיגִי-קִי קִינְסוֹמְיָאה   לה לַאנְגוֹסְטָה פּוֹאי אִין טַאנְטָה קַאנְטִידָאר · קִי
לוֹס מִצְרַיִים לוֹאינוּ :   קַאבְזוֹ גְרַאנְדִי אִיקְקוֹרִירַאר :

חֹשֶׁךְ   מַכַּת בְּכוֹרוֹת
אֵיסְקוּרִידָאר   פֵירִידָה דֵי מַאיוֹרֵיש

טְרֵיס רֵיאָם דִי טִינְייְבְלָה אִי אִיסְקוּרִירַאר · אִי   פּוֹר לוֹס פְּרִימוֹג׳יניטוֹס טוֹדוֹס לֵייוֹרַאבַּאן · קִי
לוֹס ג׳וּדְייוֹס קוֹן גְרַאן קְלַארִירַאר :   מוֹאִירְמוֹה לה מַאנְייָאנָה לוֹס אֵלְייַאבְּאן :

רִבִּי יְהוּדָה הָיָה נוֹתֵן בָּהֶם סִימָנִים · דְּצַ״ךְ · עֲדַ״שׁ · בְּאַחַ״ב :

רבי

רכי   רִבִּי יְהוּדָה אֵירָה בָּאן אִין אֵילְייָאש שֵׁינְייָאלֵישׁ · דְּצַ״ךְ · עֲדַ״שׁ · בְּאַחַ״ב :

רכי

opening verse; and as the men sang and the women danced, Miriam lifted her voice in response: 'Sing ye to the Lord, for he hath triumphed gloriously; the horse and his rider hath he thrown into the sea.' (*Ex.* 15:21.) If an easterly wind were blowing that day, the voices of the singers would have been heard on the Nile.

The crossing of the Red Sea. A fresco from the French church of St Sauvin sur Gartempe, 10th–11th century.

NOT UNTIL 3,300 years later did the children of Israel return to Goshen. During the 1973 Yom Kippur War, an Israel army force crossed the Suez Canal and captured the territory between Ismailia and the Gulf of Suez. The troops called it Goshen. I tried to convince them that biblical Goshen lay somewhere further to the north, in the swamps of the delta, a district referred to by the local inhabitants as al-Tina (Arabic for swamp). But my explanations were of little avail. They listened to me with deep interest – but the name remained.

The first to reach 'Goshen' were the paratroops. On 16 October, at 1.20 a.m., I received a signal: 'Danny's force is in the water.' (Brigadier General Danny Matt was commander of this paratroop brigade.) In the thousands-of-years interim, the methods of crossing had changed. Instead of parting the waters with the aid of a divine rod, we put into service rubber boats, rafts, and pontoon bridges. Only names remained from the distant past. Our motorized rafts were called *timsachim* (Hebrew for crocodiles).

The new Goshen bore no signs of the riches and greatness it boasted in the days of Pharaoh Rameses II. Miserably poor peasants were living in wretched shacks; rank water trickled slowly along the irrigation ditches; and the cattle grazing at the sides of the roads looked as if they had come out of the pharaoh's dream of the seven gaunt cows, 'poor and very ill-favoured and lean-fleshed'.

The relations prevailing in our own generation between Israel and Egypt remind me somewhat of pharaonic times. It took four wars, resulting in four Egyptian defeats, to get the leaders of Cairo to agree to a Geneva peace conference with Israel.

In the 1967 Six Day War, although Egypt lost her finest army formations and the whole of Sinai, she refused to recognize her defeat. Her president, Gamal Abdul Nasser, replied to Israel's offer of peace with: 'no recognition of Israel, no negotiations with Israel, no peace with Israel.' General Zacharov, commander of the armed forces of the USSR, Egypt's ally, promised Nasser that he would teach the Egyptian army how to fight and conquer Israel. Nasser relied on this and promptly began to prepare for the next war. In the meantime, both he and Zacharov passed from this world, and it was the new Egyptian president, Anwar Sadat, who launched the next war. In this one, too, the Yom Kippur War, Egypt was defeated, and it ended with Israel's forces being closer to Cairo than in the previous wars. Sadat learned something from that. He nullified his alliance with Russia, sought closer relations with the United States, and announced that he favoured peace. Perhaps this time there really will be an end to Egyptian-Israeli armed conflict. Perhaps this time Egypt's rulers will not undergo a change of heart, as they did in the biblical past, and will not again rush into battle against Israel.

If peace is ever attained between the two countries, we shall almost certainly have to give up most of Sinai. If this happens in my lifetime, I shall welcome the peace but regret the farewell to Sinai. There, in a bygone age, our forefathers found freedom. In our own day it gave us the feeling of space. Israel is a wonderful country, but it is small. Whenever I travel westwards from El Arish and southwards from Eilat, I feel as if I were given wings, as though I were lifted from the enclosing walls of built-up cities and the strangling network of asphalt and carried off to a free, wide and open expanse without barrier. This sense of limitless distance in Sinai is true not only of space but also of time. The passage of thousands of years has not erased the traces of the ancient past. Some may have been covered by sand, but they have not been lost or obliterated, and frequently brought to

In their hasty exodus, the Israelites 'baked unleavened cakes of the dough which they brought forth out of Egypt'. This is commemorated by Jews in the Passover Festival by eating *matza*, which is unleavened bread. Bedouin in Sinai bake a similar kind of flat bread in the ancient way.

light are the remains of antiquity – fortresses, turquoise quarries and copper mines in the clefts of a mountainside, inscriptions and drawings on rock and stone at the side of an ancient by-way.

When I first visited the area of the quarries and mines in the Wadi Maghara, I was aided by *Researches in Sinai* written by Sir Flinders Petrie, the archaeologist and Egyptologist who discovered the temple to Hathor at Serabit el-Khadem. His book was published in 1906, but I had no later material at hand. From Petrie I learned that most of the rock-inscriptions and reliefs carved above the entrance to the mines had been sliced away and removed to the Cairo Museum. I therefore expected to find none on my visit. However, my Bedouin guide, Abu Yusuf, told me there were still two at the top of the mountain. It was early, so I decided to climb up and see.

I cannot claim that it was an effortless ascent without huff or puff. But I did get there, and was rewarded by the sight of inscriptions and reliefs. They were stylized representations of an Egyptian king wearing the crown of Upper and Lower Egypt in the symbolic act of forcing the submission of a local ruler – by striking his head with a cudgel.

I offered silent thanks to Petrie for having left them there. In a museum, they would just be part of a collection of ancient artefacts. Here they were reality itself – not mute witness of what had happened but the events themselves, with the seal of the pharaoh marking his control of the quarries and mines and the access highways. The inscriptions and pictorial reliefs were not a description of the battle for control but a mark of the battle itself, or rather the highpoint of the battle – victory.

The name of the Egyptian emperor was carved on the stone: Sekhemkhet. The local chieftain he subdued, kneeling in surrender, was an unnamed nomad. All my sympathies were with him. In the struggle between the Egyptian rulers and the nomads of Sinai, I belong to the descendants of the nomads. True, the drawings and inscriptions ante-date even the period of the Hebrew patriarchs – they are more than 4,600 years old. But the heart sets no boundaries round time.

Myself, I do not believe in the accuracy of this rock carving: I think the portrayal is an example of pharaonic boastfulness. I do not believe the local nomad was subdued. I do not dispute that the kings of Egypt did indeed conquer this place and brought in slaves to quarry precious stones and mine copper; but I do not think they either defeated or captured the local nomadic chiefs. These almost certainly escaped to the mountains. At the first glimpse of the imperial troops, they would have folded their tents, harnessed their camels and driven their herds eastwards, to the valleys between the granite mountains. The Egyptians, like all the foreign conquerors, eventually abandoned this region and returned to their own land, to the land of the Nile and their irrigated fields, leaving behind only inscriptions and drawings carved out of the rock. The nomads would then have returned to Wadi Maghara, re-opened the blocked wells and set up their tents anew. It was these camel-riding, sheep-rearing nomads who were the victors, winners of the last battle, and the true rulers of the desert.

A common scene in the Negev today

In the vicinity of the Sekhemkhet inscription were heaps of huge rocks and boulders which had slid down the steep mountainside. Abu Yusuf told me that beneath the stones was the hidden entrance to a cave. An old Bedouin woman from his tribe related that when she was a little girl, she was tending her father's flocks in this very place when suddenly one of the young goats disappeared between the rocks. She had gone to recover it and found it standing near the opening to a cave. She had ventured inside and found it filled with sculptures and tall stone slabs with carvings of humans and animals.

This was not the first story I had heard from Arabs of wondrous and mysterious caves; but I believed this one. There could well have been an Egyptian temple or tomb in one of the caves in these parts, the entrance to which had been sealed and covered by a landslide. So we stayed on for a while looking for it. We crawled about on the rocks and moved heavy boulders in the hope of discerning some sign of the hidden entrance. But we found nothing. However, my faith remained – and remains – unshaken. I am convinced that the old woman spoke the truth. Such a cave exists. And it will yet be discovered.

8
The widow and the well

AFTER BEING SAVED from Egyptian pursuit by the closing of the parted waters, Moses and the children of Israel continued their trek eastwards, making for the wilderness of Shur which was to be their first staging area. They had eluded the pharaoh's army; but this was not the end of their troubles. These were just beginning.

For three days they journeyed in the desert without water; and when they finally reached some wells, the water was bitter. The people complained. Moses threw a tree into the waters and they became sweet. Their thirst quenched, the people then faced hunger, and again they complained. They recalled their 'good days' in Egypt and cried out to Moses: 'Would to God we had died by the hand of the Lord in the land of Egypt, when we sat by the flesh pots, and when we did eat bread to the full; for ye have brought us forth into this wilderness to kill this whole assembly with hunger.' (*Ex.* 16:2.)

In the desert, as in Egypt, the Lord heard their cries of affliction and came to their help. He gave them 'bread from heaven' in the morning, and meat in the evening. In the morning, 'when the dew that lay was gone up, behold, upon the face of the wilderness there lay' a fine, flake-like thing, 'as small as hoar frost on the ground. . . . And the house of Israel called the name thereof Manna: and it was like coriander seed, white; and the taste of it was like wafers made with honey.' (*Ex.* 16:14, 31.) At the closing of the day, the people were given the flesh of birds: 'quail came up, and covered the camp.'

I do not know what exactly was manna, the 'bread from heaven' which our forefathers ate in the wilderness. Nor is the meaning at all clear of 'it was like coriander seed, white'. It was probably some kind of berry. And it must have had an attractive taste, for whatever is meant by 'wafers made with honey', it was assuredly not bitter.

Quails, on the other hand, are not unfamiliar to me. I came across them frequently in northern Sinai. With the coming of autumn, birds of the northern countries migrate south and the quails embark on their expedition. From central Europe they fly to Turkey, where they gird themselves for a mighty effort: crossing the Mediterranean in a single night. It is a flight of crushing fatigue. Not only do they have to cover a great distance, but they must also maintain a high speed – fifty miles an hour. Any bird that lags ends up in the sea. At first light, the quails are already approaching the coast; and when they suddenly spot the patches of green – the palm groves – they lose altitude, but do not reduce speed. From

The Israelites receive manna from heaven.
From a medieval manuscript illustration.

a height of two yards above the waves, they continue their flight like flashing darts. Only when they reach the coast do they land, exhausted, drained, with just enough strength to make for the shrubs. There, under cover, and in the shade, drawing in the warmth of the sands and the soft rays of the autumn sun, and caressed by the light sea breeze, unmoving, their wings folded, eyes closed, every muscle and sinew relaxed, they give themselves over to total rest. Within hours, they regain their strength and vigour – if only given the chance.

The Bedouin who dwell near the coast used to await the arrival of the quails with eager joy (until the Israel government prohibited quail-trapping). They put up fences of fish-netting all along the shore, and the fatigued quails, hastening to reach dry land, flew into the nets and were trapped before their feet touched the ground. The nets were placed a few hundred yards from the water's edge. If they were put any closer they got ripped by the powerful impact of the fast-flying birds, and so the trap was set only when the quails reduced their speed before landing. Two, three and even four sets of netting were put up, one behind the other to ensure a maximum haul, so that birds escaping one trap would be caught by the next. In the past, when the coastal region had only a sparse population, the landing grounds of the quails stretched all the way from Jaffa on the coast of Israel right down to Alexandria in Egypt. Over the generations, the trappers got the better of their victims and almost wiped them out. Now only a few flights remain, and they seek sanctuary in the central stretch of northern Sinai, between El Arish and Romani, the portion of the coast that is still relatively free of settlement – or at least so it appears from above through the ingenuous eyes of the luckless quail.

EVEN WHEN Moses was not having to cope with the awesome problems of hunger and thirst, he had little rest. He was available to the people at all times. They stood about Moses 'from the morning unto the evening', coming to him 'to enquire of God' and to settle disputes 'between one and another'.

When his father-in-law Jethro visited him and saw how much Moses was taking upon himself, he gave him the following counsel: 'The thing that thou doest is not good. Thou wilt surely wear away, both thou, and this people that is with thee; for this thing is too heavy for thee; thou art not able to perform it thyself alone.' He advised Moses to choose able and trustworthy officials and to place such men over the people 'to be rulers of thousands ... of hundreds ... of fifties, and ... of tens. And let them judge the people at all seasons ... every great matter they shall bring unto thee, but every small matter they shall judge: so shall it be easier for thyself, and they shall bear the burden with thee.' (*Ex.* 18 : 17–22.)

THE CONGREGATION of Israel journeyed to Rephidim in the wilderness of Sin, and there they faced a new trial – battle. They were attacked by the Amalekites. It was the Israelites' first military encounter. Up to then, they did not even have an army. Moses called on Joshua, the son of Nun, to select able-bodied men from among the people and go out and fight the attackers.

The Amalekites were camel-riding desert nomads, highly mobile, and the Israelites had to exert their full strength to defeat them. Moses went to the top of the hill which overlooked the battlefield with 'the rod of God' in his hand, the rod which performed wonders. Whenever 'Moses held up his hand . . . Israel prevailed; and when he let down his hand, Amalek prevailed.' But Moses was no longer young and his arms grew weary. So Aaron and Hur, who were with him, 'took a stone, and put it under him, and he sat thereon'; and they themselves supported his arms, one on either side. So Moses' 'hands were steady until the going down of the sun. And Joshua discomfited Amalek and his people with the edge of the sword.'

The Amalekites attacked the Israelites who had reached Rephidim from Egypt because they sought to safeguard their control of the water wells, the groves of date palms, and the grazing grounds in the valleys. The Amalekites were the descendants of Esau, who had settled in mountainous Edom, south of the Dead Sea. From there, they had pressed westwards and southwards with their camels and their herds and had spread across the entire face of the Sinai Peninsula, from the Negev of Canaan right down to the Red Sea. Swiftness of movement was their distinctive characteristic in raid or battle. Their fighting men were trained from youth to wield a bow and hurl a javelin from the back of a galloping camel.

As the source of life to the desert dweller, the well is understandably associated with notable episodes in the biblical account of early Israel. Abraham forged a covenant with King Abimelech over wells, and wells were the cause of Isaac's contention with the local shepherds. Jacob met his future wife at a well, and wells were the sites of Moses' miracles. Now it was over wells that the Amalekites battled with the Israelites.

The wells in Sinai have not lost their importance. I had a friend among the Bedouin of northern Sinai, Sheikh Abu-Ali, who to me was truly representative of the desert way of life. With the prosperity brought by the Israelis after their conquest of Sinai, the sheikh moved his tribe and tents and settled in the vicinity of El Arish. He was close to the market, where his sheep, salty goat's cheese, and the labour of his camels fetched good prices. He was well over seventy – he himself did not know his precise age – and had evidently been tall and strong as a young man. He was now frail and all that was left of the earlier man were his stature and his dignity.

When we first met, he had with him his young wife, who had just given birth to the 'child of his old age', Ibrahim. He already had three married sons from previous wives, and they ran their own independent households. Members of the tribe told me that the sheikh was very wealthy in livestock and palm-groves.

I was informed one day that the sheikh had died after a brief illness, and I went to pay my respects to the mourning family. I thought this would be my last contact with them. But not long thereafter, a frightened young Bedouin woman with a child in her arms appeared at the office of our military governor of northern Sinai seeking refuge. It was the sheikh's young widow and the infant Ibrahim. She said the sheikh's grown-up sons were out to kill her.

As in patriarchal times, a Bedouin woman draws water from a primitive well in Sinai.

It transpired that shortly before his death, the old sheikh had come to write his will, but by then most of his property had already been distributed among his married sons. Little was left for his young wife and child. She had then consulted with her family and they advised her to ask her husband to bequeath the water wells to her and her son. The sheikh had agreed, and the will was duly notarized. After his death, the family of the widow had promptly established control over the wells, which until then had provided water for the sheep, camels and plantations belonging to her stepsons, and for their families. All now had to come to the young widow and drink from her cupped palm – or give her and her son a portion of the inheritance.

Some time later I asked our military governor whether there was any news of his ward, the mother of Ibrahim. 'Whenever she comes to visit me', he said, 'she is full of complaints. But her eyes sparkle with joy. After all, she has the wells!' Victory was assured.

9

The law-giver

THE GREATNESS of Moses lies not only in his qualities as liberator of the children of Israel from Egyptian bondage, and as their leader throughout the journeyings in the wilderness, but above all as law-giver. It was through him that the *Torah* (the Pentateuch, the first five Books of the Old Testament) was given to the nation of Israel, with the Ten Commandments as its foundation pillars. 'And Moses came and called for the elders of the people, and laid before their faces all these words which the Lord commanded him. And all the people answered together, and said, "All that the Lord hath spoken we will do."' (*Ex.* 19:7, 8.)

Moses spent forty days and forty nights on the top of Mount Sinai receiving the *Torah* and all the ordinances, as well as instructions on such matters as the fashioning of the Tabernacle and details of ritual worship. All this time the Israelites waited below, their patience wearing thin as day followed day without the return of their leader. They had no notion of what had happened to him, and they finally gave up hope of his reappearance. They thereupon 'gathered themselves together unto Aaron, and said unto him "Up, make us gods, which shall go before us; as for this Moses, the man who brought us up out of the land of Egypt, we wot not what is become of him."'

Aaron responded to their plea, took 'the golden earrings which are in the ears of your wives, of your sons, and of your daughters ... and made it a molten calf'. (*Ex.* 32:2–4.)

Moses eventually came down the mountainside, saw the people dancing round the golden calf, and angrily flung the *Torah* tablets from his hands so that they broke. He then ground the golden calf to powder, and set about restoring the law among the unruly people. Standing 'in the gate of the camp', he cried out: 'Who is on the Lord's side? let him come unto me. And all the sons of Levi gathered themselves together unto him.' Moses then ordered them to slay the sinners. They did so, 'and there fell of the people that day about three thousand men'. (*Ex.* 32:26, 28.) There was a further punishment from the Lord – plague.

After this episode, Moses returned to Mount Sinai with two new tablets of stone for another forty days and forty nights, and came back to his people bringing them all 'the words that were in the first tables' inscribed anew on the fresh ones. And as he came down the mountainside 'with the two tables of testimony' in his hand, watched by 'Aaron and all the children of Israel ... behold, the skin of his face shone'.

top Moses receives the Tablets of the Law on Mount Sinai.
bottom He expounds the Law to the Israelites.
From a 9th-century Carolingian manuscript.

TO ME, DAVID BEN-GURION was the Moses of our time, which witnessed the resurgence of the nation of Israel and its restoration to its land. Like Moses, Ben-Gurion set the people of Israel a dual objective: to return to their homeland; and to be 'a moral nation'.

Like Moses, Ben-Gurion was a unique figure: he towered above his fellow men, was possessed of far-sighted vision, and stuck unswervingly to his course. He, too, gave himself over completely to his people without ever giving in to them. He never yielded to their weaknesses, never compromised over his principles. 'I do not know what the nation wants,' he once told me, 'but I believe I do know what is desirable for it.' Ben-Gurion's rule, like that of Moses, was marked by clashes with his people. They recognized his outstanding leadership, admired him greatly, accepted his injunctions and the goals he had set them with a 'we will do'; but they also 'grumbled' and 'murmured', flung at him a 'Who made thee a prince and a judge over us?', and turned to the golden calf.

I had met Ben-Gurion in my youth, but we became particularly close after my appointment by him as Chief of Staff of the Israel defence forces in 1952. He was then Prime Minister and Minister of Defence, and my activities under his direction went beyond purely military bounds. The infant State of Israel at that time had just taken its first steps, and heading Ben-Gurion's major concerns were two projects he considered of supreme urgency.

One was mass immigration. Hundreds of thousands of Jews, mostly from Islamic countries – North Africa, Yemen, Iraq, Syria, and Lebanon – were anxious to come to Israel. We had to help them leave their countries of oppression, bring them to our country, and welcome, rehabilitate and establish them when they arrived, affording them work and housing.

Ben-Gurion's second concern was land settlement, particularly of the desolate areas. There was the extensive Negev desert, which had not been settled; and there were numerous Arab villages in the centre and south of the country which lay empty. They had been abandoned by their occupants, totalling several hundred thousand, during the 1948 War of Independence. Their mud shacks had collapsed, water wells were blocked or destroyed, fields were covered with thorn and bramble. Figs and grapes which had ripened had not been picked, and swarms of hornets had spread through the orchards. 'If we do not prevail over the devastation', said Ben-Gurion, 'the devastion will prevail over us.'

Ben-Gurion did not think that the way to get the nation to do what was required of it lay solely through the exercise of governmental authority. The government could take decisions. But that was not enough. It was up to the people, especially the young, to apply themselves voluntarily to fulfilling the needs of the nation. The War of Independence was over, and the youth of the country should now leave their homes in towns, and even in veteran moshavim and kibbutzim, and establish settlements in the Negev, in areas abandoned by the Arabs, and on State lands elsewhere in the country.

On 10 June 1954 Ben-Gurion addressed a special gathering of some eight thousand upper-grade high school pupils from all over the country who assembled

Dayan with David Ben-Gurion in 1972.

in the open air amphitheatre of Sheikh Muneis in northern Tel Aviv. He explained to them the supreme national importance of settling the Negev Desert and underlined the political and military dangers facing Israel if the Negev and other empty spaces were not settled quickly. Established settlement was the answer to terrorist raids organized by the neighbouring Arab States; to the demands of Arab refugees to return to the villages they had forsaken; and also to mounting political pressures from international powers to give up territory we had captured in the War of Independence. Issuing his call to the young people gathered before him, he told them they had to choose between dedication and opportunism, between a life of mission and one of personal advancement, between devotion to national aims and the pursuit of private gain.

He ended his speech with this appeal, his voice charged with emotion: 'If our young people declare, "Yea, we will go up," Jewish history will respond: "You can – and you will – succeed."'

Jewish history was silent that day. The high school pupils remained unmoved. There was no rush to volunteer for national tasks. Indeed, many of them seemed to pay little attention to the Prime Minister's words. It was heartbreaking to watch Ben-Gurion, white mane fluttering in the breeze, eyes flashing, trying to

78

The village hall at Nahalal.

enthuse his listeners with the glow of his vision, while the boys and girls sat largely indifferent, chattering and joking among themselves, glancing at their watches, wondering when it would end and they could all go home.

The next day Ben-Gurion went to another gathering called for the same purpose. This time it was a conference of members belonging to moshavim, and it was held at my village, Nahalal. Ben-Gurion's mood was understandably low after the Sheikh Muneis assembly. He had also fallen sick, and was in fact under treatment at the Tel Hashomer hospital, but insisted on leaving. I went to see him and urged him to rest and not go to Nahalal. I myself would be attending the conference and I assured him that I would do my best to persuade the young members of the veteran moshavim to go down to the Negev. But Ben-Gurion would not hear of staying away. 'For such a purpose', he said, 'I am quite well.' He was very worried by the thought that the moshav members, too, might prove disappointing. He left his hospital bed and travelled north.

The Nahalal conference was held in the village hall, spacious enough but sombre, its walls unplastered concrete, the seating hard wooden benches. Ben-Gurion mounted the platform leaning heavily on a cane. His introduction was short and pertinent. A number of new villages had been established in the Negev, settled by new immigrants mostly from North Africa. They knew nothing of farming, and being new in the country were unfamiliar with defence matters. The sons of the moshav, experienced farmers and trained soldiers, should therefore leave their well-developed and by now flourishing farm-villages in the Valley of Jezreel and the Sharon plain, and move to the new moshavim. There they could guide and instruct the new immigrants in farming, in handling the administration of the village, and in defending it from attack by Arab saboteurs. The young women of the veteran moshav should also go out to the new immigrant villages as teachers in the local schools and nurses in the rural clinics.

The weekend conference lasted two days, and Ben-Gurion sat through it all, listening intently to the participants in the discussion, young and old. At times, however, he seemed to isolate himself from what was going on and sink into private thought, eyebrows contracted, forehead creased, chin jutting, lips firmly pressed together. I could not fathom the secret of his reflections, but his expression denoted an iron adherence to his decision. He knew what he wanted and was certain of his course.

This conference was unlike the gathering at Sheikh Muneis. Despite the burdens of running the farms at Nahalal, Kfar Vitkin and others, the sons of the moshavim decided to go down to the Negev to help the new immigrants. Many announced that they would sell the cows and chickens, which needed a good deal of attention, to make it easier for their parents to manage the farms without the children's help. The moshav members were joined by several young members of kibbutzim. At first sixty went to the Negev and soon the number grew to two hundred and ninety.

The conference concluded with Ben-Gurion again at the rostrum. He had discarded his walking-stick and appeared to have recovered. He spoke quietly, but his delivery was emphatic and incisive, each phrase a hammer blow on stone. The communal hall was crowded, for during the day, the Sabbath, young men and women had flocked to Nahalal from many parts of the land, drawn by news of the volunteering response. Lightning charged the air. All eyes were clamped on the speaker. No one moved. There was not a rustle in the room. Then came Ben-Gurion's closing words, uttered from the depth of his soul: 'Verily, the presence of God resides here.'

ONE OF THE MOSHAV VOLUNTEERS who left for the Negev was Varda Freedman, a girl from Kfar Vitkin in the Sharon plain. She went as a youth guide to the new immigrant village of Patish between Gaza and Beersheba. A few months after her arrival she organized a festive celebration. The occasion was the marriage of a young immigrant, and Varda had suggested to his family and the village council to mark the happy event with communal rejoicing. 'Everyone needs it,' she said. 'We should all get away occasionally from the humdrum, day-to-day routine, and fill the village square with light and song and dance and gaiety.' All agreed, and the celebration took place on a Sabbath eve early in March 1955.

At the height of the festivities, a band of Arab terrorists who had infiltrated

Bedouin tents in the desert.

from the Gaza Strip broke into Patish and attacked the celebrants. (At that time, a year and a half before the Sinai Campaign, Gaza was still under Egyptian control.) The saboteurs opened up with machine-gun fire and flung grenades into the midst of the wedding party. Twenty-three persons were hit. Twenty-two of them, villagers from Patish, received bullet and grenade wounds. One was killed – Varda Freedman. The wounded eventually recovered and returned from hospital to their homes in Patish. Varda was brought for burial to Kfar Vitkin, the village where she was born.

Ben-Gurion summoned me to an urgent meeting on the military implications of the attack. He thought we should drive the Egyptians out of the Gaza Strip. This meant capturing the Strip and putting it under Israeli control.

His words surprised me. We had often discussed the problem of Gaza, and Ben-Gurion had consistently taken the firm position that despite the acts of sabotage carried out by the *fedayun* from the Gaza Strip, the operational base for Egyptian-directed terror raids, Israel should not seize this territory. It held some three hundred thousand hostile Palestinian refugees, and Israel could do without them. It was better for us if the Strip and its inhabitants remained outside the borders of Israel.

Ben-Gurion had now changed his mind. He explained that all the earlier considerations were still valid, but against them we had to set the human reality: the danger to the Jewish immigrants who had come to redeem the Negev, and to the young veterans who had left their established settlements in order to help the newcomers. We had also to remember that the re-born State of Israel was still in its infancy. Whatever the implications for the distant future, what now had to be done was to give protection to the young villages, help their inhabitants to strike roots, and inspire them with confidence and faith in our strength. We had to get the Egyptians out of Gaza so that the immigrants could build their new homes without harassment.

The government did not endorse Ben-Gurion's proposal. (During part of that year, 1955, the Prime Minister was Moshe Sharett and Ben-Gurion was Defence Minister.) I, too, was opposed to it – I for military reasons, members of the government for political reasons. Each considered the problem from the point of view of his public function. Ben-Gurion, deliberately, ignored all these external considerations. His heart was wholly with the new immigrants who had come to the Negev desert and were beginning to make it bloom. He was their spokesman, leader of the nation, the Moses of our times.

IN THE CENTURIES since the Roman period, there has been wide acceptance of the tradition, particularly in the Christian world, that Jebel Mussa (the Mountain of Moses) is the biblical Mount Sinai. At its foot stands the sixth-century St Catherine's Monastery, which has attracted pilgrims throughout the ages. Merchant caravans and passing travellers would also stop there to offer prayer.

Mount Sinai can be reached from two directions: from the east, along the mountain track from Dahab on the Gulf of Eilat; and from the west, by the route that

The mountains of Southern Sinai, the awesome landscape encountered by the Israelites on their Exodus trek.

starts at Abu Rodeis on the Gulf of Suez. The western route passes through Wadi
Firan, which holds the largest desert oasis in the peninsula, the Oasis of Firan.
It is blessed with an abundance of water, thousands of date palms, and large
stretches of lush green. This was therefore the principal route to Mount Sinai.

The north-western entrance to Wadi Firan is approached through Wadi Mukhatab. Thousands of drawings and writings are inscribed on rock and stone along
both banks of this 'Valley of the Writings'. The inscriptions are mostly in the
Nabatean language and belong to the first and second centuries AD; the later ones
are in Greek, Latin and Arabic. The drawings are primitive representations of
camels, asses and ibexes, as well as human figures. Most of the writings also follow
a standard pattern. They bear the name of the writer and his supplication to be
remembered with favour by the powers above.

Scholarly researchers engaged in deciphering these writings have been dis-
appointed. There were no world-shattering discoveries. I am no researcher, and
my own efforts to read some of the inscriptions have not proved very rewarding.
Nevertheless I am greatly drawn to them, for I see in them the people who wrote
them, simple folk – shepherds, pilgrims, traders, and the mercenaries who escorted
the caravans. During the rest intervals, when the wayfarer group would stop to

Wadi Firan, the desert oasis on the main approach route to
Mount Sinai, is evergreen with palm trees (*opposite*).
above The filigree pattern of palm roots.

refresh themselves, one of them would wander off alone to entreat the protection of the All-High. If he were a young man, he would remove his sandals and climb to a tall rock that dominated the route. Older travellers would make do with a stone closer to the caravan track. The route was long and dangerous, and much privation and misfortune at the hand of man and nature threatened the traveller. It was natural, therefore, to wish to offer a prayer, to scratch upon the Nubian sandstone a blessed plea, each in his own tongue, each to his own god, and seek his mercy and his aid to so-and-so, the son of so-and-so, 'who should be remembered with favour'.

The rock drawings of animals served a similar purpose. They were intended as propitiatory symbols to protect the supplicant from evil – rather like the talisman worn round the neck, or amulet ring on the finger. Whoever journeyed in the wilderness needed the mercy of heaven.

A large stone bearing Nabatean inscriptions lies in the garden of my home in Zahala. It comes from the area of the Valley of the Writings. It was brought to me some time after I left the Ministry of Defence by a young man who worked on road construction in Sinai. He told me he noticed the stone when the heavy bulldozers were gouging out a path through the mountains and had thrust the rocks to the side. 'I immediately saw,' said the young man, 'that here was an Egyptian [*sic*] inscription, and I decided to bring it to you as I was driving my truck home to Herzlia' [a few miles from Zahala].

I thanked him warmly, and agreed to his request not to mention his name so as not to get him into trouble with his employer. He said that the contractor 'doesn't like us to meddle with such things. If we come across antiquities we are to bury or hide or destroy them, for otherwise government officials come out and stop all work and it upsets all our plans.'

We hoisted the stone from the truck, drank coffee, and just before he left I asked him discreetly, so as not to insult him, why he thought the inscription was Egyptian? 'Can't you see it's hieroglyphic writing?' he said. 'It's all over the place, no top and bottom. Hieroglyphic, one hundred per cent!' I did not have the heart to correct him.

I cannot visit Sinai every day, but I can get a daily glimpse of the inscribed Nubian sandstone from Sinai by looking through my window. In winter it absorbs the rain and turns dark. In summer its colour is bright and its sand grains sparkle in the sun. The inscribed scrawls and rough drawings which score its surface by no means mar its appearance. Both they and the stone are an integral part of Sinai.

The stone from Sinai with Nabatean inscriptions, now in Dayan's garden at Zahala.

PART THREE
THE PROMISED LAND

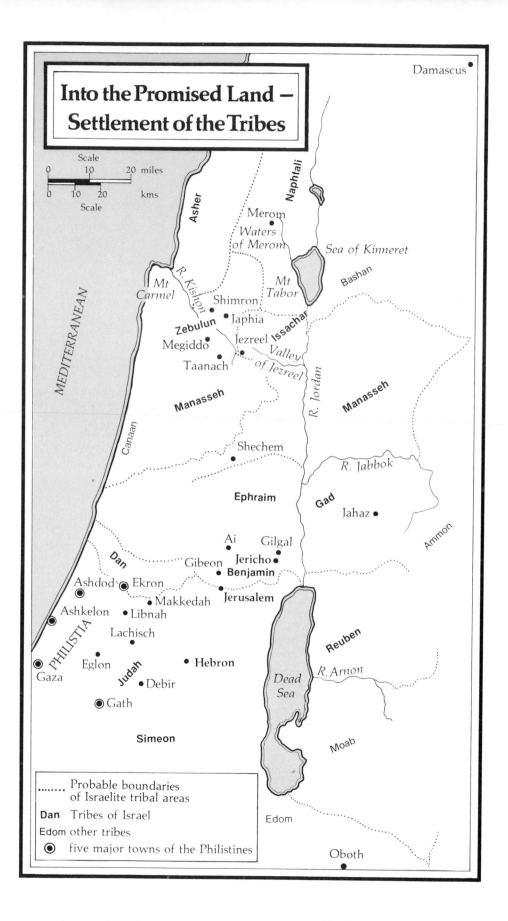

Into the Promised Land – Settlement of the Tribes

Scale
0 10 20 miles
0 10 20 kms
Scale

Damascus

MEDITERRANEAN

Asher

Naphtali

Merom

Waters of Merom

Sea of Kinneret

Bashan

Mt Carmel

R. Kishon

Shimron

Mt Tabor

Zebulun

Japhia

Jezreel

Issachar

Valley of Jezreel

Megiddo

Taanach

Manasseh

Manasseh

R. Jordan

Canaan

Shechem

R. Jabbok

Ephraim

Gad

Jahaz

Ammon

Ai

Gilgal

Gibeon

Jericho

Benjamin

Dan

Ashdod

Ekron

Makkedah

Jerusalem

Ashkelon

Libnah

Lachisch

Reuben

R. Arnon

PHILISTIA

Eglon

Judah

Hebron

Dead Sea

Gaza

Debir

Gath

Moab

Simeon

Edom

Oboth

10
Sword and ploughshare

THE TIME HAD COME to go up and take possession of the land of Canaan. The children of Israel had wandered in Sinai for forty years, and a new generation had arisen, born free in the desert, who had known no bondage. Their backs had not been bent under harsh slave labour, nor their spirits bowed by the humiliating whip of a taskmaster. These Hebrews who now sojourned in Kadesh Barnea were not the Hebrews who had dwelt in Goshen. Oppressive Egypt had been left far behind. They were now at the eastern end of Sinai, at the edge of the Negev, and they could already glimpse the land of the patriarchs, the land of their fathers Abraham, Isaac and Jacob.

The men selected by Moses 'to spy out' (*Numbers* 13:17) this land were twelve 'heads of the children of Israel', each a leader of his tribe. Their mission was not only to explore the Canaanite cities and discover whether the inhabitants were strong or weak, few or many, their prime purpose was to get to know all that could be known about the land which the Lord had given to the children of Israel, 'whether it be good or bad ... fat or lean, whether there be wood therein, or not. And be ye of good courage,' Moses told them, 'and bring of the fruit of the land.' (*Num.* 13:19, 20.)

And, indeed, the twelve returned bringing with them pomegranates and figs, and a huge cluster of grapes which hung from a pole carried by two men. It had been cut down at the banks of a brook near Hebron. The 'land whither thou sent us', they told Moses, 'floweth with milk and honey; and this is the fruit of it.' (*Num.* 13:27.)

After their years in parched and arid Sinai, the Israelites longed for a green and pleasant land, whose skies poured forth rain and whose fields yielded wheat and barley, a land of vineyards, fig trees and pomegranates. It was, as the twelve had said, a land of milk and honey; but they had been smitten by fear of the local peoples, the Amalekites, Hittites, Jebusites, Amorites, Canaanites, and above all by 'the giants' they had seen in Hebron, 'the sons of Anak'. (Anak is Hebrew for giant.) Moreover, their cities were fortified 'and very great'.

Only two of the twelve representatives remained uncowed. They were Joshua the son of Nun and Caleb the son of Jephunneh. 'Let us go up at once', they said to Moses, 'and possess' the land, 'for we are well able to overcome it'. (*Num.* 13:30.) But their ten companions held to their view. 'We be not able to go up against the people,' they said, 'for they are stronger than we.'

The first Israelite attempt to break into Canaan by the shortest and most direct

previous pages Mount Tabor in Jezreel, scene of the decisive battle in which the Israelites led by Deborah and Barak defeated the Canaanite forces.

93

The twelve men sent by Moses to 'spy out' the land of Canaan brought back pomegranates, figs, and a huge cluster of grapes.

route was a failure. The Canaanite king of Arad in the northern Negev, together with the Amalekites from the hill country near the Sinai border, went forth to meet the Israelites, attacked them from the heights while they were making their laborious way along the winding uphill track through Atharim, and routed them. They also 'took some of them prisoners'.

The Israelites had been engaged in no military action since their early skirmish with the Amalekites at Rephidim. During their subsequent desert years they had learned how to handle sword and bow; but they were untried in battle. Even those who marched at their head had no combat experience. If all had been as daring as Caleb of the tribe of Judah, they might have vanquished the king of Arad. But they were not. The Canaanites got the better of them, and the Israelites fled for their lives. They returned to the desert, to their tents in Kadesh Barnea.

The king of Arad and his people were men of war, equipped and arrayed for battle at all times. Their city was close to the fringe of the desert. Behind it lay the fields of grain, and on the horizon the hilltop garden greenery of Hebron. The cities in this region and on the Negev plateau were border settlements. They were strongholds protecting the land of Canaan from invaders and marauders pressing up from the south, from Mount Seir and from the wilderness of Paran. These were fast-moving nomads who swept in from the desert like a sandstorm to plunder their crops and carry off their flocks.

The young Canaanite lads tending the herds of camels also served as scouts. At the approach of an enemy, they would jump on their camels and race to alert

94

their people. The city gates would promptly be closed, and the men would gird their swords, hang their bows on their backs, and rush forth to meet the attackers. In their ill-fated engagement, the Israelites, weary from their long trudge through the reluctant sand, and confused by terrain unknown to them, were outclassed by the warriors of Arad and were beaten. They bewailed their dead, bound their wounds, and retired.

The tribal leaders met with Moses and Joshua. This was not the way to conquer the land. The fortified border cities should be bypassed, and they should avoid engaging the strongholds along the fringes of the desert. They would turn eastwards, even though this would lengthen the march, take the roundabout route through the lands of Edom and Moab, and from there penetrate into Canaan.

In the event, they had to bypass not only Arad but also Edom in the east. Repeated requests by Moses to the king of Edom to grant passage through his territory were rejected. The Israelites found themselves once again trekking through desert. They moved south as far as Eilat and Ezion-geber at the northern end of the Red Sea, and from there turned north-eastwards, going all the way round Edom. The journey was long and rigorous. The people hungered and thirsted, and many died of snake bite.

Moab too, like Edom, had to be bypassed, the Israelites skirting its eastern border as they proceeded northwards. But they gradually came closer to their yearned-for destination, the land of Canaan. They passed through Oboth and the valley of Zared at the southern end of the Dead Sea, and reached the brook of Arnon, which marked the northern border of Moab and the southern border of the land of the Amorites. Here, too, Moses sent messengers to the Amorite king, Sihon, with the request: 'Let me pass through thy land: we will not turn into the fields or into the vineyards; we will not drink of the waters of the well; but we will go along by the king's high way, until we be past thy borders.' (*Num.* 21:22.)

Sihon turned down the request, mobilized his people, and went out into the desert to engage the Israelites. This time, however, the Israelites were prepared for battle. They arrayed their forces in strategic positions at Jahaz and awaited the enemy. When the Amorites appeared they came under concentrated attack and were routed. The Israelites took possession of their land, from the Arnon brook northwards right up to the River Jabbok.

After Sihon, king of the Amorites, came Og, king of Bashan. From him, the Israelites did not even seek prior permission to pass through his territory. They entered it and kept on marching. The king and his people tried to stop them, and in the ensuing battle at Edrei were wiped out. Bashan, too, was taken over by the Israelites.

The conquest of the country had begun. The children of Israel had paid the price and learned the lesson of their earlier defeat. They would not again undertake direct assaults on fortified cities, or act impetuously and fall into the ambushing arms of the enemy. Furthermore, their warriors were now thoroughly trained in their weapons – the sword, bow, sling, javelin and shield.

The Israelites did not themselves settle down within fortified cities, did not seek refuge in the shade of city walls, did not shut themselves in behind gate and bolt. Their strength lay in constant movement. Their watchword was mobility: stay on the move; move and conquer. In the wake of the vanguard, the fighting men, came the rest of the nation, the shepherds with their flocks, and the camels and asses bearing the aged, the women and children, the tents and the considerable enemy spoil. Thus did the twelve tribes move and fight and capture, seizing every well and grazing area, conquering and settling.

Israel had come up from the desert, their eyes set on their country. Who would stop them?

THE FIRST TRIBES to establish themselves in permanent settlement were Gad, Reuben, and half the tribe of Manasseh. The territories they received were the kingdom of the Amorites, Bashan and Gilead on the east bank of the River Jordan which the Israelites had conquered. But Israel faced a formidable campaign – the conquest of Canaan, the land west of the Jordan. So 'Moses said unto the children of Gad and to the children of Reuben, "Shall your brethren go to war, and shall ye sit here?"' (*Num.* 32:6.) They promised him that their combat men would cross the Jordan westwards with the other tribes, and fight with them there; but their families would remain. 'We will build sheepfolds here for our cattle, and cities for our little ones. But we ourselves will go ready armed before the children of Israel, until we have brought them unto their place: and our little ones shall dwell in fenced cities because of the inhabitants of the land. We will not return unto our houses, until the children of Israel have inherited every man his inheritance.'

THIS PRACTICE of the sons of Gad and Reuben is not strange to the citizens of Israel today. In our own generation, too, security and land settlement are intertwined. Whenever a piece of land became available and passed into our possession, we promptly established a settlement thereon. The finest of our young men and women went out to locations near the border and established homes there, creating kibbutzim, moshavim and ordinary villages. These men and women, like those of Reuben and Gad, rushed to the help of the nation in time of danger and emergency. They left their homes, their children, their parents, their crops, their livestock, girded their weapons and went off to join their brother-troops at the front. The battles over, they returned to their homesteads, laid aside their swords and took up their ploughshares, sowed, planted, and re-possessed their land.

One such man is Meir Har-Zion. He was brought up and educated in Kibbutz Ein Harod in the valley of Jezreel. At the age of eighteen, when he became eligible for national service, he joined the army; and a year later, in 1953, he volunteered for the commando unit, Force 101, commanded by Arik (Major General Ariel Sharon). He fought with this unit until he was seriously wounded towards the end of 1956.

I first met him when I was on the general staff as chief of operations, and had gone down to the area of Nitzana on the Sinai border to inspect Force 101. Har-Zion at the time was a platoon commander, a tall, lean and wiry youth, with a frank and open countenance and piercing eyes. It was a pleasure to be with him. He exuded confidence and integrity. We had a long talk. It transpired that Har-Zion knew every inch of the country, had walked its length and breadth, and was familiar with everything that was upon it, inanimate as well as living, both the flora and the fauna. Even in the area where we were at the time, he knew of a promontory which concealed a pair of eagles who were building a nest. We drove out there. As we approached the nest, an eagle emerged, took off, and circled above, flying in wide circles higher and ever higher. Har-Zion, leaning with one arm on a rock, followed the flight. His eyes never left the eagle. It was evident that he was meticulously studying the movement of the bird's wings, as though he were trying to learn from the eagle how to take off and fly heavenwards.

In those years between the end of the War of Independence in 1949 and the Sinai Campaign of 1956, Israel was the target of numerous attacks by Arab terrorists from the neighbouring states. Bands of men, trained and equipped by Arab governments, infiltrated into Israel and carried out acts of sabotage and murder, killing civilians, mining highways, sabotaging water and electrical installations. Without declaring war, Egypt, Syria and Jordan were in fact conducting guerrilla warfare against Israel.

The Israel Army, through its ordinary units, did not manage to neutralize the terrorists and force a halt to their activities. A change was wrought with the establishment of the special Force 101. Only then did Israel gain the upper hand.

Har-Zion's unique qualities became evident throughout the four years he served in this unit. He was the most courageous soldier and the finest reconnaissance man in the Israel army. He was the only man whom I promoted to officer rank, within my authority as chief of the general staff, without his having to take an officer's training course. I met him frequently and closely followed his progress. His remarkable accomplishments in battle were due not only to his doing everything better than anyone else but to his doing it differently. This sprang from his intimately close relationship with the land of Israel, and to his special talent in combat. On his reconnaissance patrols throughout the country and across the borders, in daylight or in the darkness of night, heading a small squad and at times alone, he would choose the perfect route. And he did so with the instinct of one who had lived here thousands of years ago, when humans walked over the face of the land and were familiar with all its tracks like the wild animals, the jackal and gazelle.

In combat, Har-Zion sought close contact with the enemy, face-to-face, hand-to-hand, a struggle of life and death. He preferred battle with close-quarter weapons, with sub machine-gun and grenade, to long-distance warfare conducted with sophisticated devices.

I recall a specific reprisal action against Hebron which could not have been carried out without Har-Zion. In January 1954 an Arab band from Hebron – which was then under Jordanian control – infiltrated into Bet Govrin, in Israel, and murdered a number of Jewish civilians. It was a particularly cold winter, and Mount Hebron was covered in snow. None of us believed that in such weather our troops, carrying weapons and heavy packs of explosives, could manage in a single night to march twenty-one kilometres, much of it up the steep, trackless, snowy mountain slope, to break through the Jordanian guard of Arab legionaries, attack their military target, and get back to Israel before first light.

At dawn, the four-man squad led by Har-Zion returned to base. They had reached Hebron, stormed their way through to their objective and blown it up. The fighting on the spot was not particularly tough; but as they were returning they were pursued by a body of armed Arabs, and only when they had killed most of them were they able to leave the city, evade the guard units and patrols, and reach Israel. They were utterly exhausted after their grim march in the bitter cold across the snow-covered slopes, climaxed by combat, and the equally hazardous march back, forty-two kilometres in all. But in the Israel army, and in the war that was being conducted at the time against terror, the action in Hebron became a symbol of what was militarily possible: no place in the rear of the enemy was beyond our reach.

Har-Zion took part in most of the engagements that were undertaken during his army service. He commanded several of the operations and was always at the head of his men. The most important actions in those years were breaking into the army camp at El Burj on the outskirts of Gaza; the operation in Kibia following the murder of a Jewish mother and child in Yehudiah; the attack on Nahlin after the murder of Jews in Kisalon; storming the Arab Legion camp at Azun, capture of the Egyptian army outpost near Kisufim; capture of a Jordanian army patrol on the Beth Horon road; and the operation which cleared the east bank of the Sea of Galilee of its Syrian fortified positions.

Har-Zion's last action was the attack at the beginning of September 1956 on the Jordanian police fort at Rahawah on the Hebron–Beersheba highway. Shortly before, he had been wounded twice; the first was a bullet in the hand, the second an injury to his leg. If fate issues warnings, these were sent very clearly to Har-Zion. But despite his injuries he continued to battle, and in the action at Rahawah he was gravely wounded with a bullet in his throat. His life was saved by the medical officer who accompanied the unit. He crawled to Har-Zion under fire and performed a tracheotomy with his pocket knife, enabling him to breathe. Back at the base hospital it transpired that he had lost the power of speech, one hand was paralysed, and the nerves in the other had been damaged.

I visited him soon after in hospital, and later when he was convalescing. His doctors then told me that there was nothing known to medicine that could return him to health. They may well have been right. It was not medicine but strength of will and faith that cured Har-Zion and got him back on his feet. He gradually learned to speak anew, and his body regained its vigour. One hand is still fairly useless but the other makes up for it.

After his recovery Har-Zion returned to the village of his youth, Kibbutz Ein Harod, became a shepherd, and married Ruthie, a girl from Kibbutz Geva. The

The multi-coloured rock-strata in the Sinai mountains.

A well in Sinai.

army gave the wedding reception. All his friends wished to attend, but there was room only for two thousand. It was held in a paratrooper camp, where a huge marquee was put up, and aircraft hangars were cleared to make room for the buffet tables bearing enormous quantities of the standard refreshments – cakes and lemonade.

His unit gave Har-Zion as a wedding present the battalion's mascot – Eli, a small donkey that roamed free around the camp. It was solemnly resolved that the army would henceforth fight without its mascot, while Eli would be the mainstay of Har-Zion's farm.

Shortly thereafter Har-Zion decided to build a home for himself, and he established a cattle ranch on the ridge of 'Star of the Winds' – Kaukeb el-Hawa, near the site of the Crusader castle Belvoir. He named his ranch 'Shoshana', after his sister, who was murdered by Bedouin while hiking near En-Gedi.

'Star of the Winds' towers on a promontory on the Heights of Issachar above the western bank of the River Jordan between Beth-shan and the Sea of Galilee. Its eastern slope which drops down to the river is covered with basalt rock, unfavourable for crops but offering abundant pasturage. Lying on the east bank of the Jordan, opposite 'Star of the Winds', is the land of Gilead, the territory which 'the children of Reuben and the children of Gad' chose for their inheritance; for, as they told Moses, they 'had a very great multitude of cattle' and the land of Gilead 'was a place for cattle'.

Half the tribe of Manasseh also settled in Gilead. After battling the Amorites, 'Jair the son of Manasseh' took over their ranch-land and made his home there, calling it 'Havoth-Jair', the farm of Jair. (*Num.* 32:41.)

The estate of Jair and the 'Shoshana' ranch of Meir Har-Zion are separated by three thousand years and the River Jordan – separated but not divided.

11
Stratagem

ORTY YEARS after the original Passover on the night of the exodus from
Egypt, the children of Israel crossed the Jordan into the promised land. They
had left the deserts of Moab on the east bank of the river and moved to
the west bank, encamping at Gilgal in the plain of Jericho. The generation that
had departed from Egypt had died in the wilderness. Only two members of that
generation were still alive: Joshua, the son of Nun, and Caleb, the son of Jephunneh. Moses and Aaron were also dead. Aaron at the age of 123 was 'gathered
unto his fathers' on Mount Hor on the border of Edom. Moses died in the land
of Moab at the age of 120, his eyes undimmed, his natural force unabated. He
was succeeded by Joshua.

The first three engagements fought by the Israelites under Joshua upon entering
Canaan were the battles of Jericho, Ai and Gibeon. Their victories gave Israel
a considerable military advantage, particularly their conquest of Gibeon, which
was not only a large city but one sited on a dominant hilltop position. While they
had still been in the territory east of the Jordan and had defeated Sihon, king
of the Amorites, and Og, king of Bashan, news of their prowess had sown fear
in the hearts of the neighbouring inhabitants. Balak, the son of Zippor, king of
the Moabites, had so dreaded war with the Israelites that he sent for Balaam,
the son of Beor, a noted soothsayer, to subdue Israel through magic and witchcraft.

Before crossing the Jordan, Joshua sent two spies into Canaan to reconnoitre
the area in and around Jericho. The imminent battle for that city was doubly
significant to Joshua. It would be the first action against a local Canaanite
kingdom; and the first under his command since the death of Moses. It was thus
of supreme importance that he should be victorious.

The two spies returned from their reconnaissance with the encouraging news
that 'truly the Lord hath delivered into our hands all the land; for even all the
inhabitants of the country do faint because of us.' (*Joshua* 2:24.) In presenting
their report to Joshua, the two men were quoting almost literally what they had
heard in Jericho from Rahab the harlot. She had told them that the people of
Canaan had 'heard how the Lord dried up the water of the Red Sea ... and what
ye did unto the two kings of the Amorites, that were on the other side Jordan. ...
And as soon as we had heard these things, our hearts did melt, neither did there
remain any more courage in any man, because of you.'

And, indeed, the battle for Jericho was not difficult. The city 'was straitly
shut up because of the children of Israel: none went out, and none came in'.

above Jericho, site of Joshua's
first and most famous battle in
the conquest of Canaan.
right A shofar, the biblical ram's
horn, prominently associated
with the battle of Jericho.

(*Josh.* 6:1.) It was under siege for six days, and on the seventh day the Israelites circled the walls and blew their *shofarim* (rams' horns) and climaxed this with a powerful blast. The walls of Jericho collapsed. The Israelites stormed in and captured the city.

The next action, against Ai, was less simple. The first attack failed. The warriors of Ai came out of their walled city to meet the Israelite troops, thrust them back and pursued them down the mountain slope, killing thirty-six of them. This casualty figure was not high, but Joshua was worried by the defeat, concerned about its impact on morale: 'the hearts of the people melted, and became as water'. (*Josh.* 7:5.) He promptly put in a renewed attack, using a stratagem this time. One Israelite assault force 'made as if they were beaten' (*Josh.* 8:15) and simulated flight. The men of Ai were taken in, and, as before, left their city and pursued the apparently retreating attackers, leaving their gates open and their walls un- defended. At this point, another Israelite force of some five thousand went into action. They had stealthily approached the other side of the city during the night and lay hidden in the valley between Bethel and Ai. As soon as Ai had been emptied of its fighting men, they rushed in and set it on fire. The troops of Ai, seeing the smoke, broke off their pursuit of the 'fleeing' Israelite unit and hurried back. But they now found themselves caught between the two Israelite forces, the one that had fired the city and the one that had staged the mock retreat. They were attacked from the front and rear and wiped out.

By capturing Ai, the Israelites had reached the half-way point in their ascent up the central mountain range. The next move was to go on to the top, for whoever held the ridge controlled the region. This was well recognized by the local Canaanite rulers of fortified cities which dominated the ridge at the time, notably Gibeon, Jerusalem and Hebron. They thereupon 'gathered themselves together, to fight with Joshua and with Israel, with one accord'.

However, after the fall of Ai, the men of Gibeon realized that they would be the next Israelite target, and they were panic-stricken, even though 'Gibeon was a great city, as one of the royal cities ... and all the men thereof were mighty'. (*Josh.* 10:2.) Determined to avoid combat – and destruction – they consulted with the elders of the city and decided on surrender. But they doubted that Joshua would accept it, and so they hit upon a ruse. They despatched messengers to him at his camp in Gilgal, and these arrived tattered and dusty as though after a lengthy journey, and said they had come 'from a far country' to conclude an alliance with the Israelites. Joshua responded sympathetically and 'made a league with them'. (*Josh.* 9:15.)

When this news reached Adonizedec, king of Jerusalem, he alerted four of his allies, Hoham, king of Hebron, Piram, king of Jarmuth, Japhia, king of Lachish, and Debir, king of Eglon. Together they marched on Gibeon, seeking to seize it and deny the Israelites so strong a foothold on the mountain heights. The Gibeonites sent an urgent appeal for help to Joshua: 'Come up to us quickly, and save us.' (*Josh.* 10:6) Joshua promptly led his troops on a night march from Gilgal and fell upon the armies of the five kings who were besieging Gibeon. The

Canaanites fled, hurrying down the slopes through the pass of Beth Horon towards the coastal plain. Joshua's men pursued them, overtook and killed them. The Israelites were also aided by a providential storm of huge hailstones which battered the heads of the retreating Canaanites.

It was indeed a great victory. The commanding city of Gibeon had fallen to the Israelites, the forces of the five Canaanite kingdoms had been routed, and the five rulers themselves were trapped in a cave, taken forth, slain, and left hanging upon five trees until eventide.

Joshua sang his hymn of praise to the Lord in the presence of all Israel: 'Sun, stand thou still upon Gibeon; and thou, Moon, in the valley of Ajalon. And the sun stood still, and the moon stayed, until the people had avenged themselves upon their enemies.' (*Josh.* 10:12, 13.)

Possession of Gibeon and the victory over the five kings opened the mountain region to Joshua. The Israelites then turned southwards and maintained their advance, capturing in turn Makkedah, Libnah, Lachish, Eglon, Hebron and Debir. The whole of the south was now in Israelite hands – the mountain range, the foothills and the northern Negev. The coastal strip remained beyond their power of conquest. The 'Way of the Sea' was controlled by Egyptian forces and by the local Canaanite occupants who possessed powerful formations of iron chariots.

ISRAEL'S WAR OF INDEPENDENCE, unlike the Joshua campaigns, was fought when the Jews were already settled in the land. The battles were conducted from and within the country itself. The directions of Israel's advances were also the reverse of those in Joshua's day. Jewish settlement was mainly concentrated before the war in the coastal plain, and from there the Jewish troops struck out to the north, the south and the east – to the Galilee, the Negev and the foothills. Furthermore, the War of Independence started with a combined Arab assault on the Jewish community, and only as the campaign developed did Israel go over from defence to attack.

On 29 November 1947, the United Nations Assembly adopted its Partition Resolution whereby the land of Israel was to be divided between the Jews and the Arabs and two states established, a Jewish state and an Arab state. The Arabs rejected this UN decision and launched a series of bloody attacks. The first occurred in Jerusalem. An Arab mob headed by bands of armed irregulars broke into the Jewish commercial centre, looted it and set it on fire. The British government, which was the mandatory power in Palestine at the time, announced that it would be terminating the mandate on 15 May 1948. On that date, the British administration and the British armed forces would leave the country.

At 4.30 p.m. on Friday, 14 May 1948, the eve of the Jewish Sabbath, David Ben-Gurion read out the Proclamation of Independence and declared the establishment of the state of Israel. (This followed a decision of the Jewish National Council of Palestine.) Seven and a half hours later, at midnight, the neighbouring Arab territories announced that their armies had invaded the new-born state.

Seven Arab countries – Iraq, Lebanon, Syria, Jordan, Egypt, Saudi Arabia and Yemen – established a joint command and sent their expeditionary forces to conquer the land of Israel.

These regular Arab armies joined the irregular Palestinian bands and attacked Jewish settlements. At first, Israel was compelled to apply her entire armed strength to the defence of her villages and cities. But as the weeks went by, she secured more arms, increased the size of her army, and was able to take the military initiative. The first Jewish attack was 'Operation Nahshon', which broke open the road to Jerusalem. The Arabs had blocked this highway and placed Jerusalem under siege. This action was carried out on 3 April 1948, a month and a half before the British withdrew, before Israel proclaimed her statehood, and before the invasion by the Arab armies.

At a special session of the Jewish National Council of Palestine, on 14 May 1948, David Ben-Gurion proclaims the establishment of the State of Israel.

Chaim Weizmann, Israel's first President, in Jerusalem, December 1948, accompanied by Dr Dov Joseph, civilian governor, and Moshe Dayan, Jerusalem military commander at the time.

The War of Independence lasted about a year and a half – from 29 November 1947, when the UN adopted its Partition decision, to 20 June 1949, when the Israel–Syria Armistice Agreement was signed. (Similar agreements had been signed earlier that year between Israel and Egypt, Lebanon and Jordan.)

The Arab armies were vanquished on all fronts, and the existence of the state of Israel was now not merely the product of a proclamation but a practical reality. She was a state with confidence in her leader – David Ben-Gurion – and in her army, the Israel Defence Forces.

The first phase of Israel's War of Independence was marked not only by successes but also by failures and critical situations. The turning point came on 15 October 1948 with 'Operation Joab', and with it came the opening of the decisive and victorious phase. The objective of this operation was to drive out the Egyptian forces from the south and thereby prevent repeated enemy attempts to cut off the Negev from the rest of Israel.

'Operation Joab' was launched against the background of recommendations by Sweden's Count Bernadotte, who had been appointed by the United Nations as mediator between Israel and the Arabs. His proposals were blatantly anti-Israeli. The worst of them was the recommendation that the Negev be severed from Israel. Bernadotte was shot dead on 17 September 1948 when he was on a visit to Jerusalem. His assailants were members of Lehi, one of the dissident Jewish underground organizations, and it was feared that Bernadotte's proposal might well be transformed into a 'political will and testament'.

'Operation Joab' went well. On 21 October Israeli forces drove the Egyptian invasion troops from Beersheba. Shortly afterwards they entered Ashdod, on the coast. The Egyptian army was badly mauled and in utter disarray.

Following Bernadotte's recommendations but before the 'Joab' operation, Ben-Gurion had turned his eyes to the east – to the eastern part of Jerusalem and to Mount Hebron, which were held by the Jordanians. The war was drawing to its close. Israel's future was in the process of being fashioned. The Israel army had become strong, and was capable of continuing its advance. This was the time for action. If not now, when?

Ben-Gurion brought his plan before the Cabinet on 26 September 1948: Israel forces were to capture the Old City of Jerusalem and Mount Hebron; an Arab enclave was to be left stretching from and including Nablus down to Jericho; and the entire land of Judah was to come within the boundaries of Israel, including the whole of Jerusalem, Hebron, the western shore of the Dead Sea, and the Jordan fords opposite Jericho.

Ben-Gurion's proposal was not accepted. Five members of the cabinet supported it; seven voted against. The rejectors envisioned gloomy consequences of such military measures. The United Nations 'upon whom we are dependent', they said, would react with the utmost severity to armed action initiated by us, particularly after the murder of Bernadotte. The United States would impose sanctions, and prohibit American Jewry's financial aid to Israel. And the Arabs would renew their attacks on all fronts.

Ben-Gurion said the Cabinet rejection would be 'mourned for generations'. By leaving the current situation unaltered, the kingdom of Jordan would continue to hold sway over the Judean hills, the Old City of Jerusalem, and the roads leading to it from the north, east and south. This Cabinet decision, he added, brought shame to the ministers who had opposed action; and it would lead to political and strategic disaster.

Ben-Gurion was right in deploring the decision. But he erred in his forecast. The 'mourning period' did not last for generations. Less than twenty years later, Mount Hebron was captured by Israel.

On 22 May 1967 President Gamel Abdul Nasser of Egypt blocked the Straits of Tiran to Israel navigation. One week later, on 31 May, King Hussein of Jordan flew to Cairo and asked to join the Arab front against Israel. Nasser agreed, signed a military pact with him, and appointed Egyptian General Abd el-Munam Riad commander of the eastern front and of the Jordanian army. On 5 June, at the outbreak of the Six Day War, Jordan went the way of Egypt and Syria. Her forces attacked Israel. They shelled and mortared the Jewish parts of Jerusalem and opened fire with artillery and light weapons all along the armistice lines. Jordan's war with Israel lasted only two days. On the third morning, the Israel army captured Jerusalem, and in the afternoon Hebron, Nablus and Jericho surrendered.

The war with Jordan ended. Who can tell what would have been the fate of Jerusalem and the West Bank if King Hussein had not joined in the fighting. Neither Egypt nor Syria had asked him to come in with them. It was the king himself who had chosen to do so. He had boarded his Caravelle and flown off to Nasser, piloting the aircraft himself as his forbears had jumped on their horses and galloped off into the distance.

Messengers of virtuous deeds are unharmed. The plane landed in Cairo without mishap, Hussein went to war, was defeated, and Jerusalem, Samaria and Judah passed to Israeli control.

After the war a Jewish city, Kiriat Arba, rose at the side of Hebron. In 1970 *The Book of Hebron* appeared, published by the Council for the Community of Hebron. It opened with a preface by David Ben-Gurion, called 'Sister to Jerusalem'. It ended with these words:

It should not be forgotten that the greatest of Israel's kings started his public life in Hebron, the city to which the first Hebrew, Abraham, had come some eight hundred years before King David. We would be guilty of the most fearsome error if we failed to establish a large and growing Jewish settlement in the shortest possible time in Hebron, neighbour and predecessor of Jerusalem. This will also bring blessings to its Arab neighbours. Hebron is worthy of being sister to Jerusalem.

I visited the West Bank frequently after it came under our control. 'Small Israel', as it had existed before the Six Day War, had long been intimately familiar to me. I had spent my childhood and early youth in the Jordan valley and the Valley of Jezreel. I got to know the Negev when I served as GOC southern command. And I criss-crossed Sinai during the 1956 Sinai Campaign when I was chief of staff. Now there was opened before me the central mountain range that soars above the spine of the country, stretching from Shechem (Nablus) in the north to Hebron in the south, the heart of ancient Israel, of Judah and Samaria.

The archaeological remains of bygone ages when this was a wholly Jewish region belong largely to the period of the Second Temple (sixth century BC to first century AD). They include mosaic floors of synagogues; stone sarcophagi with Hebrew names and inscriptions; oil lamps decorated with reliefs of Jewish ritual articles – the *menorah* (replica of the holy candelabrum that stood in the Temple), the *shofar* (ram's horn) and the *lulav* (palm branch), as well as Jewish coins.

I was delighted to see these objects. I loved to read the words on the silver coins written in ancient Hebrew script: 'Israel Shekel'; 'Jerusalem the Holy'; 'Year Two of the Freedom of Israel'; 'Year One of the Freedom of Jerusalem';

Dayan's 12-century BC earthenware jug in the shape of a cow, found near Jericho.

and so on. However, I felt drawn more to the earlier periods, to the times of the patriarchs, the Joshua conquest, the kingdom of David. A great number of archaeological objects belonging to these periods were unearthed – pottery vessels, bronze swords, figurines. Many of these were pre-Israelite. They may also have been used by the Israelite settlers, but the style and workmanship of some and the evident ritualistic pagan associations of others, such as the figurines, stamped them as Canaanite artefacts. This did not bother me. I became attached to them. I found great charm in their shape, form and colour. They were crude, but functional. And I took delight in the burnished red linear decorations coating the ancient jars, and in the fashioning of the fertility images, the incense pans, and the vessels moulded in the form of animals.

On one occasion, Dajani, an Arab dealer in antiquities from the Old City of Jerusalem, brought me a large earthenware jug in the shape of a cow. The mouth, ears and horns were slightly chipped, but this did not mar its excellence. I could hardly take my eyes – and hands – off it. It was a superb vessel belonging to the twelfth century BC (just after Moses and Joshua, and early in the period of the Judges). It had been found wedged in a hole of a ruin near Jericho. I had seen nothing like it, either in archaeological illustrations or in any museum.

The price was pretty steep, so I rang up the manager of the Soldier's Bank, Dov David, and asked if I had enough cover for the cheque. No, said he, but write the cheque anyway, and we'll manage somehow. I signed, and offered blessings for the Canaanite family that had taken the trouble to place the jug in a recess caused by a fault in the wall, so that it was well and wholly preserved for more than three thousand years.

More complicated was the episode with the incense burner which I acquired from Abu Ali. Abu Ali is an uncommonly tall Bedouin – his nick-name is Al-Tawil, Arabic for 'the high one' – from the Ta'amrah tribe that dwells in the Judean desert, between Bethlehem and the Dead Sea. He runs a variety of enterprises, among them antiquities. I do not think anyone has ever succeeded in duping him by trying to sell him a fake antique or a counterfeit coin. Whenever I bought anything from him, I could always be sure that it was authentic. I knew where it had been found and how often it had changed hands – and which hands – until it had ended up in the possession of Abu Ali.

One day I received a message from him telling me that he had a beautiful earthenware censer that he was sure would interest me. We arranged to meet in Jerusalem and there I saw it. It was indeed beautiful. It was also unique. It was shaped like a goblet with a dish set in its upper part, and the rim of the dish was decorated with representations of human faces. The vessel was found with a few pieces missing and some broken. It was repaired, and the missing parts replaced with plaster. I bought it, and asked where it had been discovered. Abu Ali said it was found in a cave south of Bethlehem. I asked him to take me there. I wished to see what kind of cave it was, whether a burial cave, a dwelling, or one used for pagan rites.

He promised to do so and we fixed a date. But shortly before we were due to meet, he informed me that he was very busy and asked for a postponement. He postponed the next meeting too on some pretext or other. I refrained from interrogating too closely one so much smarter than I, and I just went on waiting. The hoped-for day finally arrived and we set out for the cave.

We passed Bethlehem, and about half way along the road to Hebron we turned off westwards along a dirt track in the direction of the foothills. We reached the end of the track after about four kilometres, left the car, and continued on foot up a steep path between boulders and thick olive trees. There is something human about a very old olive tree. Its trunk is creased and furrowed, boughs and leaves droop and lose their freshness, their colour fades; yet if anything its dignity is enhanced. Not even its plaited roots spread over the surface of the ground, nor its bowed branches, nor yet the open gashes revealing its hollow trunk, can diminish its splendour. Men, regimes, kingdoms, empires, have risen and fallen all around it. Customs, faiths, cultures, have flourished and disappeared. Only the olive tree continues in eternal tranquillity, bearing the message of peace through its branch, shedding radiance through its oil, and offering pleasurable nourishment with its choice fruit.

The cave had been scooped out of the rock, and no one who had not known

The earthenware censer, found in a cave south of Bethlehem.

of its existence would have noticed it. Its entrance had been half-closed by huge stones, and the thick growth of weeds in front of it had been neither cut nor trampled.

This had once been a burial cave. The remains of skeletons were still there. But in the course of time it had been used as a sheepfold and as shelter for shepherds in heavy rains. There was evidence of recent digging, and it was this which had brought to light ancient pottery vessels.

Now that my curiosity about the cave had been satisfied, I asked Abu Ali why he had kept postponing our visit. 'O *Wazir*', he replied, 'this cave was being used at the time by a band of PLO saboteurs. It was they who began digging "in their spare time" and they who unearthed the ancient vessels and put them on the market. How, then, could I bring you here, you who are minister of defence? I had to wait until they moved elsewhere. Imagine what would have happened if I had brought you while they were still here. Either they would have opened fire on you, in which case your soldiers would have shot me; or you would have shot them, in which case their comrades would have suspected me of betraying them and delivering them into your hands, and then they would have murdered me and my children.'

Antiquities were one thing, terrorists another. To reach old age in such circumstances, you had to know how to wiggle through between the raindrops and keep dry. How else would the Ta'amrah tribe have held out through the convulsive changes that have so often marked this region?

12
A king's possession

AFTER HIS CONQUEST of Mount Hebron and the northern Negev, Joshua went back to his Jordan valley base at Gilgal, near Jericho. The Canaanite kings who ruled the north of the country heard that he had returned from his victorious campaign in the south, and they judged that he would now proceed northwards to the conquest of their cities. Jabin, king of Hazor, accordingly did what Adonizedec, king of Jerusalem, had done before him; he called on his neighbouring rulers to band together and undertake joint military action against the Israelites. The principals in this military alliance were four kings: Jabin himself, whose city, Hazor, 'was the head of all those kingdoms ... Joab king of Madon ... the king of Shimron, and ... the king of Achshaph'. (*Josh.* 11:1, 10.) They were joined by the Canaanite kingdoms just south of the Sea of Galilee and on the Mediterranean coast, and by 'the Amorite, and the Hittite, and the Perizzite, and the Jebusite in the mountains, and the Hivite [who dwelt in the north] under [Mount] Hermon in the land of Mizpeh'. It was a great host, 'much people, even as the sand that is upon the sea shore in multitude, with horses and chariots very many.' All these armies met together in the northern Jordan valley and went on to deploy for battle 'at the waters of Merom, to fight against Israel'.

Joshua did not wait until Jabin and his allied armies launched their attack. He and his men descended upon them, taking them by surprise, storming their positions, inflicting heavy casualties, and throwing them into disarray. The Canaanites fled, and the Israelites 'chased them unto great Zidon ... and they smote them, until they left none remaining. And Joshua ... houghed their horses, and burnt their chariots with fire.'

Joshua fought a lengthy war against the Canaanites. 'There was not a city that made peace with the children of Israel, save the ... inhabitants of Gibeon: all other they took in battle.'

Joshua was now 'old and stricken in years'. The campaign of conquest had ended. The country 'rested from war'; but there remained 'yet very much land to be possessed'.

THE CANAANITE KING whose estate I possessed was the 'king of Shimron-meron' mentioned in the Book of Joshua (12:20). It was upon the property in the Valley of Jezreel which was his some three thousand three hundred years ago that there arose the cooperative farm village of Nahalal where I was brought up. When I came to Jezreel as a child with my parents, the site of ancient Shimron-meron

boasted a few mud shacks and a large grove of fig trees. The Arabs called the place Simonia (a corruption of biblical Shimron), and the spring at the foot of the *tel* – the archaeological mound containing the remains of early settlement – was known as the Spring of Simonia.

The mound itself, Tel Shimron, is a narrow, lofty hill with a steep eastern slope, and its summit towers above its surroundings. Our village teacher, Meshulam, explained that the origin of the biblical name Shimron is '*shmor*', Hebrew for 'guard' or 'protect', and here was the height which guarded the Valley of Jezreel. This was a common form of nomenclature, he used to tell us: Mount Lebanon was so called because it was 'the white mountain – '*lavan*' is Hebrew for 'white'; Mount Hermon was 'the holy mountain' – '*herem*' is one of the Hebrew words for 'consecrated'; and the River Jordan (Yarden in Hebrew) stemmed from '*yored*', which means 'descend', as it was the river which flowed down to below sea level.

This was the language pattern of the Canaanites and the ancient Hebrews; this was how they named their surroundings. It is probable that the '*meron*' part of 'Shimron-meron' derives from '*mareh*', Hebrew for 'view', for the hill offered a commanding view of the valley, just as other biblical sites of high elevation were often named '*mitzpeh*', Hebrew for 'watch-tower' or 'observation post'.

The Valley of Jezreel today is dotted with farm settlements and criss-crossed with tarmac roads. But when I first got there, fifty-seven years ago, it looked much as it did in Joshua's day, with hilltop villages, and cattle and sheep pasturing in the valley below.

The two villages closest to Shimron and mentioned in the Bible were Nahalal and Japhia. (*Josh.* 19:12, 15.) The names still lived: the local Arabs called these villages Ma'alul and Ya'apha. They, too, stood on summits which looked out over the valley, and they also had springs at the foot of the hills which nourished the greenery – fig trees, mulberry bushes and vines.

The land bought for the Jewish settlement of Nahalal was divided among its members by lot. The field that fell to my father adjoined Tel Shimron, and was very superior land, choice grey soil, light and soft. The Arabs called such land 'soil of ruins', since it was a mixture of ashes and decayed vegetation swept down from the high mound by the wind and the rain.

The site of the *tel* had held successive large settlements for thousands of years. Scattered near it are the remains of these early ages, potsherds belonging to various early periods ranging from the Middle Bronze, some 3500 years BC, to about 300 AD in the Roman period. After the Joshua conquest at the end of the thirteenth century BC, the Shimron region was allotted to the tribe of Zebulun. Nahalal and another three cities were detached from Zebulun and assigned to the Levites. The tribe of Levi, it will be recalled, was not granted a territorial region of its own, but its families were distributed and lived among all the other tribes of Israel. Nahalal, Yokneam, Karta and Dimona were given to the Merari clan of the tribe of Levi.

When we were learning this at the village school, I saw in it the tracing of the

The Jezreel valley, seen from Mount Tabor.

finger of God. According to our family tradition, we belong to the Levites. My only difficulty at the time was how to explain to my classmates why the family name Merari had undergone the transformation to Dayan!

A further problem arose when we continued our studies and learned from the Book of Judges that the tribe of Zebulun failed to capture Nahalal and the Canaanites continued to live there. Actually, this did not trouble me. The Canaanites were not strangers to me. I reckoned it had been possible to live with them and maintain good neighbourly relations, just as we in Nahalal lived with our Arab neighbours at Ma'alul and Ya'apha, and with the el-Mazarib Bedouin who dwelt behind Tel Shimron.

At all events, Shimron and Nahalal had eventually passed into the hands of the Israelites. One day during the ploughing season I found a jar-handle from the Israelite period and on it was the inscription in ancient Hebrew writing: 'For the king'. The rest of the inscription had been worn away. Gideon Chen, the young son of our neighbouring farmer, also found a relic of the Israelite past – a large stone bearing the representation of a *menorah*, the seven-branched candelabrum which is the symbol of the state of Israel today. It may have been a tombstone belonging to the Second Temple period. There is no better evidence of our early

The view from Tel Shimron, the biblical hill of Shimron-meron, where the founding families of Nahalal lie buried.

116

settlement here than these stones. None can deny their truth. As Joshua said to the children of Israel: 'Behold, this stone shall be a witness unto us; for it hath heard all the words of the Lord which he spake unto us.' (*Josh.* 24:27.) These stones were here in Joshua's day. They saw and heard what happened then, and today they bear witness thereto.

The eastern shoulder of Tel Shimron was set aside by Nahalal as the cemetery. The area was cleared of its basalt boulders, its perimeter fenced and planted with trees. When a grave was being prepared, the diggers would occasionally come across bits of skeletons and potsherds belonging to the period of the patriarchs, for in ancient times, too, the local inhabitants would bury their dead on this hill. This is where the children of Nahalal come in winter to pick flowers. Anemones and chrysanthemums cover the hill of Shimron with a tapestry of red and yellow. In summer the area is barren and desolate, with the acacia trees providing the only patches of green. But summer or winter, this is a unique spot, with its prospect of the Valley of Jezreel, the Carmel range, the mountains of Manasseh and the hills of Nazareth. Close by lie the villages and fields of Nahalal, Beth She'arim, and the Kibbutzim Gvat and Sarid. Cutting into the rustle of nature are the sounds of tractors at work with the plough, and of planes taking off from the nearby airfield of Ramat David.

In this cemetery, together with their comrades, lie my grandfather Abraham and my grandmother Sarah, my father Shmuel and my mother Dvorah, my brother Zohar and my sister Aviva. Here, too, will I be buried. This is the place where I would wish to lie in eternal rest, on this hill looking out upon Jezreel, the biblical hill of Shimron-meron.

13
The song of Deborah

JOSHUA DIED at the age of 110. He was mourned by the children of Israel and buried 'in the border of his inheritance in Timnath-serah, which is in mount Ephraim, on the north side of the hill of Ga'ash'.

At his death, Israel was left without a leader who could unite the nation. Joshua's men of war, who in his time were encamped at Gilgal and from there would go out to battle in the north and the south, were now dispersed, each dwelling in his own tent. The tribes had begun to settle the territories that had fallen to them by lot, and were building their homes. Reuben, Gad, and half the tribe of Manasseh returned to the eastern bank of the Jordan, to the cities on the heights of Moab in Bashan and Gilead. Judah and Simeon went south, to Mount Hebron and the Negev. Naphtali and Asher settled in the north, between the Sea of Galilee and the Mediterranean. Zebulun had its possession in the Valley of Jezreel and its environs. Issacher and the other half of the tribe of Manasseh were in the centre of the country. Dan was in the stretch of the coastal belt near Jaffa and in the foothills to its east. And Ephraim and Benjamin were established in the central hill region, in Shechem and Bethel, north of Jerusalem.

The Israelites did not at that time take possession of the whole of the country. The Sidonians and the Hivites remained 'on Mount Lebanon' in the north; 'the five lords of the Philistines' dwelt in the south as rulers of Ashdod, Ashkelon, Ekron, Gath and Gaza; and within the tribal territories were small scattered enclaves of varied local inhabitants – Canaanites, Hittites, Amorites, Perizzites and Jebusites.

The weakened military power of the Israelites through tribal dispersal and the absence of national leadership prompted action by their enemies. The first to strike was 'Chushan-rishataim king of Mesopotamia', and he maintained mastery over Israel for eight years. Then 'the Lord raised up a deliverer ... Othniel, the son of Kenaz, Caleb's younger brother', who 'judged Israel, and went out to war' and defeated the Mesopotamian army. Othniel was the first of the *ad hoc* leaders who emerged in time of crisis and who are known in the Bible as 'Judges'.

The next attack came after forty years of quiet. The enemy this time was Eglon, king of Moab, who 'gathered unto him the children of Ammon and Amalek, and went and smote Israel'. Eighteen years of subservience followed, until there arose another judge or liberator, 'Ehud the son of Gera'. Ehud slew King Eglon by a stratagem, called his people to battle against the now leaderless Moabites, and routed them. 'And the land had rest fourscore years.' (*Judges* 3:30.) It was broken

Mount Tabor, scene of the
dramatic episode in the story of
Deborah the Judge.

by the Philistines. Ehud by now was old and weak, and the danger was met by
a young hero, 'Shamgar the son of Anath'. He neutralized the enemy, in the course
of which he 'slew of the Philistines six hundred men with an ox goad: and he
also delivered Israel'.

Then came the decisive Israelite campaign against the Canaanites. After the
death of Ehud, 'the Lord sold' Israel 'into the hand of Jabin king of Canaan,
that reigned in Hazor; the captain of whose host was Sisera'. Under his command
was a force of 'nine hundred chariots of iron; twenty years he mightily oppressed
the children of Israel'. Deborah, a prophetess from the hill country of Ephraim,
'judged Israel at that time'. (*Judges* 4:4.)

Deborah summoned Barak, the son of Abinoam, from Kedesh-Naphtali and
told him that 'the Lord God of Israel commanded' them to revolt against Sisera.
Barak was to conduct the campaign. He was instructed to draw Sisera and his
army to the River Kishon, and the Lord would 'deliver him into thine hand'.
Deborah and Barak well knew that they faced a very hard war. It would not be
possible this time for the enemy to be defeated by a single tribe. All the tribes
of Israel would have to join together again, as they had done in Joshua's day,
in order to overcome the Canaanites.

Joining Barak were ten thousand men from Zebulun and Naphtali, tribes close to Hazor who had suffered under the mastery of King Jabin. Barak assembled his men on Mount Tabor, its slopes unscaleable by iron chariots and offering a fine vantage point from which to follow the movements of the Canaanite army.

Sisera reacted by mobilizing his entire chariot force and setting off to crush the Israelite rebels. His vehicles could move only over level ground, so he was compelled to lead his men on a deep detour, driving through the Jordan valley and the Valley of Beth-shan and round to 'Taanach by the waters of Megiddo' at the western end of the Valley of Jezreel. There they prepared themselves for battle, and moved against the Israelites deployed on Mount Tabor at the other end of the valley.

The fighting took place at the foot of the mount. As Sisera's vehicles coming from Megiddo approached Tabor, the combatants of Naphtali and Zebulun rushed down the slopes, shouting and trumpeting and sending their arrows into the midst of the enemy horses and charioteers. There was utter confusion in Sisera's forces as the frenzied animals ran amok and chariots crashed into each other. The enemy troops abandoned their vehicles and fled on foot towards their base at Haroshet-hagoiim, with Barak's men in hot pursuit: 'and all the host of Sisera fell upon the edge of the sword; and there was not a man left'. (*Judges* 4:16.)

Sisera himself 'fled away on his feet to the tent of Jael the wife of Heber the Kenite', seeking refuge. She gave the exhausted man a drink of milk and covered him with a rug. When he had fallen asleep, she 'took a nail of the tent, and took

The archaeological site of Megiddo, gateway to the Valley of Jezreel.

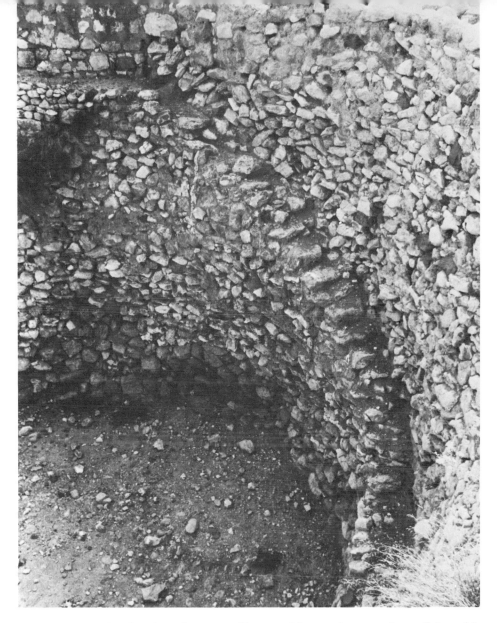

Megiddo's 9th century BC shaft with steps leading down to the water tunnel.

an hammer in her hand, and went softly unto him, and smote the nail into his temples, and fastened it into the ground: for he was fast asleep and weary. So he died.'

On that day, 'God subdued ... Jabin the king of Canaan before the children of Israel.'

THIS BATTLE, with its resounding victory for the Israelites, was the last one they fought against the Canaanites, and it remained engraved on the memory of the nation for generations thereafter.

'Then sang Deborah and Barak the son of Abinoam on that day', and what follows in chapter 5 of the *Book of Judges*, known as the 'Song of Deborah', is one of the most beautiful poems in the chronicles of Israel, and one of the most powerful – more powerful indeed than the battle it describes. It bears instructive witness of the condition of the people of Israel at that time, when 'the highways were unoccupied, and the travellers walked through by-ways. The inhabitants of the villages ceased, they ceased in Israel, until that I Deborah arose ...' (*Judges* 5:6, 7.) The Israelite tribes, split and divided over the face of the land, were hard-pressed by their strong neighbours, and were forced to shut themselves in behind fortified city walls. When they did emerge, they avoided the main routes and kept to the by-ways. There was only one course for the tribes to follow if they were to stand up to their enemies: come to each other's assistance, unite and go forth jointly to battle.

Not all the tribes took part in the war against Sisera. The tribal territories of Judah and Simeon were far off to the south, and Deborah and Barak did not even ask for their help. But Reuben and Dan were called, and they failed to respond. The tribe of Reuben, who had settled on the east bank of the Jordan, had been suspected even in Moses' day of tending to separate themselves off from the tribes west of the river. In the 'Song of Deborah', the scornful prophetess reprimands the Reubenites for not sending their sons to fight in Israel's battles, preferring the easy life: 'Why abidest thou among the sheepfolds, to hear the bleatings of the flocks?' The Danites, too, sealed their tribal ears against Deborah's appeal. Settled along the coast near Jaffa, they went about their normal business, sailed their boats and fished: 'why did Dan remain in ships?' The tribe of Asher also 'continued on the sea shore', in the north, and did not join the combatants.

The majority of the nation, however, behaved differently. The fighting men of Issachar, Ephraim and Benjamin, in the central hill country, heard Deborah's call to arms and went off to battle. So did the clan of Machir, the son of Manasseh, east of the Jordan, as well as the men of Zebulun and Naphtali in Galilee. Deborah had high praise for these volunteers, mentioning each tribe by name as shining examples of noble behaviour, to be remembered with glory by the nation of Israel. 'Praise ye the Lord,' sang Deborah in her opening verse, for when Israel was in distress, 'the people willingly offered themselves'.

From the time of the Judges until our own day, throughout all the vicissitudes of our nation, this verse from the 'Song of Deborah' has been our guiding light.

SEVERAL YEARS after routing Sisera, the Israelites found themselves gravely troubled by the Midianites, who came up from the Arabian desert in great numbers, together with 'the Amalekites, and the children of the east'. They ranged over the countryside plundering the crops, making off with the livestock, and leaving 'no sustenance for Israel, neither sheep, nor ox, nor ass'. (*Judges* 6:4.)

Israel was delivered from the hand of Midian by Gideon, the son of Joash, from the tribe of Manasseh. Gideon dwelt in his father's house in Ophrah, and like all Israeli farmers at the time he hastened to gather in the harvest from the fields and put it out of reach of the looters. As he 'threshed wheat by the winepress, to hide it from the Midianites', an angel of the Lord appeared 'and said unto him, "The Lord is with thee, thou mighty man of valour ... Go in this thy might, and thou shalt save Israel from the hand of the Midianites."'

Gideon prays for victory in battle. From a 15th-century German illustration.

The 'Spirit of the Lord came upon Gideon, and he blew a trumpet' and called the people to battle. The first to follow him were the men of his own Abiezer clan, but other tribes also rallied to his appeal. He 'sent messengers unto Asher, and unto Zebulun, and unto Naphtali; and they came up to meet them', their numbers reaching thirty-two thousand.

Gideon assembled his force along the southern edge of the Valley of Jezreel on the slopes above the Well of Harod. The enemy were encamped in the valley itself between the Hill of Moreh and Mount Gilboa. They were a mixed force made up of the 'children of the east' from the deserts of Arabia, Amalekites from Sinai and the Negev, and Midianites whose origin was the wilderness of Moab south of the Dead Sea. They were a huge motley, 'like grasshoppers for multitude; and their camels were without number, as the sand by the sea side'.

Gideon, like Barak in Deborah's day, sought victory by sowing confusion in the enemy camp. But his method was different. Gideon knew that the Midianites on camels were not like the Canaanites on iron chariots. Camels would not panic at the sound of trumpet blasts and would not stampede like chariot-horses and gallop off in all directions. Crouching at ease and chewing the cud, the camel herds would not move without a command from their trained riders. If the Israelites were to break into the Midianite encampment in broad daylight, they would be overwhelmed by the sons of the desert, masters of sword and bow, and fleeter than the gazelle.

At midnight, 'in the beginning of the middle watch' just after the change of

guard, Gideon 'came unto the outside of the camp' of the enemy. With him were only three hundred picked men, whom he divided into three equal companies. He had sent home the remaining thousands of volunteers. The men in the three companies carried a trumpet in the right hand and a pitcher containing – and concealing – a flaming torch in the left hand. They silently ranged themselves round the north, west and south sides of the encampment. At a signal from Gideon, the men of all three companies uttered a great shout, 'The sword of the Lord, and of Gideon', blew their trumpets, broke their pitchers and waved their fiery flares about in the air; but no man moved from his fixed position. 'And they stood every man in his place round about the camp'. And, indeed, they had no need to do anything else. Consternation struck the enemy encampment, the Midianites believing they were under massive Israelite attack. In the darkness within the camp, they could not distinguish between allied friend and foe, and every man's sword was set against his fellow. Then began a panic flight, the Midianites escaping eastwards to Beth-shittah, and from there continued south-wards to the Valley of Beth-shan and on 'to the border of Abel-meholah'.

The tribes of Naphtali, Asher and Mannasseh were alerted, and their fighting men pursued the enemy. Gideon anticipated that the Midianites would try to

The spring of Harod, where Gideon selected his 300 commandos to fight the Midianites.

cross the River Jordan, and he 'sent messengers throughout all mount Ephraim' to urge its people to set up ambushes at the river fords. The men of Ephraim did so, and managed to trap part of the enemy force. Gideon crossed the Jordan with his men in the wake of the main body of the fleeing Midianites, passed through Succoth and Penuel, climbed the heights of Ammon, and continued 'by the way of them that dwelt in tents' until they reached the Midianite base at Karkor. And the Israelites 'took the two kings of Midian, Zebah and Zalmunna, and discomfited all the host'. Gideon killed the two Midianite chieftains with his sword.

'Thus was Midian subdued before the children of Israel, so that they lifted up their heads no more. And the country was in quietness forty years in the days of Gideon.' (*Judges* 8 : 28.)

THE CAMPAIGNS of Barak against the Canaanites and Gideon against the Midianites gave Israel the two greatest military victories in the period of the Judges. Both are recorded in biblical song and story which shed special light on the history of our people in those times.

The two campaigns took place in the Valley of Jezreel, and the places mentioned in the biblical reports are there to this day. I grew up with them. The waters flow forth from the spring Ein Harod and the Kishon stream as they did then; Taanach and Megiddo seal the valley from the south west; and Mount Tabor soars above its surroundings and dominates the fields spread out below as in the days of antiquity.

The names of the local Arab villages preserve the memory of early Israel. The village at the foot of Tabor is called Daburiah, after Deborah the prophetess. Hirbet-shittah, near Beth-shan, is the very Beth-shittah through which the Midianites fled.

For me, the Valley of Jezreel is not a battlefield which evokes personal war memories. From the moment when I first came to it as a child to this very day, it has symbolized for me honest manual labour and the blessings of the soil, fields of corn and fruit orchards, gushing springs and herds of cattle, the farmer walking behind his plough, the harvester gathering the stocks for the threshing-floor.

The clashes which occurred in the Valley of Jezreel and in which I took part were on the whole the contentions of peacetime, mostly with our Arab neighbours but at times with nomads who came in from the east and south. Peasants from the Hauran (Syria) and Bedouin from Transjordan and the Negev would cross the borders and enter the country in time of drought. Group after group of Hauranians would make their way along the railway line from Damascus towards the port of Haifa, where they might find work as stevedores. They would walk along singing songs of dull monotony, each verse rendered by a soloist and repeated by the group in community song. They would rest at night at the side of the track and then try to enter and steal from the orchards and chicken coops. When they were caught and brought to the village guardroom, they would sit hunched on the floor, neither remonstrating nor pleading for mercy, starvation

in their eyes. The village guard would give them a few smacks, in token perform-ance of duty, and send them on their way, shouting at them in a tone of faked anger not to show their faces again, and privately wondering whether those bags of skin and bones would reach Haifa.

The Bedouin raids were more serious and more difficult to cope with. True, they did not descend upon the country like the Midianites 'as the grasshoppers for multitude', but we could never get rid of them without a clash. The Sagar Bedouin from across the Jordan came searching for pasture mostly with flocks of sheep. The Azazme tribe from the Negev and Sinai had goats and camels. I had difficulty in understanding their guttural Arabic, and I also found their man-ners and customs different from those of the Israeli Bedouin. They took pride in their hair, which they wore long and in plaits and which they washed in camel-urine to keep it soft and shiny. Their bodies were swathed in shirts of white cloth tightly tied with criss-crossed leather straps. They would brazenly bring their

126

herds into the cultivated fields among the crops and fodder. When caught, the grown-ups would feel the weight of our fists, but for the most part they would take to their heels when they saw us coming and leave their cattle in the charge of their little brothers. There was sheer artistry in the way they fled. They would first prod the camel to get it going, and mount it while it was on the move by first jumping on its neck and then crawling on to its hump; or they would seize one of its hind legs, get a grip on its protruding kneecap with their bare toes, and haul themselves up by their finger nails on to the back of the galloping beast. We would pursue them on horseback or in one of the police tenders, and when we managed to catch them there would be a scuffle. They were rough fighters, and used stones and knives. When we alone were involved, we of sober Nahalal, the clashes would end merely with fisticuffs and shouting. But when they encroached on the fields of our neighbours at Kfar Baruch, where there were a number of impetuous and hot-blooded youngsters, the engagements often required the intervention of police from Nazareth and ambulances from the central hospital.

After we had pushed them off our fields and driven their herds beyond the River Kishon, relations between us would improve. There was something strange, wild and free about them that captured my heart. They made their bread, deliciously crisp, from ears of grain cut straight from the stalks in the field, the kernels roasted whole, unground, over the fire, and the bread baked in the embers. Their principal food was the produce of their herds. They carried a wooden bowl into which they would milk the camel and drink from it. The cheese was made from goat's milk. They would let it ferment, then knead it into balls, and dry them on the tent cloths. They would carry the dried cheese balls on their journeys, and before eating would soak them in water. The food they liked most, however, were dates, the fruit on which they were brought up. Wherever they went, they were never without their *hajvah*, preserved dates pressed into large chunks, which were kept in goatskin wrapping. To roam over the desert, stretch out on the warm ground beneath the blue sky, munch dried dates, goat's cheese and toasted corn wafers – what else could a man want?

In 1936 I was called on to serve as a guide to a British army unit in the Valley of Jezreel. Armed Arab bands were sabotaging the Iraq Petroleum pipeline, and British troops had been sent to guard it. The pipeline ran from the Iraq oilfields through the Valley of Jezreel to the port of Haifa, crossing the Jordan opposite 'Star of the Winds', skirting the village of Ein-Dor (biblical Endor where Saul consulted the 'witch') between Mount Tabor and the hills of Moreh, and thence along the River Kishon.

Battalion headquarters were at Afula, the site of biblical Ophrah (according to archaeologist Yohanan Aharoni), the dwelling place of Gideon the Judge. The British army received me with open arms, lavishing upon me a wooden folding bed and three blankets, a corner of a NAAFI (or PX) tent and a mess-tin. The rifle, handsome uniform, and monthly wage of eight Palestine pounds I received from the police force. The uniform was that of a *ghaffir* (supernumerary policeman), tailored according to the finest Turkish traditions, with long baggy pants, and topped by headgear that was a joy to behold – a high-crowned astrakhan-type hat which fell over my ears. When I saw myself in the mirror, I could not help recalling the biblical description of what my forebears, the priests, were to wear upon their heads: 'And for Aaron's sons ... bonnets shalt thou make for them, for glory and for beauty!'

The system of protecting the pipeline was based on patrol and ambush along the line itself and along the access roads. My task was to guide the British troops through the dirt tracks and paths in the area, and also to serve as interpreter with the Arabs and the Jews. The operations of this unit of the King's Own Scottish Regiment were carried out mainly at night. But for all their activity, they never captured the Arab saboteurs and did not bring a halt to the sabotage. The troops always gave away their positions. They patrolled in 'iron chariots' – noisy armoured cars – and when they waited in ambush they smoked and cursed. The Arabs, who could hear them from far off, simply bypassed them, got close enough to the pipeline to shoot it up and set the oil on fire, and vanished into the darkness. The flames of the burning oil leapt high into the sky, illuminating all the surroundings, and could be seen from miles away. At sight of the blaze, the *shebab* (street-corner layabouts) in the Arab towns of Shechem and Jenin would celebrate the victory of the saboteurs, and crowds would throng the streets clapping hands and singing '*Al tirat ve-al debabat mah yagdush le-al asabat*' ('the planes and the tanks were unable to vanquish the saboteur bands').

I felt uncomfortable over these events. I was on the side of the British; yet the art of night operations as conceived by Gideon – carried out with intelligence by a few picked men – was being followed by our enemies, the Arab bands, while I was riding in an 'iron chariot'.

The Scottish regiment was replaced by the Yorkshire Rifles. The new battalion commander was a balding, ginger-whiskered officer – the ends of his moustache were tightly twirled into sharp points – who displayed a deeper interest in the bottle than he did in my recommendations for more sophisticated ambush tactics. One day, when we were passing Ein-Dor, he told me to call the village *mukhtar*. The headman duly appeared, full of bows and smiles. 'Tell the bastard,' said the commander to me, 'that if there is further sabotage of the pipeline, I'll blow up his house; and if sabotage is repeated, I'll go on blowing up the rest of the houses in the village.'

That night the pipeline was again sabotaged, and next morning the *mukhtar*'s house was blasted. The mutual blastings went on for some time, but eventually the Yorkshire Rifles gained the upper hand. 'I did not come here,' the battalion commander explained to me, 'to teach British soldiers how to crawl in your bloody country. I am here to teach the bloody Arabs how the British operate.'

To each generation, its own 'deliverer'.

THE LAST OF THE JUDGES and 'mighty men of valour' who 'delivered Israel' in time of stress was Samson, and then came the establishment of the monarchy.

For forty years the Philistines had held dominion over the Israelites until Samson arose and saved them. And Samson 'judged Israel in the days of the Philistines twenty years'. (*Judges* 16:20.)

His predecessors, Barak the son of Abinoam and Gideon the son of Joash, came from the northern tribes, Naphtali and Manasseh. Their battles were with the Canaanites and Midianites, and took place in the north of the country and in the Valley of Jezreel. Samson belonged to the tribe of Dan, whose territory lay to the south east of Jaffa, and he fought the Philistines who occupied the southern coastal belt.

He delivered his first blow against them in Ashkelon, one of the five cities of the 'lords of the Philistines'. His bride, 'a woman in Timnath of the daughters of the Philistines', revealed to her kinsmen the solution to the riddle Samson had set them as a wager at his wedding feast. The stakes were 'thirty change of garments', which Samson now had to pay them, since they had 'guessed'. Samson's 'anger was kindled' by the betrayal and the deceit. 'And the Spirit of the Lord came upon him, and he went down to Ashkelon, and slew thirty men of them ... and gave change of garments unto them which expounded the riddle.'

From now on there was war between him and the Philistines. He attacked them from time to time and put fear into their hearts. Samson did not summon the other tribes of Israel to his aid, nor even members of his own clan or family. He conducted a lone struggle. His own people bowed down in subservience to the masters and lacked the courage to revolt. The greatness of Samson lay not only in his physical strength, but in the spirit of freedom that flamed in his breast and inspired him to rise up against the enslavers of his nation.

After his wife's betrayal at the wedding feast, Samson had sent her back to her father's house at Timnath. Later, 'in the time of wheat harvest', he decided to visit her, but when he arrived, her father would not let him enter her chamber. He said to Samson: 'I verily thought thou hadst utterly hated her; therefore I gave her to thy companion.'

Samson used this as an opportune pretext to strike another blow at the Philistines. He caught three hundred foxes, tied firebrands to their tails, and sent them running through the Philistine fields and orchards, burning 'the standing corn, with the vineyards and olives'. The Philistines came after him, but he eluded them and went 'and dwelt in the top of the rock Etam', a promontory in the Judean desert south of Bethlehem, beyond the reach of his enemies.

The Philistines thereupon came up 'and pitched in Judah' and demanded of the Israelites that they hand over Samson to them. The weak-hearted men of Judah went out to the Etam rock and called to Samson: 'Knowest thou not that the Philistines are rulers over us? What is this that thou hast done unto us?' Samson replied: 'As they did unto me, so have I done unto them.'

But the Israelites preferred to give him up to the enemy rather than suffer Philistinian retribution for his actions. 'We are come down to bind thee', they told him, 'that we may deliver thee into the hand of the Philistines.' Samson agreed, came down from the rock, was bound 'with two new cords' and brought to the Philistine camp at En-hakkore, near the Sorek stream. A great roar rose up from the Philistine midst as the bound prisoner was handed over, when suddenly 'the Spirit of the Lord came mightily' upon Samson, and 'the cords that were upon his arms became as flax that was burnt with fire, and his bands loosed from off his hands'. Finding 'a new jawbone of an ass' nearby, he took it and with it slew a thousand Philistines. 'With the jawbone of an ass', he cried, 'with the jaw of an ass have I slain a thousand men.' (*Judges* 15:14–16.)

Samson's relationship with the Philistines was ambivalent. He fought them, but he also sought their company. Even after smiting them with the animal's jawbone, he went to pay court to a harlot in Gaza – and Gaza, like Ashkelon, was one of the five major Philistine cities!

Samson's downfall came about through love of a lady – 'a woman in the valley of Sorek, whose name was Delilah' and who betrayed him. She received 'eleven hundred pieces of silver' from each of 'the lords of the Philistines' to discover the source of Samson's strength. Day after day, Delilah urged and pressed and cajoled Samson until she finally elicited the secret: 'There hath not come a razor upon mine head' since birth, and 'if I be shaven, then my strength will go from me'. She then summoned the Philistines to come up surreptitiously and lie in wait. And when they came 'and brought money in their hand', she went to Samson, 'made him sleep upon her knees' and had 'the seven locks of his head' shaved off. She then cried out, 'The Philistines be upon thee, Samson. And he awoke out of his sleep, and said, I will go out as at other times before ... And he wist not that the Lord was departed from him' and that his strength had ebbed.

The Philistines rushed upon him, seized him, put out his eyes, brought him to Gaza, bound him with brass, and set him to grinding corn in the prison. Meanwhile, 'the hair of his head began to grow again'.

To celebrate the capture of their prize enemy, the Philistines assembled in a great gathering to offer sacrifice to their god Dagon; and they had the blind Samson brought from the prison house to the temple to 'make us sport'. Inside the building, 'Samson said unto the lad that held him by the hand' to guide and set him between 'the pillars whereupon the house standeth, that I may lean upon them'. He then 'called unto the Lord ... strengthen me, I pray thee, only this once, O God, that I may be at once avenged of the Philistines for my two eyes'.

As he ended his plea, he 'took hold of the two middle pillars upon which the house stood, and on which it was borne up', one with his right hand and the other with his left, and cried out: 'Let me die with the Philistines!' So saying, 'he bowed himself with all his might; and the house fell upon the lords, and upon all the people that were therein. So the dead which he slew at his death were more than they which he slew in his life.' (*Judges* 16:30.)

The Philistines were associated with the Israelites – as their sworn enemies – throughout the period of the Judges and the early years of the kingdom of Israel. Samson's life from birth to death was almost wholly bound up with them. He fought the Philistines and made friends with them, defeated them and was vanquished by them and, eyeless in Gaza, in the last of his heroic deeds, he wrought dramatic vengeance. Then came 'his brethren and all the house of his father ... and buried him between Zorah and Eshtaol in the burying place of Manoah his father'. But his life was spent and his feats, battles and death took place in the land of the Philistines.

I CAME TO the 'land of the Philistines' from the mountains. During the latter part of the 1948 War of Independence I was commander of Jerusalem, and had my home there. I continued living there for a time when, after the war, I was appointed GOC Southern Command. I would leave early in the morning for my headquarters in the south, and as I drove down from the cold mountains, crossed Delilah's Valley of Sorek, and reached the coastal belt, I always had the feeling that I had come to another land. It was a land of springtime every day of the year, caressed by a breeze as soft and smooth as swan's down, favoured by a warm sun, with green fields and a treasury of multi-coloured flowers, and bordered on the west for the entire length of the coast by a flashing stretch of golden dunes. No wonder Samson loved to walk in the land of the Philistines, not only to battle but also to feast with friends. The village where he was born, Zorah, lies at the foot of the Jerusalem hills and at the edge of the coastal plain. Above it to the east soar the mountains. Below it, stretching southwards and seawards, lies the flat and fruitful plain, unmarked by boulder or fissure. Stout trees, like the oak and terebinth, flourish in the mountains; but the palms of honeyed dates, and the lilies with their intoxicating perfume, glorify the Vale of Sharon and the Shephelah.

After our War of Independence came immigration and settlement. The cactus hedges were torn up, shacks cleared, the mounds which held the remains of abandoned Arab villages levelled, and on these sites arose Jewish settlements. Immigrants from Yemen, North Africa, Iraq and Europe built their homes and cultivated the land in the Sharon, the coastal foothills and the Negev.

If one looked out only upon the surface, the view at that time was of a new landscape, the landscape of the state of Israel that had again come into being. But an additional landscape was being exposed in those days, the landscape of the past. Bulldozers preparing ground for construction and cultivation brought to light remains of ancient settlement. Channel-cutting over the length of the country to bring the waters of the Jordan in the north to the Negev in the south also brought forth the days of antiquity. Every phase in the development of an infra-structure which involved excavation – foundations for buildings, pits for electric pylons, the opening of quarries, laying networks of roads, sewage, telephone lines – all, as though by magic, raised parts of the thousands-of-years-old mantle which covered the face of the land.

Most of the pottery artefacts that were unearthed were bits of broken jugs, plates, flasks and oil lamps belonging to the Canaanite period. These were the primitive vessels of poor peasants, the local inhabitants. But occasionally the excavating bulldozer would turn up something special. Such were the Philistine artefacts, of a splendour of colour, form and decoration which reflected a spirit of joy in living.

I received an urgent call one day from Aryeh, a young friend still in his teens who shared my interest in archaeology. He lived with his family in the village of Azor, just south-east of Jaffa, close to a small *tel* which was within an area then being levelled for the erection of housing estates for new immigrants. When the first bulldozer began excavating, it threw up several ancient vessels. Aryeh was there, and he spotted them, showed them to the driver, told him they looked like important antiquities, and asked him to stop work. 'Nonsense', said the driver, and told him not to 'bother me with these bits of old rubbish and let me get on with the job. The immigrants are still living in temporary shacks and we've got to get them into proper houses before winter.' That was when Aryeh had telephoned me.

I went with him to the *tel* late that afternoon. It was evident that people had buried their dead here throughout the ages, as far back as the Canaanites, three thousand seven hundred years ago. During one period, roughly three thousand years ago, the Philistines too had used this as a burial site. At the side of the corpse they placed a pot containing the meat of a goat or lamb, and dainty flasks of oil and perfume. They may not have done the same with every burial, but this was what I saw in the tombs that had been opened by the blade of the power-shovel.

I collected a few unbroken vessels and a large number of potsherds. The vessels bore the figure of a swan, the characteristic decoration on Philistine cooking pots and on vessels with strainer spouts which archaeologists call 'beer jugs'. The special features of the Philistine swan are its graceful lines, particularly when it is depicted with arched neck, its head meeting its wing.

Next day the government antiquities department ordered all construction work to stop, and some time later carried out a 'salvage dig' on the site to rescue what was left after the operation of the earth-moving equipment. This was good, right and proper. But I confess I was less happy at having to part with the vessels I had collected. It was with no ease of heart that I handed them all over to the antiquities department. I was left with only a few shards, and the memory of the sliced-up mound.

Years passed. The area became covered with roads, houses and public buildings reaching right up to Jaffa. But the *tel* was fenced and protected, and so it remains to this day. I never pass it without seeing with the mind's eye rows of Philistine graves beneath the surface, the resting place of the Sea People who came from the Aegean region, Crete, Rhodes and Cyprus, and invaded this country. These strangers brought with them their lively culture. They continued here their pattern of domestic life, duplicating the atmosphere in their island homes with a welcoming wine jar, decorated with swans against a painted background of red and white, exuding gladness and joy.

The loveliest Philistine swan I have ever seen was the one I found in Ashdod. Of the five biblical cities of 'the lords of the Philistines', the three on the coast have been preserved in name throughout thirty centuries: Ashdod, Ashkelon and Gaza. The identity and location of the other two, Gath and Ekron, have not yet been established with certainty.

The Philistine shard with the decoration of a swan, which General Dayan found in Ashdod.

Our War of Independence ended with Gaza in Egyptian hands, and Ashkelon and Ashdod in ours. The Arab inhabitants of Ashkelon stayed put, but Ashdod was abandoned and destroyed.

One winter day I drove past the archaeological mound of Ashdod and saw bull-dozers at work clearing the ruins of the adjacent village and preparing the ground for cultivation. Towards the end of the week it rained heavily, and there was no let-up on the Saturday, our Sabbath.

I am not superstitious. Nor am I a believer in the prevision of dreams. But on that Sabbath morning I woke up early with the thought that the heavy downpour immediately following the bulldozer must assuredly have exposed a tomb in the wall of ancient Ashdod. It may be that what I had dreamed was a montage of the ruined brick wall of Ashdod that I had passed earlier in the week, and a vision of the biblical story of the Philistines nailing the body of King Saul to the wall of Beth-shan.

In any event, I set off for Ashdod. Leaving the car at the side of the road, I trudged through the mud and climbed the *tel*. Before I had reached the top, I was certain I would find what I was looking for. Strewn on the slopes were pieces of a large jar which had undoubtedly been washed down from the summit of the mound by rainwater. When I got to the wall, I saw bones from a human skeleton, and beside them two jugs and a flask. They were lying in the sludge of a hollow scooped out at the bottom of the wall. The jugs had been crushed by the weight of the earth that had been pressing on them throughout the centuries; but the small flask, with three handles, and tapering down to a sharp point, was perfectly preserved. The base of one large jug was in its original place; the rest of it had been swept down the slope – they were the pieces I had seen on my way up.

The jugs and flask, about 3500 years old, were not unique. Nor was there anything grand about the tomb itself. It was the simple grave of a Canaanite male who had been buried at the foot of the wall.

My eye suddenly lighted upon a potsherd painted white with black stripes. Washed by the rain, its colours stood out clearly. It was evident that this was a piece of Philistine pottery that had been swept down from a later stratum. I followed the channel furrowed by the rushing rainwater and indeed, against a bush at the top of the mound, I found a heap of similar potsherds. They were partly covered by mud, but the complete head of a swan was clearly visible on one of the pieces. I scratched around and collected all the fragments that belonged to the same vessel. I was wet to the bone, but the Philistine swan warmed my heart.

I returned home, washed and dried the potsherds, matched, fitted and glued them together. When the reconstruction was complete, it constituted only about a quarter of the vessel, enough to identify it as belonging to the type known as 'jug with spout and strainer'. They have a single handle on the right side, and are thought to have held wine. One drank straight from the spout, the right hand holding the vessel by the handle and the left hand supporting it from the base.

What interested me, however, was not the wine but the swan. It appears on the portion of jug in my possession in all its glory, a full-bodied, three-toed, stylized bird, wings spread backwards, beak straining forward, drawn in black and white.

The Philistines reached Ashdod when the city had already been settled for several centuries, and they replaced the earlier cultures with their own. Their styles, patterns and art forms in turn gave way in later centuries to the Persian, Hellenistic and Roman. But of them all, Philistine pottery decorated with their incomparable swan takes pride of place. To me, there is nothing like it. Should you ever visit the Israel Museum in Jerusalem, ask to see my 'swan of Ashdod'.

Why was the swan-figure so widely used as an embellishment by the Philistines? Its grace and beauty would have been sufficient reason; but it may also have symbolized their attachment to the sea – their ship's prow was often crowned with the figure of a swan. And I have heard the theory that the Philistines regarded the swan as the ideal creature: it could fly, swim, and waddle on land.

Though the swan was the most widespread motif in Philistine pottery, it was not the only one. I had the good fortune to discover a piece of a rare Philistine vessel in the form of a lion's head. The complete object was what is known by scholars as a ryton. This was a large goblet for ordinary wine-drinking or it may have been used in ritual ceremonies. The part I found with the head of a lion is identical with the lower section of a vessel unearthed at Megiddo. I discovered it, broken, in a field near the archaeological mound of Tel es-Safi, located in the coastal plain halfway between Gezer and Lachish. The field is not part of the *tel*. It lies to its west, across the wadi that encircles es-Safi, but apparently at one time it was also the site of a Philistine settlement.

The globular shard was lying on the surface of the slope that runs down to the wadi. In the summer months the pawing of the sheep that pasture in this area crumbles and powders the soil, which is swept into the wadi with the coming of the rains, leaving the ancient shards exposed. Had it not been for the decorative coloured stripes on the lion's face I might not have noticed it. Only when I had washed and cleaned the pottery piece did I realize its quality. In the evening, after reading up on the archaeology of the region, I learned that the current scholarly theory identifies Tel es-Safi with Gath of the Philistines. Even if this theory is not accepted by all, it was most acceptable to me, at least on that day of discovery. What could be more symbolic than the broken head of a Philistine lion rolling round the fields of Gath – especially when it was not far from 'the vineyards of Timnath' where Samson tore 'a young lion' in pieces 'as he would have rent a kid'?

PART FOUR
THE KINGDOM OF ISRAEL

The Kingdom
of Israel
in David's Time

MEDITERRANEAN

HAMATH

PHOENICIA

ARAM

• Damascus

Mt Gilboa

Bezek •
Aphek •
• Eben-ezer

R. Jordan

• Jabesh Gilead

Joppa

Shiloh

AMMON

Ramah •
Gibeah •
• Michmash

• Rabat Ammon

Cave of Adullam

Jerusalem

Gaza •

Valley of Elah

• Keilah

Hebron •

MOAB

• Beersheba

EDOM

PHILISTIA

• Sela

Scale

0   20   40 miles

0   20   40

kms

Eilat   Ezion-geber

▲▲▲▲▲ Boundary of the kingdom

14
The daughters of Shiloh

A S THE PERIOD of the Judges drew to an end, the sceptre of authority passed from the 'deliverers' – all but one, valiant men of war – to the priesthood. This authority, in the middle of the eleventh century BC, was vested in 'Eli the priest'. His ministry was at Shiloh, which held the Ark of the Covenant and was then the Jewish centre of worship. Eli 'judged Israel forty years', and after him came Samuel of the tribe of Levi, brought up from infancy by Eli in 'the house of the Lord in Shiloh'.

Eli had been kind to Samuel's mother, Hannah. She was the wife of Elkanah, a 'man of Ramathaim-zuphim, of mount Ephraim', and she had been childless. On their annual pilgrimage to Shiloh, Hannah petitioned the Lord to give her a child, but 'she spake in her heart; only her lips moved, but her voice was not heard'. (1 *Samuel* 1 : 13.) Eli watched her and 'thought she had been drunken'. But when he learned the truth, he comforted her. Hannah vowed that if she were blessed with 'a man child, then I will give him unto the Lord all the days of his life'. When Samuel was born, she waited until he was weaned and then fulfilled her vow by entrusting him to the care of Eli.

Samuel eventually succeeded Eli as priest. He was also a prophet, the greatest since Moses, and 'he went from year to year in circuit to Bethel, and Gilgal, and Mizpeh, and judged Israel in all those places. And his return was to Ramah [Ramathaim, his birthplace] for there was his house, and there he judged Israel; and there he built an altar unto the Lord.' (1 *Sam.* 7 : 16, 17.)

The Samuel period was of fateful moment in the early history of Israel. This was a troubled period when the tribal confederacy was proving inadequate to meet the external pressures, and the nation was moving towards a united kingdom. There is recurring biblical comment, pithy and painful, on the situation in the country during this time: 'In those days there was no king in Israel: every man did that which was right in his own eyes.'

Eli wore the crown of leadership not by virtue of any personal distinction or charisma, as was the case with his predecessors, the Judges, but through his membership of the priestly dynasty and his official religious function. In the same way, and in the normal course of events, one of his sons would inherit the high office. He had two sons, Hophni and Phinehas. Both were 'priests of the Lord' in Shiloh; but they did not 'walk in the ways of the Lord'. Both were corrupt, wicked men who exploited their positions by exacting gifts from those who came to sacrifice and worship. Their aged father, shocked at the reports he heard of their 'evil

previous pages The river Jordan.

dealings', did indeed speak harshly to them and sought to restore them to the path of righteousness. But they 'hearkened not unto the voice of their father'.

Samuel was to have the same problem in his day with his own sons. He also had two, Joel and Abiah, and he appointed them 'judges in Beersheba'. But they, too, were corrupt. They 'turned aside after lucre, and took bribes, and perverted judgement'. Yet Samuel behaved as had Eli: he, too, heard reports of his sons' evil-doing, yet he allowed them to remain in their posts.

Israel at that time was afflicted not only by internal troubles; she also suffered serious blows from her neighbours. During Eli's ministry, 'Israel was smitten before the Philistines' at the battle of Ebenezer, near Aphek, ten miles north-east of Jaffa, and lost 'about four thousand men'. The Israelites were at a loss as to what to do. They had no outstanding military commander, no one to lead them. In their perplexity, they despatched messengers to Shiloh to bring the holy Ark to the battle front. They hoped that its presence would inspire the fighting men, stiffen their morale, guide them in combat, and 'save us out of the hands of our enemies'. But in this battle, too, Israel was roundly beaten, suffering grievous losses. They 'fled every man into his tent: and there was a very great slaughter; for there fell of Israel thirty thousand footmen'. Among them were Eli's sons. And Eli himself died upon hearing the news. The Ark of the Lord was captured by the Philistines and taken to the temple of their god Dagon in Ashdod.

The effect on Ashdod was disastrous. The idol Dagon fell from its pedestal and was shattered, and the people of the city were struck by misfortune. Instead of its being a blessing, the Ark brought a curse upon the heads of the Philistines. After seven months of misery, they said: 'Send away the ark of the God of Israel, and let it go again to his own place, that it slay us not, and our people.' They thereupon set the Ark upon a specially made wagon which was drawn by two milch kine 'on which there hath come no yoke', and sent it on its way, driverless, across the border into Israel. And it came to rest in the field of Joshua in Beth Shemesh.

The country was untroubled by external foes for the next twenty years, and then the Philistines launched another campaign, attacking the Israelites at Mizpeh. This time, however, they were badly beaten, and the Israelite troops pursued the fleeing Philistines, 'and smote them', and subdued them; 'and the hand of the Lord was against the Philistines all the days of Samuel'. There was also 'peace between Israel and the Amorites'.

Israel had neutralized her enemies, received back the Ark of the Covenant, and the 'cities which the Philistines had taken from Israel were restored to Israel, from Ekron even unto Gath'. Nevertheless, the Israelites sought an end to the existing regime and its replacement by a permanent system of national leadership. 'Then all the elders of Israel gathered themselves together, and came to Samuel unto Ramah, And said unto him, Behold, thou art old, and thy sons walk not in thy ways: now make us a king to judge us like all the nations.'

Samuel's response was an angry rebuke, and he warned them what their lot would be under a monarchy. The king would press their sons and daughters into

A medieval Old Testament miniature, showing (top panel) Samuel exhorting the Israelites to destroy 'the strange gods'; and (lower panel) aided by Samuel's prayer, the Israelites repel the Philistines.

his service, impose heavy taxes on their farm produce and livestock, and even take the choicest of their fields, vineyards and olive groves and give them to his officers. But the people refused to heed his words. 'Nay', they replied, 'but we will have a king over us; That we also may be like all the nations, and that our king may judge us, and go out before us, and fight our battles.' And the Lord said to Samuel: 'Hearken unto their voice, and make them a king.' Samuel thereupon assured the elders that he would do as they wished, and sent them home.

Separate tribal existence was about to cease. A monarchy was to rise in Israel, its watchword national unity.

SHILOH FLOURISHED as the religious centre of Israel during the period of the Judges. It came to an end when that period ended. It was from Shiloh that the Ark had been brought to the Ebenezer-Aphek battlefield and captured by the Philistines. But when they sent it back to Israel on the driverless wagon which came to rest 'in the field of Joshua' at Beth Shemesh, it was not restored to Shiloh but was installed in 'the house of Abinadab' in Kirjath-jearim. (1 *Sam.* 7:1.)

The Bible does not explain why. But archaeological excavation carried out at the site of ancient Shiloh revealed that it was destroyed in a great fire in the middle of the eleventh century BC. Scholars suggest that when the Philistines vanquished Israel at Ebenezer, they went on to capture and destroy Shiloh.

The city is first mentioned in the *Book of Joshua*. After the conquest of Canaan, 'the whole congregation of the children of Israel assembled together at Shiloh, and set up the tabernacle' which held the Ark of the Covenant. (*Joshua* 18:1.) Thereafter, Shiloh appears frequently in the biblical record as the site of notable national events. It was there that seven of the tribes received their territorial allotments: 'and Joshua cast lots before them in Shiloh before the Lord: and there Joshua divided the land unto the children of Israel'.

Shiloh was also chosen as the site to re-establish unity following an inter-tribal clash. The grim episode of the concubine at Gibeah, victim of mass rape by 'certain sons of Belial' of the tribe of Benjamin, prompted all the other tribes solemnly to swear that 'There shall not any of us give his daughter unto Benjamin to wife'. Later, after a bloody battle against the Benjaminites, they regretted their oath, as this would lead ultimately to the elimination of one of the twelve tribes of the nation. But since their oath could not be revoked, a solution was found involving the annual 'feast of the Lord in Shiloh' which also celebrated the grape harvest. They told the Benjaminites: 'Go and lie in wait in the vineyards; And see, and, behold, if the daughters of Shiloh come out to dance in dances, then come ye out of the vineyards, and catch you every man his wife of the daughters of Shiloh, and go to the land of Benjamin.' (*Judges* 21:21.)

However, the most memorable events that occurred in Shiloh were those associated with the prophet Samuel. The heartbreaking plea of the childless Hannah, the compassion of Eli the priest, the revelation of the Lord to the boy Samuel, the death of Eli and his two sons, and the loss of the Ark of the Covenant, are all part of the spiritual tradition of Israel.

top The Ark of the Covenant.
bottom David plays his harp.
From a 9th-century manuscript.

They were frequent themes in the works of the two poets who were my favourites when I was a boy – Rachel of Deganiah, and Shlonsky. Rachel often wove into her poetry allusions to biblical events and characters, linking stories of the national past with her personal present, her being, her experiences, sensations, emotions, her own childless state. Her poem 'Barren' was very much in vogue in the country at the time. Its grace of expression and depth of feeling breathed new life into this human story of antiquity:

> *If only I had a child,*
> *a child of my own.*
> *Curly-haired, clever, and dark.*
> *To hold by the hand as we slowly*
> *strolled through the park.*
> *A child.*
> *Of my own.*
>
> *Uri, I'd call him, Uri my own.*
> *Gentle his name and clear,*
> *a droplet of a stream.*
> *To the dark child of my dream,*
> *'Uri,'*
> *I'd call.*
>
> *Like Rachel our Mother I am bitter still.*
> *Still pray as Hannah prayed, her womb a stone.*
> *Still, still I await*
> *my own.*

(Translated by Robert Friend)

The poetry of Shlonsky was quite different. His work was far more complex, more sophisticated, full of symbolism, elusive suggestions, and brilliant word-play. It was not – or so it seemed to me in my youth – idyllic and pastoral like Rachel's. Shlonsky had come to Israel from Russia after the First World War, had lived through and been influenced by the 1917 revolution, and his work was imbued with the spirit of rebellion. In my village of Nahalal, the spiritual guides were the 'constructive' writers and poets, Bialik, Tchernichovsky, Rachel and Brenner.

The new spirit of iconoclasm, of which Shlonsky was the standard-bearer, was rather frowned upon by the veterans. And so it was without the knowledge of the village cultural committee that I travelled specially to Tel-Aviv one day, on behalf of the Youth of Nahalal Literary Society, to invite Shlonsky to come and lecture to us and read his poems. Shlonsky accepted, and the entire village, old and young, gathered in the communal hall to hear him. Shlonsky was then a young man with delicate features, a soft voice, and a formidable mane crowning his head. Microphones were not then known in Israel, and Shlonsky had to raise his voice. This proved no difficulty, for he soon warmed with enthusiasm to the magic of his words and read in ringing tones.

The finest poem he recited that evening had as its theme the young Samuel in the shrine at Shiloh, awakened at night by the voice of the Lord – he thought he was being called by Eli the priest. It is entitled 'Revelation', and is the opening poem to his collection *Just so*:

> 'Now Eli was very old ... and the sons of Eli
> were worthless men ... and the child
> Samuel ministered unto the Lord'.
>
> (1 *Sam.* 2:12, 18, 22.)

> *'Hear me!' someone called.*
> *Someone called my name.*
> *What was near?*
> *Who came?*
> *Eli said: 'Lie down again.'*
> *Eli said: 'In vain.'*
> *Eli said: 'No vision comes because my eyes grow dim.'*
>
> *But 'Hear me!' someone called again.*
> *But I was called by name again.*
> *And how was I to answer,*
> *'I am here!'*
>
> *Midnight. And Eli on his bed*
> *wept, 'My sons, my sons!'*
> *And already the universe crouched*
> *in me, wounded like a sunset sky*
> *midst the corpses of my clouds.*
>
> *And I knew, my people, the Lord was coming,*
> *was coming in a storm to kiss your wounds.*
> *And Eli's sons were evil, and Eli very old.*
> *And I was still a child.*
>
> *But the universe was roaring.*
> *Suffering pain and singing.*
> *And where the east turned red,*
> *a finger of lightning beckoned,*
> *and I said:*
>
> *'Speak, Lord, for thy servant hears!'*

(Translated by Robert Friend)

I was enthralled. I listened to the poet and heard the voice of youth's revolt against 'crabbed age', the voice of the young Samuel to Eli the elderly priest carried through the ages right down to our own day in the village hall of Nahalal.

I asked my parents for their impression when we got home after the lecture. My mother remained silent. She was in tune with the spirit of dissent and sympathetic towards the ideals of the Russian Revolution; but she was then unfamiliar with Hebrew literature, particularly traditional Hebrew writings. My father, however, was well versed in ancient Hebrew works, and knew well what Shlonsky was doing. I asked him what he thought of the poem 'Revelation'. 'Yes,' he said. And after a pause he added, 'Very nice.' I forbore from further questioning. It was evident that he was referring to the biblical story and not to Shlonsky's interpretation.

THERE IS NOW no human settlement on the site of Israelite Shiloh. There is, however, more than a hint of the preservation of its original name: the archaeological mound where the ancient city stood is still known by the local Arabs as Khirbet Silon (the Ruins of Silo). It is possible to identify the location by the precise details given in the *Book of Judges* (21:19): it lies 'on the north side of Bethel, on the east side of the highway that goeth up from Bethel to Shechem, and on the south of Lebonah'.

This was an area I missed on my youthful hikes during the British mandatory period. I first visited Khirbet Silon only after the 1967 Six Day War. I remember going there from Shechem – getting to it from the opposite direction to that taken by the Benjaminites who went northwards to ambush the daughters of Shiloh dancing in the vineyards. I had gone to Shechem to see Abu Romel, a dealer in antiquities, having heard that he had acquired some interesting mosaic tablets, parts of the floor of a Byzantine church. They had been discovered by peasants in Lebanon, smuggled into Jordan, and from there brought to the West Bank.

I found Abu Romel at his home in Hawara, a residential suburb on the southern outskirts of Shechem along the highway to Jerusalem. It is so named because its inhabitants came originally from Wadi Hawara, a swampy area twenty-seven miles away to the west, between Nathania and Hadera. The swamp lands had been bought by the Jews, dried out, cultivated, settled, and renamed Emek Hepher (the valley of biblical Hepher). Time and events leave their mark, some slight, some deep. Nations go to war; populations shift. Settlements are destroyed and abandoned; others rise in their place. Shiloh has undergone only a slight corruption of name in the Arabic Khirbet Silon. But a suburb of Shechem has become Hawara, and Hawara is once again the Hebrew Hepher.

The mosaics of Abu Romel were no special bargain. I bought three of the tablets, two bearing the design of birds, and the third a picture of a girl with doves on her shoulders. I drank sweet tea and bitter coffee, thanked and blessed my host, and continued on my way.

The entrance to the Valley of Shiloh lies about twelve miles south of Shechem. We left the Jerusalem highway and turned east along a dirt track. The archaeological *tel* of Shiloh is shaped like an elongated oval, pointing north. I was told that the valley adjoining the mound is variously called by the local Arabs Marj el-Id and Marj el-Bint (Arabic for the Valley of the Festival and the Valley of the Girls). I was tempted to think that the names were a holdover from antiquity; but they were no doubt conceived by some Western archaeologist probing the site and familiar with the biblical story, and the names stuck.

Little remains of the scholarly excavations. The few ruined buildings that still stand on the *tel* are late Arab. The sole relics from ancient Shiloh are, as usual, potsherds – bits of flasks, bowls and plates fashioned by potters thousands of years ago. Among them are also handles of jars – which may well have been held by 'the daughters of Shiloh' – and parts of sooty oil lamps which illuminated the houses of the city in antiquity.

Thistles, weeds, and wild oats sprouted between the boulders strewn over the mound, all that remains of walls and structures that have long been destroyed. The soldiers who were with me asked about the history of the site, and I told them. 'And that's all that can be seen of this now,' they observed ruefully. There was indeed nothing of note to be seen on the surface of the ground. But echoing in my mind as I stood there were two of the most moving verses ever uttered, both by leading personages associated with Shiloh. One was by a prophet to a king – Samuel's rebuke to Saul: 'Hath the Lord as great delight in burnt offerings and sacrifices, as in obeying the voice of the Lord?' (1 *Sam.* 15:22.) The second was from a man to a woman – the words of love and comfort from Elkanah to his wife Hannah, who so grieved because she was childless: 'Am not I better to thee than ten sons?' (1 *Sam.* 1:8.)

15
The tragic Saul

THE PROPHET SAMUEL had been opposed to the establishment of a monarchy. 'And ye have this day rejected your God, who himself saved you out of all your adversities and your tribulations', he told the elders of Israel who were demanding a king. But eventually he too realized that there was no other course. The tribes were scattered throughout the land of Canaan, from Mount Hermon and Mount Lebanon in the north to the tip of the Dead Sea in the south; and two of them, Gad and Reuben, dwelt in the mountains of Gilead east of the Jordan.

The Israelites at that time could almost hold their own against the enemies who lived within their tribal territories, but not against the enemy peoples round their borders. The Philistines occupied the coastal plain and the foothills. The Sidonians were in the north, the Amalekites and the Edomites in the south, and the Ammonites in the east. None of these bordering nations was allied to Israel. All seized every opportunity to attack and invade her. No single tribe alone could withstand their provocation, and enemy pressure mounted against neighbouring Israel, particularly from the Philistines.

Samuel the prophet went up to Zuph to 'sacrifice ... in the high place', and the Lord revealed to him that 'Tomorrow about this time I will send thee a man out of the land of Benjamin, and thou shalt anoint him to be captain over my people Israel, that he may save my people out of the hand of the Philistines; for I have looked upon my people, because their cry is come unto me.' When Saul, the son of Kish, met Samuel next day, the Lord said to the prophet: 'Behold the man whom I spake to thee of!' (1 *Sam.* 9:16, 17.)

Yet not only Samuel but also the very people who had demanded a king showed no haste in recognizing Saul as their master. When the young man encountered and joined an itinerant band of prophets shortly after his meeting with Samuel, he was mocked: 'the people said one to another, "What is this that is come unto the son of Kish? Is Saul also among the prophets?"' (1 *Sam.* 10:11.) Even after Samuel anointed and crowned him and declared publicly that the Lord had chosen Saul to be king over Israel, there were 'worthless fellows' who said, 'How shall this man save us?' And they despised him.

Saul held his peace, making no reply to his detractors. He returned to his home in Gibeah and to his labours, ploughing and sowing his father's fields. He knew that he had been anointed ruler in order to take military command in the war against the nation's enemies, and that day would come.

Saul's first battle was not, as expected, against Israel's closest neighbours, the

The mountains of Moab, looming over the Dead Sea.

Philistines, but against Ammon. 'Nahash the Ammonite came up, and encamped against Jabesh-gilead' on the east bank of the Jordan. When the Israelites of Jabesh sought surrender terms, Nahash set the condition 'that I may thrust out all your right eyes, and lay it for a reproach upon all Israel'. The shocked elders of Jabesh sent 'messengers unto all the coasts of Israel' seeking help; but none responded. Then they came to 'Gibeah of Saul', and upon hearing their tidings, 'all the people lifted up their voices, and wept'.

When Saul came in from the fields and heard the report of the Jabesh messengers, 'his anger was kindled greatly'. He was incensed not only with the Ammonites but with those tribes of Israel who had failed to go to the help of their brothers. In the presence of all, he took his 'yoke of oxen', slaughtered them, 'hewed them in pieces, and sent them throughout all the coasts of Israel' by messenger, with the warning signal: 'Whosoever cometh not forth after Saul and after Samuel, so shall it be done to his oxen.' (1 *Sam.* 11 :6, 7.)

Saul did not behave as had his predecessors, the Judges. He did not request and he did not plead. He did not echo Deborah's call: 'the people willingly offered themselves'. Saul ordered and threatened. He gave notice to the tribes that anyone failing to join him in battle would have good reason to be sorry. The Israelites had not heard such language before. 'And the fear of the Lord fell on the people, and they came out with one consent.' (1 *Sam.* 11 :7.)

Saul mustered them at Bezek – west of the Jordan, opposite Jabesh-gilead – and took command. Every tribe had responded, and the total strength was formidable: 'the children of Israel were three hundred thousand, and the men of Judah thirty thousand'. This was the first time since the Joshua conquest that all the tribes of Israel went jointly to war as a united force. Saul called for the messengers from Jabesh and told them to inform the elders of their city that 'tomorrow, by that time the sun be hot, ye shall have help'. (1 *Sam.* 11 :9.) On the morrow, before dawn, Saul launched a three-pronged surprise attack on the Ammonite camp. By 'the heat of the day', the Ammonites were cut down, and the survivors who fled 'were scattered, so that two of them were not left together'.

Two years later came the turn of the Philistines. Saul selected three thousand picked men, sending home the rest of the militia, and divided his force into two formations. One, numbering two thousand men, he put under his own command and deployed at 'Michmash and in mount Bethel'. The remaining thousand troops were placed under the command of his son Jonathan and despatched to 'Gibeah of Benjamin'. At a given signal, Jonathan attacked and defeated the Philistine garrison at Geba, and Saul 'blew the trumpet throughout all the land, saying, "Let the Hebrews hear." And all Israel heard say that Saul had smitten a garrison of Philistines.' This opening move launched the campaign against the Philistines.

The enemy mustered a huge force to crush the Israelites: 'thirty thousand chariots, and six hundred horsemen, and people as the sand on the sea shore in multitude.' When they had moved up to the pass of Michmash, they were thrown into disarray by a raid behind their lines carried out by Jonathan and his armour-bearer. Spotting 'a sharp rock' – one of two cliffs which bounded a deep gully,

Jericho; the view from the river Jordan.

and on which stood a Philistine outpost – Jonathan went through the defile and reached the rock in the rear of the enemy. He then 'climbed up upon his hands and upon his feet', his aide behind him, broke into the outpost and wiped it out.

'And that first slaughter, which Jonathan and his armour-bearer made, was about twenty men' – no great number; but the surprise was great, and the loss of the outpost which commanded the pass was a strategic disaster for the enemy. Panic erupted in the Philistine camp – 'the earth quaked'. Amidst their confusion, Saul and his force launched the main assault, and after a bitter battle put the enemy to rout. 'So the Lord saved Israel that day; and the battle passed over unto Bethaven.'

Following this campaign, Saul 'fought against all his enemies on every side, against Moab, and against the children of Ammon, and against Edom, and against the kings of Zobah ... whithersoever he turned himself, he vexed them. And he gathered an host, and smote the Amalekites, and delivered Israel out of the hands' of all who sought to plunder her.

The wars with Israel's enemies were not the only ones the first king of Israel had to fight. Saul faced contenders and adversaries even among his own people. The principal opposition came from the priests. His immediate predecessors, Samuel and Eli, spoke to the nation in the name of the Lord. They presided over the sacrificial offerings, made inquiry of the 'Urim and Thummim' (thought to be a kind of priestly oracle) about affairs of State, and were the medium through which the answer – the word of the Lord – favourable or harsh, was transmitted. Even after the establishment of the monarchy and the elevation of Saul, Samuel continued to 'inquire of the Lord' and give orders to the king on the conduct of the war. When the enemy gained the upper hand, the blame was heaped on Saul. When all went well, the praises were 'for the Lord' – that is the priests. On one notable occasion (described in chapter 14 of 1 *Samuel*), 'the Lord' snatched victory from Saul over the Philistines when it was within his grasp because his son Jonathan had inadvertently violated an oath taken by his father. (The troops persuaded Saul not to punish him.)

Thus, despite Saul's victories over Israel's enemies, his prestige declined. Samuel reproved him in public, and in a final confrontation informed him 'in the name of the Lord' that because 'thou hast rejected the word of the Lord, he hath also rejected thee from being king.... The Lord hath rent the kingdom of Israel from thee this day, and hath given it to a neighbour of thine, that is better than thou'. (1 *Sam.* 15:23, 28.)

Saul was shocked and mortified. Samuel uttered these shattering words when the king returned from battling in the Negev and winning a resounding victory over the Amalekites. There had not been a military success like it since the days of Joshua. He and his men had pursued the troops of Amalek all the way 'from Havilah until thou comest to Shur, that is over against Egypt. And he took Agag the king of the Amalekites alive'. Yet he was being greeted by Samuel not with congratulation and blessing but with grim rebuke and a prophecy of doom. He was astounded.

His people were no longer a league of tribes each doing 'that which was right in his own eyes'. The entire nation of Israel accepted him as their national leader. Two hundred and ten thousand men had gone with him to war, and Samuel himself had enjoined him to 'go and smite Amalek'. His sole transgression had been to ignore Samuel's further injunction to destroy all the Amalekites as well as their possessions, including all their livestock. Saul had spared the life of King Agag, taking him prisoner, and allowed his troops to seize, and not 'utterly destroy', the 'best of the sheep, and of the oxen, and of the fatlings, and the lambs'. Saul could understand his people. Battle-worn, spent, hungry, they had been fighting hard in campaign after campaign against enemies who invaded, killed and plundered them at every opportunity. And here they were on the victorious field of combat, having inflicted a decisive blow against the enemy Amalekites – and having suffered their own casualties. Could Saul indeed deny them some of the spoils of the hard-won battle?

Yet when Samuel uttered his devastating reproof, Saul, with the dust of combat still upon him, was repeatedly driven to confess his transgression. Yes, he had not followed to the letter the priestly commands, and he was sorry. He had to abase himself before Samuel and seek the prophet's grace: 'I have sinned: yet honour me now, I pray thee, before the elders of my people, and before Israel, and turn again with me, that I may worship the Lord thy God.' (1 *Sam.* 15:30.) Was Saul's 'thy God' rather than 'our God' merely an interchangeable linguistic form, or was it the expression of an aggrieved heart?

SAUL WAS TWICE anointed king, once at Zuph and again at Gilgal. On both occasions he came to kinghood from the fields. The first was when he had been out searching for the asses of his father and had met Samuel. The second occurred after he had come in from ploughing with his oxen. He had heard the news from Jabesh-gilead, gone off to war against King Nahash of Ammon, and after the victory had gone with 'all the people' to Gilgal to 'renew the kingdom there . . . and there they made Saul king before the Lord in Gilgal . . . and there Saul and all the men of Israel rejoiced greatly'. (1 *Sam.* 11:14, 15.)

The asses of Saul's father had strayed – a not uncommon phenomenon. Asses are sociable animals and like group living. If a single one should find itself separated from the herd and home, it would always try to get back. But when all are grazing together, the whole group may easily move away from the village and wander off wherever their legs carry them. The leader may turn to the foot of the slopes to find fresh grass, and the rest will follow. Or they may hear from afar the sound of water trickling along the irrigation ditches, and all will head towards the source. They are untroubled by home-sickness, feel no attachment to their owner, have little sense of direction and soon lose their way. The important thing for them is not to be parted from the herd, to nestle close to one another, and to follow their leader. In the morning they go foraging, and at noon they seek out shade. When something frightens them, they suddenly break into a gallop, tails and ears laid back. At times they will stop in a field of loose earth or a stretch of dune, lie down and roll from side to side, rubbing their backs on the ground or wallowing in the sand. They will then get up and resume their normal practice – munching grass and moving on, without knowing where.

Saul, the son of Kish, set out with his father's servant to find the asses and turned eastwards, to Mount Ephraim. They did not know where the asses had gone, but they did know their habits: the animals would not go back on their tracks. They would keep going, their heads to the ground, tails pressed to their thighs. They would graze and walk, graze and move on, until someone would spot them, corral them and wait until the owner came looking for them. This has always been the rule with asses. It was so with the asses of Kish, the father of Saul, who dwelt in Gibeah in the territory of Benjamin more than three thousand years ago; and so it is today with the asses of the el-Mazarib Bedouin tribe that dwell behind the hill of Shimron near Nahalal. The asses of Kish were found after three days; Saul had his fateful meeting with Samuel; and he returned home to resume work in his father's fields. When the messengers from Jabesh-gilead arrived in Gibeah seeking help, Saul was out ploughing with a pair of oxen.

Ploughing is a winter job, after the rains. In the summer in Israel the ground is dry and hard, and difficult to cut through. Only the hill slopes are furrowed before the first rainfall, to ensure that when the skies open most of the water will be absorbed by the soil and not sweep wastefully down into the wadi. In winter, with its short days, the work is endless, for both the ploughing and the sowing must be completed between the first and the later rains. Early each day while it is still dark, the plough-oxen must be given their fodder. This takes time, for they chew slowly, and they must eat their fill to fortify themselves for the toil ahead. At dawn the ploughmen go out to the fields carrying a wicker basket with food for the day – a chunk of cheese, a handful of olives, and dried figs. Occasionally the housewife will add a few radishes and onions, the vegetables of winter. The hot meal is eaten at night, after the day's labours.

The wooden plough is drawn by a pair of oxen, sometimes cows. On the wealthier farms there may be two or three ploughmen, working in staggered line, one behind and slightly to the side of the other. The senior worker takes the lead, sets the pace, and determines the rest-breaks.

The ploughman's day ends when the sun begins to sink below the horizon. The animals are freed from their yoke, the ploughs left in the fields, and man and beast wend their way home. Behind them darkness creeps over the furrowed land, the product of their exertions; ahead, at the top of the hill, looms their village. Wisps of light smoke rise from the courtyards of the houses. Dinner is simmering in the cooking-pots.

This was how 'Saul came after the herd out of the field' to his home in Gibeah. (1 *Sam.* 11:5.) And this was the pattern forty years ago of our peasant neighbours who lived in the villages around us, Ma'alul, Majdal, Jedda and Aylut. In Israel today, even the Bedouin work their land with steel ploughs and tractors. The wooden plough drawn by oxen remains only in the stories of the Bible and in our memories of childhood.

Young people at work at Moshav Gamla in northern Israel.

I HAD LONG been curious as to where exactly were the two 'sharp rocks', with the defile between them, where Jonathan and his armour-bearer carried out their raid at the battle of Michmash. On more than one occasion I went exploring a wadi in the area, a dried-up river bed called Wadi Suweinit, and I think I have found the spot. Just south of the site of ancient Michmash – which is now a small Arab village called Makhmas – the wadi makes a sharp bend, almost a hairpin turn. This stretch of the wadi is indeed a deep gully – a pass or passage, as the Bible calls it – with particularly steep cliffs ('sharp rocks') on either side. This is precisely the route I would choose if I had to break into an enemy position atop one of the cliffs from the rear. Jonathan was looking for a way through to the Philistine camp, and the southern flank held the most promise, for it was only lightly guarded. It was skirted and protected by the gully, and the Philistines had no fear of an Israelite attack from this direction.

Jonathan decided to try and move through this gully. And of this passage, says the biblical record, 'by which Jonathan sought to go over unto the Philistines' garrison, there was a sharp rock on the one side, and a sharp rock on the other side: and the name of the one was Bozez, and the name of the other Seneh'. (1 *Sam.* 14:4.) It was clear to him that in crossing the wadi he would be exposing himself to the Philistines. If they ordered him to halt, and sent troops to meet him and find out what he wanted, he would have to abandon his planned raid; for even if he managed to overpower them, he would be unable to climb the steep bank under the hail of Philistine arrows. But if they were confident enough to tell him to come up to them, he could climb unmolested until he reached the top. He would then engage them, and all would be well; for he could rely on his sword, and had no doubt that he would come out best in hand-to-hand fighting.

And, indeed, the self-assured Philistines taunted the two Israelites, and behaved as Jonathan hoped they would. When he and his bearer appeared, the guards of the outpost called down to them, daring them to 'Come up to us, and we will shew you a thing!' (1 *Sam.* 14:12.) Jonathan and his aide thereupon began scaling the sheer slope, using the rock projections as hand- and foot-holds. When they got to the top and the small Philistine garrison came swaggering towards them, Jonathan promptly rushed them and set about them with his sword; 'and his armour-bearer slew after him'.

They killed a few of the enemy and the rest fled. The outpost fell; and the pass between the cliffs of Bozez and Seneh was now open to the Israelite army.

EVERY FIGHTING MAN who has ever carried out a surprise attack on an enemy position will readily sense from the biblical description the full flavour of Jonathan's lone action against the Philistine outpost – creeping through the gully, reaching the foot of the cliff, making the dangerous climb, determined, with racing heart and breath-stopping tension, to attain his objective and above all not to fall.

In 1941, during the Second World War, I fought with an Australian spearhead unit against the Vichy French in Syria. I lost an eye in this battle; but the moments most deeply engraved on my mind were those in which I crawled towards the enemy post. The exchange of fire between us had gone on since dawn, and what little ammunition we had carried in our personal packs was almost finished. The only way we could hold out until the main British forces would reach us was to capture the French position and consolidate ourselves therein. But the terrain between us and the post was open, flat, and under enemy fire, particularly by a machine-gun which kept us pinned down. Despite this, I hoped that by sticking to the ground I might manage to get close to it without discovery. The distance was not great, only about three hundred yards. I was young and wiry and I started crawling, but the pounding in my heart was pretty deafening. My own life and the fate of my comrades hung by a thread. If I succeeded in crossing the fields without being spotted and reaching a ditch that skirted the road just beneath the fortified building in which the enemy were entrenched, I could fling one of my two remaining grenades through the window of the machine-gun emplacement. If I were sighted, the enemy troops would, of course, swivel the weapon on to me and all would be lost.

The French machine-gun kept firing without pause. Its rat-tat was accompanied by the explosive reverberations of a heavy mortar and the incessant crack of rifle fire. But these were the sounds of another world, sensed at the edge of consciousness. My own immediate world was a world of silence, disturbed only by the crunch of the stubble beneath the weight of my body. And the only vision on which my eyes were fixed was of the terrain ahead, a heap of stones that would give me cover, a mound of earth I would need to skirt, a field of thorns – and then the ditch. Apart from these I saw nothing.

I got to the ditch, tossed a grenade, but missed. The second one burst through the window and silenced the machine-gun. The building was quickly captured. As Jonathan had said to his armour-bearer, 'there is no restraint to the Lord to save by many or by few'. (1 *Sam.* 14:6.) He was right. The Lord can save even with a few, but these few need strong arms and legs, and must use all their might to climb or crawl to their target.

THE WAR WITH AMALEK led to the final break between the prophet Samuel and King Saul. True, Samuel responded to Saul's plea to 'turn again with me, that I may worship the Lord'; and 'Samuel turned again after Saul; and Saul worshipped the Lord' in Gilgal. But immediately thereafter he publicly demonstrated his extreme displeasure at Saul's failure to kill Agag, the Amalekite king.

Samuel ordered that Agag be brought before him, and he then did what King Saul had declined to do. He addressed the Amalekite ruler and proclaimed for all to hear: 'As thy sword hath made women childless, so shall thy mother be childless among women.' So saying, Samuel grasped his sword and with one blow beheaded Agag. Samuel and Saul then parted. Saul returned to his home in Gibeah and Samuel to his home in Ramah, and never again did the two meet.

Samuel's remark that 'the Lord repented that he had made Saul king over Israel' gained wide currency among the people. Nevertheless, Saul continued to rule and to lead the Israelites in their battles with the Philistines.

16
Fall of a hero

THE NEXT MILITARY ENCOUNTER between the Israelites and the Philistines took place in the Valley of Elah, some six miles east of Gath. The Philistines were encamped 'on a mountain on the one side, and Israel stood on a mountain on the other side: and there was a valley between them'. (1 *Sam.* 17:3.)

The two armies faced each other for forty days, without moving from their positions. Neither side wished to risk an offensive, which entailed a descent to the valley and attack on an adversary entrenched on a hill above them. The attackers would have to make a slow climb up the steep slope, and be easy targets for the arrows of the defenders at the top operating under cover of boulder and bush. They would also be at the mercy of the sword and spear units of the defending forces, who could rush down at them in full force from the summit.

However, the Philistines took one measure which caused great anxiety to Saul and lowered the morale of his men. They sent forth each day, morning and evening, a giant 'named Goliath, of Gath, whose height was six cubits and a span' and who was armoured from head to foot. He strutted about within sight and sound of the Israelite troops and challenged them to send out a man 'able to fight with me'; but none came. Goliath taunted and vilified them. 'I defy the armies of Israel this day,' he jeered. 'When Saul and all Israel heard these words of the Philistine, they were dismayed, and greatly afraid.'

Saul promised rich rewards to anyone who would contend with Goliath; but forty days had gone by and there was still no volunteer. The situation was now serious. Saul feared that if no Israel soldier went out to meet and vanquish Goliath, the morale of his militiamen would sink to the point where they might give up, abandon the battlefield and return to their homes. Israel would become a Philistine vassal.

Help arrived on the forty-first day in the guise of a young shepherd lad, 'ruddy, and withal of a beautiful countenance, and goodly to look to'. He was David, the son of Jesse, from Bethlehem in Judah. He went out to meet Goliath, and while the rival armies on their respective hilltops looked on, he engaged the giant and killed him. 'And when the Philistines saw their champion was dead, they fled.' The Israelite army thereupon arose and pursued the enemy all the way to Ekron.

Saul took a liking to David and would not let him return to his father's house. He would live with the royal family. Later, after many more battles, Saul was outraged when 'the women came out of all cities of Israel, singing and dancing' and declaiming that 'Saul hath slain his thousands, and David his ten thousands'.

158

Top Samuel anoints David;
bottom David fights Goliath as
Saul looks on. From a medieval
illustrated manuscript.

He understood its grim significance, and said wrathfully to the men who were with him : 'They have ascribed unto David ten thousands, and to me ... but thousands : and what can he have more but the kingdom ?' This young lad from Bethlehem could capture the hearts of the people and snatch the kingdom from him. Thus, in the king's mind, the son of Jesse, too, was added to the list of his enemies, and an 'evil spirit from God came upon Saul'. He would know no quietness of soul until he saw David dead at his feet.

But this was not to be. Saul was the first to die, on the battlefield. Like Samson the strongman, he ended his own life, falling on his sword so as not to fall into the hands of the Philistines 'lest these uncircumcised come and thrust me through, and abuse me'. The battle had taken place in the Valley of Jezreel, and the Philistines were the victors, leaving many Israelites slain on Mount Gilboa, overlooking the valley. Among them, apart from Saul, were his three sons who had fought with him, Jonathan, Abinadad and Melchishua. The Philistines took the body of Saul and his sons and 'fastened' them 'to the wall of Beth-shan'.

When the inhabitants of Jabesh-gilead, on the other side of the Jordan river, heard this news, 'all the valiant men' of the city 'arose, and went all night, and took the body of Saul and the bodies of his sons from the wall of Beth-shan' and brought them to Jabesh. They remembered what Saul had done for them, how he had gone to war and rescued them from the Ammonites. Mourning his death and revering his memory, they now took the bones of Saul and his sons 'and buried them under a tree at Jabesh, and fasted seven days'. (I *Sam.* 31 : 13.)

THE PHILISTINES who vanquished Saul in Jezreel were campaigning north of their region of settlement, the southern coastal plain, with its five cities of 'the lords of the Philistines'. One of these Philistine cities was Gaza, which gave trouble to Israel even in our own day.

The spring of 1956 was particularly vexatious, with mounting attacks on our newly established villages in the northern Negev by Arab bands based in the Gaza Strip. The Strip was then under Egyptian control. Egypt's president, Gamal Abdul Nassar, had ordered his army chiefs to organize, train and arm these bands and send them into Israel on missions of murder and sabotage. These infiltrators, for the most part Palestinian refugees, called themselves 'fedayun', Arabic for 'self-sacrificers', though they avoided military camps and installations and chose only civilian targets. They would cross the armistice lines at night and plant mines in the access roads and dirt tracks to the villages, killing and maiming our people.

Israel countered Arab terrorist action in two ways. One was military – strengthening the security of border settlements and communications, and carrying out reprisal assaults on terrorist bases. The other was political. David Ben-Gurion, who was then Prime Minister and Minister of Defence, agreed to 'shuttle talks' by UN secretary general, Dag Hammerskjold, who would fly to and fro between Nasser in Cairo and Ben-Gurion in Jerusalem. He hoped to secure through Hammerskjold's mediation an agreement with Egypt to preserve the peace along the borders. In the course of these discussions with the UN representative,

Gaza.

Ben-Gurion agreed in April 1956 to halt our army patrols along the armistice lines and to pull back our forces from the border. This was in response to an urgent request by Hammerskjold, made on the recommendation of General Burns of Canada, head of the UN Truce Supervision unit. The United States President, Eisenhower, also intervened in support of the UN Secretary General. He sent a signal to Ben-Gurion urging Israel to refrain from reprisal action against Egypt, since this could lead to war.

I was army Chief of Staff at the time. My relations with Ben-Gurion were excellent. I not only followed his orders but I also agreed wholeheartedly with his judgement and decisions. I entertained a vast respect for him, as a man, as a leader of Israel, as a wise statesman and a far-sighted visionary. But on this issue, and his compliance with the UN and the American request in the face of all that was happening on the Egypt–Israel frontier, we found ourselves sharply opposed. I did not think we could restore quiet to that border through diplomatic negotiation, and it was with the gravest possible misgivings and very much against my will that I accepted Ben-Gurion's instructions to keep our patrols away from the Gaza Strip border. I ordered the army to do so, but I told Ben-Gurion at an angry and bitter meeting that this step would only encourage the Arab terrorists to intensify their murderous activities.

And, indeed, our withdrawal brought no improvement in the situation. On the contrary, soon after we had removed our forces from the border – in the latter half of April – there was a new outbreak of terror against our settlements in the south. Arab infiltrators attacked a civilian bus, ambushed farm labourers in an orange grove, broke into villages, and left killed and wounded in all these incidents. In the smallholding farm village of Shafrir, a band of *fedayun* attacked the synagogue, where children were studying the *Torah*, and opened fire on them, killing five and wounding twenty. All this violence occurred while Dag Hammerskjold was still in the Middle East. And he was still there on 29 April when Roi Rutenberg, the gifted leader of Kibbutz Nahal Oz on the Gaza Strip border, was murdered.

I had gone to Nahal Oz at midday that day to take part in a celebration: four couples were getting married in a 'wholesale' wedding ceremony. The kibbutz dining-room and entrance plaza were decorated with flowers and greenery and the whole village wore a festive air.

While the kibbutz members were putting the finishing touches to the preparations and receiving their guests, Roi rode away on his horse to drive off a group of Arabs who had crossed the border, were pasturing their flocks in the kibbutz fields and cutting the crops. When Roi reached them, he was shot dead, and his body was dragged across the border. His corpse, mutilated, was later handed over to the UN soldiers, who delivered it to us for burial.

With Ben-Gurion's agreement, I returned the army units to the border, and I instructed the troops to be tough. We could not expect the civilian settlers with their limited means to guard their fields that adjoined the Gaza Strip. Only the army could do that; and whether Hammerskjold and Nasser wished it or not,

The gates of Kibbutz Nahal Oz.

Israeli troops would be present along the border, would prevent the Arabs from crossing, would protect the settlements and their farmers, and enable them to plough, cut and gather in their harvest.

I had known Roi Rutenberg well, and had met him many times. Despite his youth – he was twenty-two when he was killed – he had filled positions of top responsibility in the kibbutz, and at the time of his death had also doubled as the military commander of the area. He was a lean young man, with blond hair and blue eyes, and full of the joy of living. I always found him uncomplaining and undemanding. Whenever we reviewed the most difficult problems facing Nahal Oz, he would always end with, 'Never mind. We'll manage.'

Roi joined the kibbutz after completing his national army service. He was born in Tel Aviv, but his parents moved to Kfar Yehezkel in the Valley of Jezreel when

The grave of Roi Rutenberg at Nahal Oz, looking towards Gaza.

he was a child, and that was where he spent his early years. He was survived by his widow, Amira, and an infant son, Boaz.

I was shocked by his murder. I had the feeling that he, like most of the Israeli population, had not grasped the extent of the dangers with which Israel was surrounded, nor the grave implications of Arab hatred.

Nahal Oz was the Israeli village closest to Gaza. All that separated the kibbutz fields from the lands of the Arabs was a mark on the ground – a furrow made by a tractor-plough. On my inspection patrols in the Negev, I would approach this border-furrow to observe what was happening on the other side. Refugee camps, built by the United Nations Relief and Works Agency, had arisen on the outskirts of the city of Gaza, housing Palestinian Arab families who had fled from their villages during our 1948 War of Independence. Through field-glasses these camps looked like ants' nests, their narrow alleys crowded with people, particularly during the noonday hours when the schoolchildren were just leaving the class-room. Thousands of youngsters, the boys in blue, the girls in black, poured out like a swollen river, branched into the alleys, and were absorbed by the slums. There was crowding even in the fields. Every inch of soil was tended and irrigated, the refugee peasants drawing water in pails from the wells, and raising vegetables in any spare plot. They cut their field crops with the sickle, and would carefully gather up each ear of corn that fell from the sheaves.

Three hundred and fifty thousand of these people lived in the Gaza Strip, a narrow sliver of land pressed between the Mediterranean and the state of Israel. Every proposal to move them and rehabilitate them in other lands was rejected by the Arab leaders. No, said these leaders, they would again make war on Israel. Their armies would defeat our army; the state of Israel would be wiped off the map; and the refugees would return to their villages and establish Palestine anew.

These thoughts were much in my mind when I attended Roi's funeral the fol-lowing day. I gave voice to them when I spoke at the graveside:

Roi was murdered yesterday. Lulled by the silence of the spring morn, he paid no heed to the men poised on the frontier-furrow to do him harm. Let us not on this day heap blame on the killers. Why rail against the hatred felt for us by Gaza? It is the hatred of people who for eight years have been living in refugee camps, watching us turn into our possession the land and villages where they and their fathers had dwelt.

We should hold ourselves responsible for the murder of Roi, not the Arabs of Gaza, for we shut our eyes to the nature of the course along which our destiny lies, and failed to comprehend the mission of our generation in all its severity. Have we indeed forgotten that this young group in Nahal Oz carry on their shoulders – like Samson of old – the heavy 'Gates of Gaza' – and that behind those gates live hundreds of thousands of hate-ridden people who pray that we be weakened so that they may then tear us apart?

Have we indeed forgotten this? We surely know that in order to stifle the enemy's hopes, we must be armed, ready and on the alert night and day. We are the biblical generation of the settlement, following the Joshua conquest, and the helmet and sword are essential requirements. There will be no life for our children unless we dig shelters, and without the barbed wire fence and the machine-gun we shall be unable to build a home, plant a tree, pave a road and drill for water. Millions of Jews who were slaughtered because they had no homeland look out upon us from their ashes, the ashes of Israel's history, and command us to settle and establish the land for our nation.

But beyond the furrow of the frontier lies an ocean of hatred and lust for vengeance. The people there look forward to the day when complacence will blunt our preparedness, to the day when we shall submit to the importuning of ambassadors of hypocrisy to lay down our arms. The blood of Roi cries out to us from his torn body: we vowed that our blood shall not be spilt in vain, yet we again allowed ourselves to be persuaded by others to drop our guard. We listened to them and we believed them. Today must be our day of reckoning. We must face up to and not be deterred by the hatred of hundreds of thousands of Arabs around us who seek our destruction, and we must resolve never to divert our eyes lest our hands become weak. That is the decree of our generation, to be armed and ever ready, strong and firm. If the sword should slip from our grasp, then would our lives be cut off altogether.

Roi Rutenberg – the young man who left Tel Aviv to build his house as a rampart at the gates of Gaza; Roi – whose eyes were blinded by the light in his heart, so that he saw not the glint of the slaughterer's knife; Roi, whose longing for peace cushioned his ears, so that he heard not the sound of murder that lurked; this was Roi. Alas, the gates of Gaza proved too heavy for his shoulders; and they prevailed.

A FEW DAYS after Roi's death I met the poet Nathan Alterman. I was on my way in to see Ben-Gurion and he was just coming out. I do not know what they talked about, but to me Alterman spoke of the murder. He asked what kind of person Roi had been, and I told him what I knew. He then asked about the general situation on the Gaza Strip border. I gave him my judgement – that without sharp reprisal actions and strengthened guard measures, we would have no rest.

Alterman was primarily interested in the mood and feeling of our people in the border settlements. 'Supposing', he said, 'we are unable to stop the terror activities. Then the real question is whether we can endure it. You know', he added, 'in the life of a nation, as in the life of an individual, spilt blood, tragic though it be, may have the opposite effect to that intended by the perpetrators. Battle in defence of the homeland tightens the link with that land, with the soil that has soaked up the blood of the fallen. The murder of Roi is dreadful; but it should forge the unbreakable will of Roi's comrades in Nahal Oz to hold on forever, come what may.'

I was greatly taken by his words. Though they were not uttered with fluency – he stammered somewhat – nor sprinkled with epigram, as were his writings, they had the ring of the visionary. He spoke like one of the Hebrew prophets, a prophet living in our own times. He looked and behaved as one of us, but his eye penetrated to the very heart of the matter, to the innermost soul of man, to the core of the nation's destiny.

Alterman to me was the greatest poet of our generation. It was not only in his general poems that he was superior and more profound than any other writer of the new Israel. He was unmatched even when expressing himself on national themes. His verses on the rounding-up of Jewish children during the Nazi holocaust, on the European survivors trying to break through the British blockade to reach Palestine, and on the combatants in our War of Independence, were masterpieces. To the young generation of Israelis they were a limpid spring from which they drew faith. Falling in battle, in the works of Alterman, was part of the struggle for our national revival, and an additional layer in the new structure.

A new volume of Alterman's poems appeared a year after Roi's death, and I began reading it the day it was published. In it was a poem called 'After the Battle'. When I read it, it was as though we were continuing our talk just after the murder of Roi. I re-read the poem in bed late that night, and I was transported to the previous year, listening to Alterman's words as he leaned against the gatepost outside Ben-Gurion's office. I read about the herald galloping to the home of Saul's mother to notify her of the king's death, and what I heard as I read was the pounding of the hooves of Roi's horse returning, riderless, thereby announcing the news of his murder. I read of King Saul thrusting his sword in native soil, and that

The Sea of Galilee.

a nation vanquished on its land will 'rise seven times as strong', and I heard the words of Alterman about Roi, whose blood seeped into the land of Nahal Oz:

Routed, they fled in a horde.
The night rang with cries of retreat.
The great king fell on his sword.
Gilboa was cloaked in defeat.
And a rider relentlessly sped.
Hooves pounded, pounded till dawn.
Nostrils foaming with blood
proclaimed how the battle had gone.
Routed, they fled in a horde.
The great king fell on his sword.
When the first light flashed through the trees
he came where his mother stood,
dumbly fell to his knees
and covered her feet with his blood.
And the dust at her feet turned red
like a battle-field after the fray.
'Arise, dear son,' she said.
And he wept as he told in dismay
how routed, they fled in a horde,
how the great king fell on his sword
'In blood the mothers stand,
but no people are vanquished long
if vanquished on their own land.
They rise seven times as strong.
An heir to the throne will rise,
though the king met his doom,' she cried,
'for on his soil there lies
the sword upon which he died.'
Her voice trembled with every word.
Thus it was. And David heard.

(Translated by Robert Friend)

Springtime in the fertile
valley of Jezreel.

PART FIVE
THE HOUSE OF DAVID

opposite 'So Naomi returned, and Ruth the Moabitess, her daughter in law . . . : and they came to Bethlehem in the beginning of barley harvest.' (Ruth 1:22).

17
The threshing floor

SAUL WAS SUCCEEDED by David, the son of Jesse, the greatest of Israel's kings. His reign brought the nation of Israel to the pinnacle of its military and political power, and the House of David was established as the Hebrew royal dynasty.

The Bible records ten generations in the genealogy of David, as was customary with monarchic records of the period, and opens with the formal 'Now these are the generations of Pharez', followed by the 'begats'. 'Pharez begat Hezron, And Hezron begat Ram'; then come Amminadab, Nahshon, Salmon, Boaz, Obed, Jesse and David. (*Ruth* 4:18–32.)

Several of these antecedents of David entered into or were the products of mixed marriages with Canaanite, Edomite and Moabite women. Pharez, the first of the line, was the son of Judah and grandson of the patriarch Jacob; but his mother was a Canaanite. After Joseph's brothers had sold him to the Midianite merchants, 'Judah went down from his brethren' who were in the Hebron region to pasture his sheep in the coastal plain. When he reached the area of Adullam, he 'saw there a daughter of a certain Canaanite, whose name was Shuah', and married her. She bore him three sons, Er, Onan, and Shelah. Judah took a Canaanite girl, Tamar, as a bride for his first born, Er. But Er died childless, and so did his brother Onan. Tamar later disguised herself and tricked her father-in-law Judah into sleeping with her. She conceived and bore twins, the first born of whom was Pharez. The descendants of Judah had been 'fruitful and multiplied', and so had their herds and flocks, and they went further and further afield for their pasturage. In the course of their wanderings, members of the tribe of Judah encountered the descendants of Kenaz, the grandson of Esau, who dwelt in the land of Edom, and assimilated them within their tribe. Salmon, the father of Boaz, was the off-spring of a Kenazite-Judahite union.

However, the most detailed account of a member of another nation entering the family of one of David's antecedents is the charming story of Ruth the Moabitess, who became the wife of Boaz of Bethlehem, the great-grandfather of King David.

The story of Ruth begins with the chronicle of an Israelite family – Elimelech, his wife Naomi, and their two sons, Mahlon and Chilion, 'Ephrathites of Bethlehem-Judah'. With famine in the land, they left for neighbouring Moab. Relations between the two countries at the time – the period of the Judges – were reasonably peaceful. They warred with each other intermittently and followed

The archaeological mound of Beth-shan, where the Philistines 'fastened' the bodies of Saul and three sons to the city wall after the battle on Mount Gilboa.

each outbreak with a truce. The Moabites were a small and weak nation who dwelt in a southern territory at the edge of the desert. The River Arnon was their northern frontier, dividing them off from the settlement region of the tribe of Reuben. Their western border was the Dead Sea, which separated them from the tribes of Judah and Simeon. The distance to Moab from Bethlehem in Judah, the dwelling place of Elimelech, is not great. On a clear day, from anywhere in Judah one can see the mountains of Moab rising like a purple wall just east of the Dead Sea, and they can be reached on foot or riding on a mule in about two days. The route is not difficult. In winter it is best to go through Hebron, skirt the southern end of the Dead Sea, and turn north. In summer, when the Arava rift is burned by the sun, it is better to go via Jericho, cross the Jordan, climb the heights of Ammon, and then swing south to Moab.

The Moabite language was similar to Hebrew. The Moabites apparently adopted the Hebraic script during the periods when Moab was under the rule and influence of Israel. In the time of Ruth – and for centuries thereafter until the disappearance of the Moabites – an Israelite arriving in Moab would understand and be understood by the people he met. The differences were largely those of dialect. For example, 'many days' in Hebrew is '*yamim rabim*'; the Moabite was '*yaman raban*'.

[Much of our knowledge of the Moabite language derives from the stele of Mesha. A stele is an upright slab of stone, usually bearing an inscription. Mesha was the king of Moab in the ninth century BC, and the inscription on his stele is the king's first-person record of how he rebelled against Israel and fought victorious battles which freed Moab from Israelite tutelage. Mesha erected his stele in his capital, Dibon, which lay just north of the River Arnon, close to the highway leading to Rabat-Ammon (today's Amman). It was discovered there in 1868. The inscription contains thirty-two lines, and anyone today with a knowledge of Hebrew can read and understand it. It is now in the Louvre.]

Elimelech and his family had gone to Moab when the territory of Judah was struck by drought but Moab had remained unaffected. This happens today, too. The clouds moving eastwards from the Mediterranean pass over Bethlehem and Hebron at a considerable height; but when they reach Moab, they come up against its lofty mountains and shed their rain. True, this rainfall is not heavy, but it is sufficient, together with the dew, to give life to barley and wheat. The grains in this southern region have adapted themselves to the local conditions and developed over the centuries a capacity for growth with comparatively little moisture. They are short-stalked, bear few leaves, but ripen early. A grainfield in Moab is not a golden sea of standing corn that dwarfs the harvester, as in the Valley of Jezreel and the coastal plain. In Moab the men and women at harvest have to stoop, and they pluck the plant together with its roots. The sheaves are short, but the ears are full, and provide satisfying bread for the sower.

Like Judah, who in his day went to Adullam and took one of the daughters of the land as a wife for his son, so did Elimelech when he came to Moab. He chose two local girls as wives for his two sons. Their fate was similar to the first

King David, from
a 15th-century mural in
the church of St Mammas,
Cyprus.

Scenes from the story of Ruth and Boaz,
from a 13th-century French illuminated manuscript.

two sons of Judah. Mahlon and Chilian, like Er and Onan, died childless. Elimelech died soon after, and his widow, Naomi, together with one of her daughters-in-law, Ruth, left Moab and returned to her people in her home town, Bethlehem in Judah.

The story of the union between Ruth the Moabitess and Boaz is a story of the threshing-floor. It begins with Elimelech's family leaving their withered fields for Moab, and ends where it began, back in Judah, with Ruth gleaning and finding her redeemer among the reapers in the now lush tracts and on the 'heaps of grain'. In the period of the patriarchs, when the Hebrews were nomads, dwelling in tents and tending their sheep, the menfolk would often meet their future wives at the well, where all would come to water their flocks. Now that they were farmers, settled on their own land, the vineyard and grainfield at harvest time took the place of the well.

It was assuredly during the *sharav*, when the air is hot and heavy, drifting in from the desert, that Naomi told her daughter-in-law: 'Behold, he [Boaz] winnoweth barley tonight in the threshingfloor.' That was the night when Ruth said to Boaz: 'spread therefore thy skirt over thine handmaid; for thou art a near kinsman'; and Boaz replied: 'thou hast shewed more kindness ... inasmuch as thou followest not young men, whether poor or rich'. (*Ruth* 3 :9, 10.) On a normal summer day, the winnowing is done in the afternoon wind. But during the daytime in a *sharav* there is not even a rustle, and the farmers wait till nightfall. After the setting of the sun the air gets cooler, a light breeze springs up, and the winnowers can take up their pitchforks to scatter the threshed grain, and leave it to the breeze to carry away the light chaff while the heavier kernels fall to the ground.

Ruth and Boaz added their own contribution to the pleasantness of the longed-for evening breeze and the sweet aroma of the threshing-floor. Boaz ate and drank 'and his heart was merry', and Ruth anointed herself with fragrant perfume and donned her festive raiment. Her mother-in-law, who knew what might await her, warned her: 'Make not thyself known unto the man, until he shall have done eating and drinking!'

All went as well as Naomi had planned. Ruth did as she had been instructed, and Boaz behaved as was expected of him. He went out to the gate of the city in the morning, saw Elimelech's next of kin, and proposed to him in the presence of ten city elders that he 'do the kinsman's part': redeem 'a parcel of land, which was our brother Elimelech's' and marry Ruth, the young widow of Elimelech's son. (This was known as a levirate marriage, where the closest kin of a male who died childless married his widow. It accorded with the laws designed to perpetuate the continuity of the family.)

Elimelech's next of kin refused the proposal – just as Onan, the son of Judah, refused to marry Tamar upon the death of his brother Er – fearing it would impair his own inheritance. He told Boaz: 'Redeem thou my right to thyself; for I cannot redeem it.' Boaz thereupon bought from Naomi 'all that was Elimelech's, and all that was Chilian's and Mahlon's.... Moreover Ruth the Moabitess, the wife of Mahlon, have I purchased to be my wife, to raise up the name of the dead

The 9th century BC Stele of Mesha, king of Moab. The language and script are Moabite, though they bear a strong resemblance to the biblical Hebrew of the period, for Moab had been under Israelite influence.

Ruth and Boaz.
A lithograph by Lesser Ury.
(1861–1931).

upon his inheritance, that the name of the dead be not cut off from among his brethren.' (*Ruth* 4:9, 10.)

And the elders of the city and all the people who were present blessed him: 'The Lord make the woman that is come into thine house like Rachel and like Leah, which two did build the house of Israel.' And they added: 'And let thy house be like the house of Pharez, whom Tamar bare unto Judah.'

So Boaz married Ruth and they had a son named Obed. Obed and Pharez were thus born of foreign women. They entered the list of progenitors of the House of David by virtue of their fathers' obligation to redeem the name of their dead kin, the reluctance of their mothers to remain childless – and their skill in capturing the hearts of their redeemers, Boaz and Judah.

IN THE EARLY YEARS of Nahalal, the threshing-floor was the centre of village life. That was where the grown-ups brought the harvest of the year's toil, and it was on the heaps of grain that we youngsters sported on the warm summer evenings.

We went in mainly for field crops in those days. We sowed wheat and barley in the winter and maize and sorghum in summer. There were no tractors or combines then. We sowed by hand, ploughed with horses and mules, reaped by scythe, and brought the produce to the threshing-floor in wagons.

The threshing-floor was in the centre of the village. Each farmer was assigned his section, and there he assembled the harvest of his field, wheat in one heap, barley in another. My father would pitchfork the sheaves from the wagon, and I would catch and stack them in two adjacent piles, ears towards each other, stalks on the outside. The threshing was done with an old German machine which groaned and creaked and worked slowly – when it worked at all, for it was always breaking down. The threshing season lasted all summer. The machine would be moved from heap to heap, swallowing the sheaves and spewing sacks of grain.

In times of Arab–Jewish tension and violence, there was considerable anxiety over the fate of the harvest. In the urban centres, the Arabs would attack the Jewish suburbs and neighbouring Jewish cities; in the rural areas they would set alight the fields and the granaries.

In Nahalal we were put on alert and the guard system was tightened. An observer was posted night and day on the water-tower to look out for any suspicious movement in the fields. When he thought he had spotted a glimmer of flame in the standing corn, he would ring a bell and riders would gallop out to douse the fire. I was fourteen in the summer of 1929 when violent disturbances broke the country's calm. Nahalal's parents, armed with old rifles and shotguns, stood guard on the homes and cowsheds, while we teenagers were made responsible for the granary in the threshing-centre. The arms we were given were a form of spear – a long-handled dagger. The village blacksmith beat out the iron weapon-heads and we attached them to sticks. I was very proud of my dagger. I sharpened its blade with the whetstone we used for the sickle and scythe, and I fashioned the handle from an oak. It was strong and hard, though heavy.

We did guard duty in pairs. One drowsed, while the other stood watch. When I was on guard, I would sit on top of the grain heap and keep my eyes in concentrated focus in the hope of spotting an Arab stealing into the granary to set it alight. I planned the action I would take if an attacker appeared, and was borne on the wings of imagination. I decided I would slide silently to the bottom of the heap, come upon the Arab from the rear, and just as he was about to touch the flame to a petrol-soaked rag, I would stab him with my dagger.

When it was my turn to rest, I would press my body between the sheaves and

Arabs loot and burn Jewish shops in November 1947, a day after the United Nations' Partition resolution.

stretch out. I had no need of blanket or pillow. The wheat stooks were more pleasant than the softest of bedding.

One night we suddenly heard rifle fire coming from the area of the vineyards. I looked out from my perch and saw the gun flashes. There was consternation in the village. The guards raced out to the scene of the shooting – with me at their heels. We met the riflemen in the vineyards. They were two policemen, a Jew and an Arab. I have forgotten the name of the Jewish policeman, but the Arab was Ahmed Jaber. This was our first meeting, and the beginning of a friendship that lasted until his death more than forty years later.

The two men reported that they had been on their *daouriah* (patrol round), when they detected the approach of three Arabs coming along the path from the direction of Zippori. They called on them to halt, but the marauders rushed into the shelter of the vineyard and opened fire. The policemen returned the fire and the Arabs fled.

The smell of gunpowder still hung in the air. Filled with excitement, I went

179

up to Ahmed Jaber and asked him whether the Arabs had not left behind their rag and can of petrol. His immediate reaction was one of surprise, which he quickly suppressed. Looking at me and seeing the dagger in my hand, he replied gravely: 'It's difficult to see in the dark. We will make a search in the morning. I really think they intended to set light to the threshing-centre. Guard well!'

Ahmed Jaber continued to serve for many years in the police station nearest to Nahalal. He was mounted, and he rode daily through his domain which extended from Zippori to Abu-Shusha (the site, later, of Kibbutz Mishmar Ha'emek). A devout Moslem, he was respected for his integrity and courage, and he hunted down murderers and robbers, irrespective of creed or nationality, with relentless zeal. He was a superb horseman, sported a luxuriant moustache, and turned up wherever there was violent contention, quickly establishing order. 'If you have complaints', he would adjure us and the Arabs alike, 'take them to the magistrate's court in Nazareth. Why come to blows? Don't you realize that you can break heads and kill with a *nabut* [a knobkerrie of oak]? Isn't God in your hearts?'

I would occasionally ask to accompany him on his visits to the Arab villages. 'Very well', he would say, 'you can come with me.' But he would add the warning: 'I only hope your father will not be angry and beat you.' I would trail after him, mounted on a grey foal I borrowed from the village guard, and listened to Ahmed's wisdom. I drank in his stories and enriched my mind with the sayings and epigrams with which he salted his speech. I was also enchanted by his police tactics. When we approached a village or a Bedouin encampment, he would surreptitiously ride up the slopes of one of the nearby hills. 'They can see', he explained, 'that I am on my way to them. They can recognize me from five kilometers away, the bastards, and if there is anyone there who is wanted by the police, he promptly leaves. You must watch for whoever is running away. Look, do you see someone there walking quickly, making for the wadi? He surely committed a burglary somewhere, the son of a bitch!'

When I was a little older and became a sergeant *ghaffir* (a member of the Palestine supernumerary police), I visited him at his home in Um el-Faham. I drove a small police truck at the time, and only with difficulty did it climb the steep rise to the village and through its alleys. The Jaber house was at the top of the hill overlooking Wadi Ara. I sat down to a meal with the members of his many-branched family, and I remember that they brought Ahmed Jaber's first-born son to show me, an infant of two whose given name was also Jaber. Ahmed introduced me to the assembled family guests: 'This is Mussa Dayan from Nahalal, the boy I told you about. He is like a son to me. If he is ever in trouble, you must help him; and if you ever need anything, he will help you. When he was small, he threw stones more accurately than any Bedouin shepherd. Now, heaven be praised, he is already a man and carries a rifle! He is like our brother.' I felt myself blushing with embarrassment, but I was delighted by his words. Um el-Faham was not my village, but Ahmed Jaber was closer to me than many of my Jewish acquaintances.

During our 1948 War of Independence, Wadi Ara, and with it Um el-Faham, were in the hands of an Iraqi army unit who arrested Ahmed Jaber and interrogated him on his contacts with the Jews. He was cruelly tortured and beaten, but was finally released through the intercession of the leading families of Jenin to whom he was related. At the end of the war, Wadi Ara passed to Israeli control.

I headed Israel's delegation to the joint Israel-Jordan Armistice Commission at the time, and I visited Um el-Faham together with Jordanian army officers to demarcate the frontier between the two countries. My first call, however, was on Ahmed Jaber. When I saw him I was appalled. He was pale and feeble, and had to support himself on a cane. He came slowly towards me, fell on my neck, and burst into tears. We kissed each other on both cheeks, and he then told me the story of his hardships. I wanted to take him with me to get him medical attention and then put him up at a convalescent home, but he declined. 'No need for doctors or rest homes,' he said. 'The pure air of Um el-Faham and my wife's cooking will restore me to health.' He also had something to say about the Iraqis, cursing and reviling them as his eyes spat fire. I found no reason to disagree.

Years went by. Ahmed's son Jaber was now a grown man and had joined the Israel police force. He was one of their best officers. The link between our families had not weakened. I would visit them from time to time, and they would come to my home in Zahala on festivals. One day about two years ago the telephone bell rang and I heard the voice of the young Jaber at the other end of the line. 'Father just died,' he said. He was to be buried that afternoon.

It was the very day when an Air France plane carrying a number of Israeli passengers had been hijacked and taken to Uganda's airfield at Entebbe, and I was busy. But I made myself free and drove to Um el-Faham. I paid a condolence visit to the Jaber home and we all then went to the funeral. The entire village turned out to pay their last respects. After the Imam had said prayers at the graveside and recited verses from the Koran which the public repeated after him, they asked me to give the eulogy. I spoke in my own language, told of my long friendship with Ahmed, of his distinguished service, and his outstanding qualities as a man and a courageous fighter. And I thanked them for inviting me to speak. I do not know whether the assembled company understood every word; but I am sure they could sense how moved I was. I am also sure that none of us, certainly not I, felt there was anything odd about an Israeli Jew speaking in Hebrew at the grave of an Arab in a Moslem cemetery. I had taken leave of a dear friend.

18
Duel at Elah

THE VICTORY of David over Goliath has become a symbol of the victory of the weak over the mighty, the victory of the spirit, of courage and faith pitted against physical strength and armour. These elements were indeed present in the uneven duel which took place in the Valley of Elah. But there was an additional element in this engagement which was of supreme importance. David had conceived a means of combat which would gain him a military advantage over the giant – in addition to the moral advantage of faith and the readiness to risk his life. Though he would be going out to battle completely exposed, and without armour, spear or sword, yet would he secure the advantage in weaponry and tactics. True, he had no experience of warfare; but he was already familiar with struggles where the stakes were life and death.

As a shepherd lad tending his father's flocks, David had fought and killed a lion and a bear. In each case, the wild animal had seized and run off with one of his sheep. He had pursued it, retrieved the victim from its jaws and saved it from being devoured. This, however, was the least dangerous part of the struggle, for the mouth of the beast was stuffed with the wool of the sheep it carried. The difficult part came when the animal had abandoned its prey and turned on David. This was the decisive moment. David had quickly grasped its beard with his left hand, and with his right hand thrust his shepherd's knife in its throat. His advantage over the beast lay in his ability to get close to it while its jaws were clamped on the victim it was busy dragging; and when it let go and bared its sharp teeth at David, the knife was already in its throat. David knew from his experience with the lion and bear that in hand-to-hand combat, what counted were a cool head, self-confidence, agility – and above all the capacity to perceive and strike at the vulnerable points of the adversary.

David had come to the Valley of Elah to bring dried grain and loaves of bread to his brothers, who were militiamen in Saul's army, and 'ten cheeses' to their commanding officer, 'the commander of their thousand'. While he was with his brothers, Goliath the Philistine appeared at the top of the opposite hill and began reviling the Israelites. David carefully observed the Philistine, noting his slow gait and his heavy and cumbersome armour, and his eyes shone. The movements of Goliath's body reminded him of the heavy and ungainly tread of the bear he had killed, and he felt he could also prevail over 'this uncircumcised Philistine' who defied 'the armies of the living God'. (1 *Sam.* 17:26.)

David looked like a carefree young land, and his older brothers Eliab, Abinadab

David and Goliath, from the 15th-century Second Nuremberg Haggadah.

and Shammah treated him as such, chiding him as they would any frivolous youngster. But David was not frivolous, or naïve, and not at all impulsive. Even after he had resolved in his heart to accept the challenge of Goliath, he did not rush to do so. He first made enquiries as to what reward would be granted the man who struck down the Philistine. The 'man who killeth him', he was told, 'the king will enrich him with great riches, and will give him his daughter, and make his father's house free in Israel.' Only after he had heard this confirmed by others did David volunteer to do battle with Goliath, and he was brought to King Saul.

Saul quickly saw that standing before him was no dreamy lad. David exuded self-confidence. Furthermore, no one else in Saul's army had offered himself for the task. The king agreed. 'And Saul armed David with his armour, and he put an helmet of brass upon his head; also he armed him with a coat of mail. And David girded his sword upon his armour.' This battle garb gave David a heroic appearance, but it produced no equivalent feeling in his heart. His hands and feet felt as if they were fettered. He had lost his freedom of movement. In such battle dress he would never have got the better of the lion and the bear.

David took off the helmet and armour and returned them to Saul. These were articles of defence, and to be on the defensive was not his purpose. He was out to attack – to run forward, use stratagem, strike, kill. He proposed to fight as he was accustomed to fight, with sling, stones and staff. These were enough. The staff was no sharp sword to stick between Goliath's ribs. But it was light and long, and had a head like a knobkerrie, thick and hard as iron. If he raised it above his shoulders in the manner of shepherds, he could land a heavy downward blow on whatever he aimed at.

David, however, put his major trust in his sling, a tiny weapon of no magnificence or splendour, but unequalled for effective stone throwing. It consisted of a small piece of leather with two thin cords of flax attached to opposite edges. The stone missile was placed on the leather and the cords drawn taut, turning the leather into a bag. Holding the ends of both cords, the slinger swung the 'bag' at great speed above his head to gather momentum, and at the right moment freed one of the cords. This released the stone, hurling it towards its target with considerable force.

Goliath had no bow. He relied for protection on his shield-bearer who walked before him. This orderly was trained to ward off the arrows of enemy archers whose flight he could follow; but he would be hard put to notice in time and parry an unexpected stone hurled from a sling. If David could outwit the shield-bearer, he could get an uninterrupted shot at Goliath before coming within range of the giant's sword.

David and Goliath approached each other, Goliath looking and moving like a walking fortress. He may not have been a coward, but he assuredly sought to keep his body intact, and protected it from all sides. His breast was armoured with mail, his legs were encased in bronze greaves, and upon his head was a helmet of bronze – all this in addition to his shield-bearer. His weapons, too, were huge and heavy; a bronze dagger, and a spear with a shaft 'like a weaver's beam' and a head that 'weighed six hundred shekels'. The total weight of weapons and personal armour almost equalled the weight of Goliath's own body. Small wonder that he walked ploddingly.

David did what he had set out to do. He ran towards the Philistine, and before the shield-bearer knew what he was about, rapidly whirled his sling and cast a stone at the exposed forehead of Goliath. Goliath collapsed and fell flat on his face. This was the moment David had expected. Rushing forward to his prostrate adversary, he drew Goliath's sword from its scabbard and cut off his head. Goliath's body remained in the field and David returned to the Israelite camp, carrying the head of the Philistine in one hand, and in the other his opponent's weapons, the dagger, spear and sword.

THE STATE OF ISRAEL, in its thirty years' existence and its victory over the Arabs in four wars, is a perfect expression of the symbolism in the David–Goliath duel.

Western Sinai in the opening days of the Yom Kippur War, October 1973.

This symbolism is to be seen not only in the triumph of little David over the giant Goliath but primarily in the difference between the war aim of the young Israelite lad and that of the pagan Philistine. 'Thou comest to me', said David to Goliath, 'with a sword, and with a spear' and with a dagger; 'but I come to thee in the name of the Lord of hosts, the God of the armies of Israel, whom thou hast defied. . . . And all this assembly shall know that the Lord saveth not with sword and spear.' (1 *Sam.* 17 :45, 47.)

Ever since it was established, Israel has had to wage a dual struggle against Arab hatred. The immediate one was military, a struggle for Israel's very survival, and it began at birth. Only hours after her Proclamation of Independence, which followed the United Nations decision on the establishment of the Jewish state in her ancient land, Israel was attacked by the armies of the neighbouring Arab countries. The Arab objective was destruction of the new state. Israel's population at that time numbered 650,000. The populations of the invading Arab states totalled some thirty million. Four wars have been fought so far in this military struggle. The last was the toughest. This was the 1973 Yom Kippur War in which the attacking Arab armies comprised one million troops, 5500 tanks, and more

than 1100 warplanes. Israel's forces amounted to less than one third of that Arab might, and in spite of these odds Israel won. That war ended with the Israeli army only twenty-five miles from Damascus and ninety-five from Cairo.

But for us, the struggle with the Arabs is not only military, and the focal question embraces far more than which side does best with planes and tanks. Israel has no desire for a relationship with the Arabs which is based on victors and vanquished. Goliath said to the Israelites: 'Choose you a man for you, and let him come down to me. If he be able to fight with me, and to kill me, then will we be your servants; but if I prevail against him, and kill him, then shall ye be our servants, and serve us.' (1 *Sam.* 17:8, 9.) David went out to battle with Goliath 'in the name of the Lord', the God of Israel, the God of righteousness, mercy, equality, with no submission and no subjugation. That is the second part of the struggle between Israel and the Arabs, the struggle for the way of life that should reign between the two peoples. The Arabs come to us with sword, dagger and

David and Saul by Rembrandt.

186

spear, while we seek to live with them in peace, side by side, on terms of equality. We come to them in the name of the Lord God of Israel.

DAVID'S VICTORY over Goliath made him a national hero. His fame spread throughout the land. He also found favour in the eyes of Saul and his son Jonathan. After his duel in the Valley of Elah he did not return to Bethlehem. The king 'would let him go no more home to his father's house' to tend the sheep, but took him to his own residence, gave him a seat at his dinner table with the royal entourage on festival days, 'and made him his captain over a thousand'. (1 *Sam.* 18:13.)

Saul's attitude changed, however, as David gained one victory after another in his engagements with the Philistines. The more successes David registered on the battlefield, giving him greater popularity, the more Saul hated him. He had promised David his elder daughter, Merab, as a bride, but now 'she was given unto Adriel the Meholathite to wife' instead. Time and again Saul sent David on forays against the Philistines in the hope he would be slain in action. When he heard that his younger daughter Michal was in love with David, he let it be known that David could marry Michal if he would bring 'not any dowry, but an hundred foreskins of the Philistines'. He 'thought to make David fall by the hand' of the enemy. But his plot misfired. David and his men went out and slew not one but two hundred Philistines.

David married the king's daughter, but there was no lessening of Saul's hostility. One day, when 'the evil spirit of the Lord was upon Saul' and David played the harp to soothe him, the king tried to pin him 'to the wall with the javelin'. David evaded the thrust, fled the king's presence, and got safely away that very night. Saul 'sent messengers' after him, and if he had not been forewarned by Saul's own children, Michal and Jonathan, he would have been seized and killed.

David made good his escape and resolved never again to return to the house of Saul. He went to Ramah to see Samuel, told him of Saul's treatment, and Samuel took him to stay with a company of prophets at Naioth. But not for long. Saul's messengers were after him, and he, a man of war, needed a sword and a sheltered place where he could make a stand and fight for his life.

He fled to Nob, a city of priests, where Ahimelech presided over the shrine, and there he found part of what he wanted. 'Is there not here under thine hand spear or sword?' he asked the chief priest. Ahimelech answered: 'The sword of Goliath the Philistine, who thou slewest in the valley of Elah, behold, it is here wrapped in a cloth behind the *ephod*: if thou wilt take that, take it: for there is no other save that here.' The sword of Goliath! Surely, thought David, the hand of the Lord was in this matter. 'There is none like that; give it to me,' said David. He took the massive bronze weapon, heavy, tough and sharp, and recalled how he had wielded it in the Valley of Elah when he cut off the head of his adversary.

David parted from his benefactor and made his way southwards to Achish, the king of Gath in the territory of the Philistines. He hoped to find refuge there, but they recognized him and wished to kill him. David feigned madness, and they relaxed their guard. He escaped. He now turned eastwards, to Judah, the territory of his birth. Here he would assemble a band of warriors and he would be their chief. He could dwell in the Judean desert, a sword at his side, and none would prevail over him, not the Amalekites in the Negev, nor the Philistines in the coastal plain, nor Saul who reigned in the hill country. David made for 'the cave Adullam'. (1 *Sam.* 22:1)

The news that he was in disfavour with Saul and had fled to the Judean desert spread through the country from Dan to Beersheba. 'And every one that was in distress, and every one that was in debt, and everyone that was discontented' went down to join David; 'and there were with him about four hundred men'. His own family left Bethlehem to join him. He seems to have sent his brothers home, but was anxious about the safety of his parents and sought refuge for them. Like Elimelech in his time, David went to Moab and said to the king: 'Let my father and my mother, I pray thee, come forth, and be with you, till I know what God will do for me.' The king agreed, and David brought his parents to Mizpeh in Moab, while he returned to his warrior band in the Cave of Adullam.

THE CAVE OF ADULLAM lies at the edge of the foothills midway between Bethlehem and Gath, at the southern entrance to the coastal plain. It served as David's headquarters. The four hundred malcontents who gathered around him no doubt lived in tents, mud shacks, and in the smaller caves nearby. I recently saw domestic utensils in one of these caves exactly as they had been left by the people who dwelt there in David's time, some three thousand years ago. It was Kassem Mantzur who led me to them.

About six years ago Giora Zeid telephoned me to say that Kassem had noticed some large jars in a cave near Khirbet Adullam, the ruins of Adullam. We arranged that the two would come to my home in Zahala the following Sabbath, and the three of us would drive down to the cave. We were a party of more than three when we left. Giora had brought his daughter Ahinoam, a sweet, comely, dark-haired young lady – her mother was a Jewess from Yemen – and Karl Singer, an old friend of his and mine, who had served as a police sergeant in Nahalal together with Ahmed Jaber. Kassem Mantzur came alone.

Giora is a childhood friend. We were in the same class at school in Nahalal. His father was Alexander Zeid, one of the early pioneers in the country and a noted 'Watchman', a founding member of the defence organization which guarded Jewish settlements. When Giora was in his teens, the family moved further west along the Jezreel valley, at the foot of the Carmel mountains. They built their house and horse stables on a hill called Sheikh Abrek, and from there Alexander would ride out on his guard duties – he was now in charge of the security of Jewish National Fund lands in Jezreel. He was ambushed and killed by an Arab band in 1938. The family remained at Sheikh Abrek. Giora, the eldest son, followed his father's vocation. He, too, was a guardsman, and he spent a good deal of time with our Arab and Druze neighbours. Our own friendship was uninterrupted. Even when I left Nahalal and went to live in Jerusalem, then in the south and

Caves in the Judean desert where David sheltered from the pursuit by Saul.

later in Zahala, we continued to meet, often with Arab, Druze and Circassian friends.

It was through Giora that I came to know Kassem Mantzur. He is a Druze from Daliyat el-Karmil, one of the two Druze villages on Mount Carmel. His house is at the northern end of the village. It is not a large house, but large enough for him and his twelve children. He makes his living as a trapper of porcupines. In his village he is known as 'the Hunter', for he used to hunt wild boar and quail; but there are few boar left, and quail trapping has been banned. In summer Kassem supplements his income by gathering fragrant herbs, mostly mint, which grow on Carmel, and extracting honeycombs from the hives of wild bees. Aromatic

plants for seasoning and wild honey are scarce and fetch high prices. His main pursuit now, however, is porcupine hunting. Its meat is red and said to be soft and somewhat sweet, and apparently appeals to the sophisticated palate. Kassem's special virtue lies not only in his mastery of the art of trapping but also in the build of his body. He is short and thin. When he detects the traces of a porcupine den, he crawls to their subterranean hole through the very tunnels they have burrowed. Wherever a porcupine can go, so can Kassem.

We drove to Khirbet Adullam, left our vehicles and climbed the hill after Kassem. Near the edge of the ridge he stopped and pointed to a small heap of earth. 'That's it', he said. 'There's the den.' He then explained the technique of the hunt, which is done with a partner. He first seals all but two of the entrances to the several tunnels leading to the den, then crawls through one of the openings, while his partner waits at the other and catches the porcupines as they emerge.

Kassem said that on his last expedition, it was when he got to the middle of the den that he saw the exposed parts of the large jars which he later reported to Giora Zeid. He would now go in again, and when he came to the jars he would knock on the ceiling of the burrow. If we listened carefully, we would hear the knocks and be able to mark the spot beneath which the antiquities were to be found.

Kassem stripped naked, started crawling through the tunnel and was soon lost to view. After a few moments we heard his thuds. We noted the spot and then

Ancient pottery vessels like those found by General Dayan near David's 'Cave of Adullam'.

began clearing the brush, boulders and earth. After a little more digging we struck a surface of stone. It was indeed the roof of a cave which over the ages had been sealed, filled and buried. The porcupines had in fact quarried their homes out of the debris inside the cave. We examined the stone roof and found it had two apertures which had been stopped up. These were chimneys which had led out from – and could now lead us into – the interior of the cave. After a few more hours of work, we could go through one of the apertures into what was now the porcupine den.

I wriggled down, and Kassem reached me through the burrow. He was right. Obtruding from the western wall of the den were the sides of three large, brown jars of characteristic Canaanite form. I scraped away enough earth from the upper portions of two of them to see that one had four handles, and one was covered with a bowl. And that was all I had time for. The hour was late, and Giora and Kassem had to get to their homes in the north. We did not even bother to fill in the pit we had dug. No one would think of exploring it.

I returned a few weeks later and went down the pit. I could not on my own clear away the debris from the entire cave. All I could do was remove the earth and stones from one patch and heap them at the side, examine what I had exposed, judge what the prospects were, restore the debris and do the same with an adjacent patch.

The large jars stood against a wall of the cave on a stone ledge which kept them raised from the floor. They were storage jars which undoubtedly had been used to keep grain. At their side on the floor lay a thin basalt stone with a slightly concave surface, together with a long cylindrical pestle, also of basalt. This was where the grain was pounded into flour. A large niche cut in the opposite wall held four jugs and five bowls. Two of the jugs were of medium size and were probably used to store oil. The other two were small, and no doubt held oil which was decanted from the larger jugs for daily use. Of the five bowls, the bottom one was large, and piled on top of it, one above the other, were four small bowls, looking much like those in which Mother used to serve us soup in our home in Nahalal.

Standing in a small alcove scooped out of the rock above the jars were two oil lamps and an incense pan. The pan may have served some ritual purpose, though I fancy it was just a tray on which the lamps were placed when they were alight.

On the floor in the centre of the cave was a mixed heap of shards from cooking pots, flasks and large bowls. The stones that had fallen through the chimneys into the cave had shattered and crushed the pottery vessels. The only unbroken article was a utensil of stone, a large, thick plate with three embossments on its underside serving as legs to keep the plate off the ground.

This was all I managed to discover that day. I had planned to return to the cave a little while later and continue my investigations; but I did not do so. When I reached home that night, I found that my feet and calves were covered with red spots. It was not difficult to trace the cause: tiny white ticks were crawling between my trouser creases, and two of them still clung to my skin. At Tel Has-homer hospital next morning, Dr Goldman asked if I had never heard of cave parasites and cave fever? It was not a malignant disease but it was extremely diffi-cult to get rid of. The ticks transmit the blood of some sick animal – a sheep or goat – to the body of the person they bite and infect him with the fever. I asked the doctor if there was any immunization against this cave disease. 'Poss-ibly,' he said, 'but the best preventive is to stay far away from caves.' As usual in such cases he gave me injections and pills. I went home and nothing worse happened to me. The truth is that what deterred me from returning to Adullam was not the doctor's warning but the loathsome sight of the white ticks clinging to my leg. Horrible.

Who had dwelt in this cave? Peasants, shepherds, warriors? All one can say with certainty is that whoever they were, they left the cave in great haste. They may have taken with them their weapons and their valuables, but their domestic utensils had been left in their accustomed places. The cooking pots, the storage jars, the small flasks in which they drew oil from the jugs, the carefully piled bowls, the basalt pestle and mortar, the lamps, were all abandoned when their owners departed, never to return. Winter came and swept earth and stones into the cave, filling it up over the centuries. Thorns covered it, and only the porcupines with their special sense discerned that beneath the rock was a stratum of loose earth, perfect for scooping out a den in which to bring forth a new generation of porcupines.

DAVID AND HIS NEW BATTALION first went into action at Keilah. He received information that the Philistines had broken into this city 'and they rob the thresh-ing-floors'. (1 *Sam.* 23:1.) They had come with their wagons and asses and plundered the produce, putting the threshed grain in their sacks, bundling the sheaves, and carrying them off.

Keilah stood on a hilltop about a two hours' march south of Adullam. At first David's men were reluctant to go into battle. 'Behold', they said to David, 'we be afraid here in Judah: how much more then if we come to Keilah against the armies of the Philistines?' They were a cowed and discontented lot. They had come south and joined David because they had been forced to flee for whatever reason from home or camp and needed a hiding place. They did not know one another, and none knew who was brave and who was cowardly. How then would they go into action as a unit when they could not trust or rely on each other?

David did not accept their refusal. But in order to inspire them with faith and confidence, he asked Abiathar, the son of Ahimelech the priest, who had fled from Saul to join him, to 'enquire of the Lord'. The divine reply was: 'Arise, go down to Keilah; for I will deliver the Philistines into thine hand.' So David and his men went to Keilah, smote the Philistines 'with a great slaughter', and took their animals. The inhabitants of Keilah were saved, and David's men emerged with stiffened morale.

The people of Keilah showed no gratitude to David for having saved them,

David cuts off the hem of Saul's
robe.
From a 13th-century
French manuscript.

fearing that Saul would 'destroy the city' which now harboured his enemy. They
accordingly sent word to the king that David was with them and that if he sent
his army, they would bolt the 'gates and bars' of the town to prevent David and
his men from leaving. The man Saul wanted would be delivered into his hands.
As at Gath, David realized the danger of remaining 'shut in'. He had best depart
instantly, make for the wilderness of Judah, and find a safe retreat in the strongholds near the Dead Sea and 'a mountain in the wilderness of Ziph'. By now
his unit was six hundred strong, and they gathered up their weapons and set off
eastward, to the desert.

Saul did not flag in his pursuit of David. In the course of it they actually met
twice, and even talked to each other. The first encounter took place 'upon the
rocks of the wild goats' (1 *Sam.* 24 : 2) in the Judean desert near the spring of En-
Gedi, on the western shore of the Dead Sea. Saul had heard that David was in
this area, and he took three thousand picked troops and went after him. David
and a few of his most trusted men were concealed in a cave in the cliff-side above
the main route, and could observe through the opening the movements of Saul's
unit.

They suddenly saw the king leave the road and climb towards the cave, and
while they moved to the deeper recesses of the cavern, Saul came in to relieve
himself. Though David could have killed him then and there, all he did was 'cut
off the skirt of Saul's robe' surreptitiously, and allowed him to depart unharmed;
and only when Saul had gone down to the foot of the slope and rejoined his troops
did David emerge from the cave and call out after him: 'My lord the King.' Saul
looked round and saw David, who prostrated himself in obeisance, then held up
the piece of Saul's garment that he had cut off, and asked the king why he pursued
him when he was innocent of any malice. 'Know thou and see that there is neither
evil nor transgression in mine hand, and I have not sinned against thee; yet thou

huntest my soul to take it... And Saul lifted up his voice, and wept. And he said to David, "Thou art more righteous than I: for thou hast rewarded me good, whereas I have rewarded thee evil."' (1 *Sam.* 24:11-17.)

Saul went home, while David and his men went to their sheltered base. But it was not long before the king renewed his pursuit. This time, too, David found himself in a position to kill him, and again he left him untouched. Saul and his troops were on their way to capture David in the wilderness of Ziph, and had pitched camp *en route*. During the night, David and his nephew Abishai, the son of Zeruiah, stole into the king's encampment and came upon Saul 'sleeping within the trench.... So David took the spear and the cruse of water from Saul's bolster; and they gat them away, and no man saw it, nor knew it, neither awaked: for they were all asleep: because a deep sleep from the Lord was fallen upon them.' (1 *Sam.* 26:7, 12.)

What followed was an exchange similar to the one 'upon the rocks of the wild goats' at En-Gedi. David 'stood on the top of an hill' and shouted to Saul: 'Wherefore doth my lord thus pursue after his servant? For what have I done? Or what evil is in mine hand?' And Saul replied, as on the previous occasion: 'I have sinned: return, my son David: for I will no more do thee harm, because my soul was precious in thine eyes this day: behold, I have played the fool, and have erred exceedingly.'

Again they parted, 'David went on his way, and Saul returned to his place.' David did not respond to Saul's invitation to 'return, my son'. He did the opposite, resolving to put even greater distance between himself and the king. There was 'nothing better for me than that I should speedily escape into the land of the Philistines; and Saul shall despair of me, to seek me any more in any coast of Israel: so shall I escape out of his hand'.

No longer would David hide out in caves and deserts. Nor would he request refuge and shelter among his brother Israelites or even in the territory of his own tribe, Judah. Together with his two wives, Ahinoam the Jezreelitess and Abigail the Carmelitess, widow of Nabal, and his six hundred men and their families, David crossed into Philistine country and went to Achish, king of Gath. Achish gave him Ziklag as a dwelling place for his family and entourage. Thus ended the chapter of Saul's pursuit and David's escape. 'And it was told Saul that David had fled to Gath: and he sought no more again for him.' (1 *Sam.* 27:4.)

THE 'ROCKS OF THE WILD GOATS' in the wilderness near En-Gedi where David eluded Saul have ever been a refuge for the persecuted. This is an arid desolate region of bare hills, accessible only over steep, tortuous and narrow paths. Moreover, from its hilltops one can spot the approach of hostile elements, while its caves, fissures and boulders provide perfect cover.

It is not only the rocks that are named in the Bible after the 'wild goats' which frequent them. (These animals are now commonly known as mountain goats, but are really ibexes.) En-Gedi, Hebrew for 'spring of the kid', probably also got its name from the young ibexes who gathered there to drink its waters. Today,

A waterfall at En-Gedi.

too, as in David's time, En-Gedi is very much an ibex centre. Like human beings who fled from their persecutors, so did ibexes seek refuge from hunters, and they found it in the waste land between the Dead Sea and the Judean wilderness.

Ibex territory stretches all the way from Ein Feshcha in the north to the tip of the Sinai Peninsula in the south. Ein Feshcha is a spring that spills into the Dead Sea about six miles south of Jericho. From here southwards, one may encounter 'wild goats' for the entire length of the ridges that skirt the Dead Sea, then along the Arava rift to Eilat, and from there all the way down the shore of the Gulf of Eilat to the southern end of Sinai.

Their need for drinking-water keeps the ibexes close to the desert oases for much of the year, since these are an abundant source throughout winter and spring and even the early summer months. As the area of vegetation becomes more extensive with the annual sprouting, the ibexes move with it and wander further afield. But with the coming of the hot weather, when the desert water sources dry up and plant life withers, the ibexes return to the hills and rocky promontories above the springs.

The ibex is a species of wild goat. The males are bearded, and long horns curve from their heads like sickles. The females are short-horned. I am not familiar with ibexes of other countries; but whenever I see ours go leaping down the mountainside to the spring at dawn, or race away in fright when I come upon them as they forage between the rocks, I feel they must be the most beautiful of all. The Israeli ibex is a tall animal, his colour is chocolate brown, and his most magnificent features are his horns. They are unusually large, and though they sprout from a small head, the whole effect is an aesthetic triumph. Near the roots they are set forward, but they soon begin to curl back until their points face the rear.

If there was ever any doubt that the ibex belongs to the goat family, it was proven by a Bedouin herdsman of the Mezaima tribe living in Dahab on the Gulf of Eilat. In 1970, while he was pasturing his goats in the valley in Sinai that leads to St Catherine's Monastery, one of the young she-goats strayed. He searched for her for days and finally gave up. He thought he had seen the last of her: she would surely perish in the desert. But three months later, taking his flock to graze in the same valley, he heard bleating, and moments later the lost she-goat sprang forth from between the boulders and rejoined her companions. The Mezaima herdsman examined her, and was astonished to discover not only that she was neither hurt nor emaciated but rather the reverse – her belly was ripe and swollen. She had left the flock a virgin, and returned pregnant!

The term of pregnancy was completed without mishap and in the spring of 1971 she gave birth to a hybrid kid, sired by an ibex. It was a dear little animal, with a chocolate skin, and taller than the other kids in the flock. It also became agile more quickly than the others, and was at once able to follow its mother. Two days after its birth, it was climbing and leaping from boulder to boulder just like a mature ibex.

It was not easy for ibexes to avoid extinction. Their skins, horns, and above all their meat attracted the hunter. They first fell victim to the bow and arrow,

An ibex, the biblical 'wild goat', in the wilderness near En-Gedi.

and in our own times to the rifle bullet. They are at their most vulnerable taking their morning drink at the spring: at first light they come down from the high ground to the water source. This has been known by hunters throughout the ages, and during the hours of darkness they would lie in wait in a concealed spot just south of the spring, so that the north wind would not carry their scent to their quarry. The thirsty ibexes would stoop to drink, and the hunter would release his arrow.

Summer after summer brought decimation to the ibexes, yet they were not exterminated. The lions, bears and leopards which had once roamed Israel's hills, forests, and the rushes of the Jordan, were all hunted down to the very last one, and became extinct; but not the ibex. Their breeding pattern may have helped somewhat. The female ibex produces a single young in the first year, and twins in subsequent years. Though some are lost to the hunter, this natural increase may make up the losses.

Their principal protection, however, is their extreme wariness. There are several ibex herds in the area of Eilat, yet they are difficult to spot. During the daylight hours they disappear behind rock and boulder, and come out to graze only at night. It is not just that they are timid; they know it is the only way to stay alive. In today's nature reserve at En-Gedi, where none can harm them, the ibexes roam at will, coming down in daylight to the lawns of the houses to munch the fresh grass, and they pay no attention to the young couples stretched out near them or even to youth groups gathered on the green in song – as long as they don't shout.

Nevertheless, their home is not the domestic lawn but the high cliffs above the Arugoth Canyon on the western shore of the Dead Sea. There they were born, there they pastured, there they hid from the hunters, and there they raised their young. It was there, too, that David and his men found a haven from their pursuers, there, 'upon the rocks of the wild goats ... in the wilderness of En-gedi'.

The common goat, belonging to the same family as the mountain ibex.

19
Brother against brother

DAVID CAME INTO HIS OWN with the death of King Saul and his three sons on the battlefield of Mount Gilboa. He realized when he heard the news that his days as a fugitive were over, and that the throne was now vacant. Yet he did not exult, nor did he celebrate. He was filled with wrath against the young Amalekite who had brought him the grim tidings, and who also reported that it was he who had given the death-blow to the dying Saul. 'Thy blood be upon thy head,' fumed David, 'for thy mouth hath testified against thee, saying, I have slain the Lord's anointed. . . . How wast thou not afraid to stretch forth thine hand to destroy the Lord's anointed?' (2 Sam. 1:14, 16.) He ordered the Amalekite to be slain.

David and his men fasted until sundown 'for Saul, and for Jonathan his son, and for the people of the Lord, and for the house of Israel; because they were fallen by the sword'. His lament over Saul and Jonathan is a war dirge. It contains the injunction to 'teach the children of Judah the use of the bow'. There is no warfare without casualties, but the bereavement and the agony must never be allowed to weaken the hands of the nation. Rather should it steel them to meet future battles, be more determined in their 'use of the bow'.

David's lament opens with the classic verse: 'The beauty of Israel is slain upon thy high places: how are the mighty fallen!' It continues in the same vein, combining tenderness and love with anguish and admiration, the pain of defeat – 'Tell it not in Gath' – with glory and splendour – 'They were swifter than eagles, they were stronger than lions.' It ends as it begins: 'How are the mighty fallen, and the weapons of war perished!' (2 Sam. 1:18–27.)

David's lament over Saul and Jonathan was 'written in the book of Jasher' to be preserved for future generations. It has indeed been preserved, a matchless masterpiece in the chronicles of our nation.

After the period of mourning, David and his men left Ziklag and returned to the territory of Judah. David did not go back to Bethlehem, the city of his brothers, but established his headquarters in Hebron, in the centre of Judah. The men who were with him, together with their households, settled in the suburbs and neighbouring villages surrounding Hebron. The people of David's own tribe of Judah accepted him as their leader, and 'they anointed David king over the house of Judah'. David also tried to bring over to his side the men of Jabesh-gilead, but they remained loyal to the house of Saul.

The kingdom split. Ishbosheth, the son of Saul, reigned 'over Gilead, and over

The Battle of Mount Gilboa, where
Saul and his sons met their death.
An Amalekite takes Saul's crown.
From the Winchester Bible.

David slays the Philistines.
From a 14th-century panel in
the church of St Etienne,
Mulhouse, France.

the Ashurites, and over Jezreel, and over Ephraim, and over Benjamin, and over all Israel. ... But the house of Judah followed David.' (2 *Sam.* 2:9, 10.)

The break between the two parts of the kingdom brought with it contention, and even the eruption from time to time of open battle. 'Now there was long war between the house of Saul and the house of David: but David waxed stronger and stronger, and the house of Saul waxed weaker and weaker.'

This 'long war' between the two houses was basically a struggle between the two rival army commanders, Joab, the son of Zeruiah, who commanded David's force, and Abner, the son of Ner, who led the army of the house of Saul. David himself had been a man of war since youth, but he had never spilt the blood of his brothers. At the start of his career, when he had been with Saul, he fought the Philistines. Later, when he fled the royal household for the territory of Achish, the Philistine king of Gath, he scrupulously avoided engaging and harming the Israelite tribes. Even when he lived as an outlaw, dependent upon his sword and on plunder, he turned south and 'invaded the Geshurites, and the Gezrites, and the Amalekites', foreign peoples who dwelt in the Negev and the Sinai Peninsula between the land of the Philistines and Egypt. When he was anointed king of Judah, he was anxious to bring the other tribes of Israel under his rule; but he sought to achieve this by peaceful means. He was distressed by Joab's attacks on the troops of Saul, which were carried out against David's will. Joab had not sought his permission. Both belonged to the house of Jesse – Joab's mother Zeruiah was David's sister. But Joab's standing both in the family and in the tribe of Judah was more solid than that of his uncle. Moreover, the army was subject to Joab's discipline and none dared to disobey him. As David was to say later, 'And I am this day weak, though anointed king.' David confessed to his servants: 'These men the sons of Zeruiah be too hard for me.' (2 *Sam.* 3:39.)

David reigned 'seven years and six months' in Judah before he became king over all Israel, seven and a half years of civil strife, with the hand of brother against brother, before the kingdom was re-united. There was one notable appeal to stop the fratricidal war. After a particularly 'sore battle', the soldiers of the tribe of Benjamin, followers of Abner, stood with him 'on the top of an hill' as he addressed the commander of David's pursuing forces: 'Then Abner called to Joab, and said, "Shall the sword devour for ever? knowest thou not that it will be bitterness in the latter end? how long shall it be then, ere thou bid the people return from following their brethren?"' (2 *Sam.* 2:27.) Joab sounded the trumpet and called off his pursuit. But the truce did not last.

The climax to the recurring violence which followed was the death of Asahel, the brother of Joab, who was killed by Abner. Joab in turn killed Abner, to the repugnance of David who 'lamented over Abner' and wept at his grave. Then came the foul murder of the lame Ishbosheth, king of Israel. David ordered his murderers to be slain.

Only then did 'all the elders of Israel' come to David in Hebron, saying, 'Behold, we are thy bone and thy flesh ... and they anointed David king over Israel.' (2 *Sam.* 3: 1–3.)

THE INTERNAL STRIFE which has on occasion afflicted our nation gave rise to some of the most painful episodes in our history. It was especially agonizing when such events occurred at a time when we were surrounded by attacking enemy forces whose objective was the destruction of Israel.

Even in our generation, during Israel's War of Independence, we proved unable to avoid an armed clash among our own people. There was only one incident; it lasted only a few hours; and the casualties were not heavy. But it took years to wipe out the hatred and heal the gash which this bloody event hacked in our national body.

I was involved in this episode, which occurred in June 1948, one month after the establishment of our state and during the brief first truce that followed the invasion of Israel by all the neighbouring Arab countries. As commander at the time of the newly formed 89th Commando Battalion, I was hurriedly summoned by the Brigade Commander, Yitzhak Sadeh. He told me that a grave crisis had suddenly arisen between the Irgun Zvai Leumi, commanded by Menahem Begin, and the government, headed by David Ben-Gurion, which called for military action.

[The Irgun was the pre-state dissident resistance organization, while the Haganah was the resistance arm of the Jewish Agency for Palestine, the official body responsible for Jewish affairs during the British mandatory administration. The Irgun had refused to accept the authority of the Jewish Agency, but it had been assumed that with the proclamation of statehood it would disband and submit to the jurisdiction of the government of newly independent Israel.]

Yitzhak Sadeh informed me that the Irgun had brought an arms ship to our shores and was proposing to equip its members, who would be operating as a private army outside the framework of the Israel Defence Forces. The ship was called the *Altalena*, the pen-name of the late Ze'ev Jabotinsky, the noted Zionist leader who had broken with the official Zionist Organization and who was the ideological father of the Irgun. While I was being briefed, the *Altalena* had begun discharging its cargo of armaments on the beach at Kfar Vitkin, a cooperative farm village some twenty miles north of Tel Aviv. (The vessel had also brought in some eight hundred and fifty immigrants, who had disembarked and been taken to a rest camp at nearby Nathania before the offloading of the arms had started.)

The Brigade Commander said that the army had received orders to seize the *Altalena*'s weapons, if necessary by force; but these orders were not being carried out by the units of the area command entrusted with this task. They were reluctant to open fire on the Irgun men. There were also stirrings of unrest in other units: some of the Irgun members who had enlisted in the army were leaving their formations to join their old comrades. It had therefore been decided to assign this mission to my battalion. Sadeh added that apparently Kfar Vitkin itself was now under Irgun control, and we would have to fight our way in to get to the shore. I informed the Brigade Commander that we would carry out the government's orders. We would go to Kfar Vitkin, recapture it, and seize the arms.

I did so with a heavy heart. I could never have imagined that we would one day be forced into a situation in which the army of Israel would be in combat against Jews. But I did not question my duty to execute this order. Ben-Gurion was not only the Prime Minister, and therefore the supreme national authority; for me, his personal authority, too, was unchallenged.

My commando battalion at the time was still in the early stages of organization. It had been established only four weeks earlier, had not yet been in action, and had not even completed its training. It comprised three companies of mechanized infantry mounted on jeeps and half-tracks, and one support company. The first three units were distinctive groups of volunteers, each drawn from a particular segment of society. One company, commanded by Uri Bar-On of Nahalal, was composed exclusively of farmers from kibbutzim, moshavim and private estates. Another was made up of Tel Avivians and was commanded by Akiva Sa'ar. The third commander was Dov Granek, known as Blondie, who had been a member of Lehi (the Hebrew acronym for the Stern Group). Like the Irgun, only smaller, this had also been a dissident underground resistance movement during British rule. The men under Dov's command were all former members of Lehi or the Irgun. I could hardly take this company on an operation against their old comrades, so off we went with two companies, the farmers under Uri and the townsmen under Akiva.

We reached Kfar Vitkin at dusk and found the gates locked. The village was in utter darkness, and enveloped in thick silence. We broke open the gates, proceeded to the village square, and entered the office of the secretariat. There we found the members of the council, worried and bewildered, sitting quietly at tables lit by kerosene lamps. They said that the Irgun commander had told them that unless they supplied them with what they needed, they would use force. The village secretary had therefore opened the commisariat and the bakery and given them all he had. But it was not this that caused them anxiety. They feared there would be a battle between the Irgun and the Israeli army, and they had accordingly ordered all the people to put out the lights and lie on the floor.

I could scarcely believe my ears and eyes. The men of Kfar Vitkin, a moshav cooperative like my own village, were very close to us. Many of them had received their agricultural training in Nahalal and I knew them well. I also had relatives among them. I told them to switch on their lights, get out of their houses and carry on with their normal life. They had nothing and no one to fear. As for the Irgun, we would deal with them.

We made our way to the beach. The company commanders reconnoitred the concentration area of the Irgun men and their stacks of arms, and quietly deployed their troops in a semi-circle round them. We then called on them to give themselves up. We received no official reply, but they opened up with a bazooka and scored a direct hit on one of our half-tracks, killing two of our men. We returned the fire, and at the end of the exchange, our casualties were the two killed and another six wounded. Irgun casualties were four killed and eighteen wounded.

The *Altalena* weighed anchor and set off for the south, towards Tel Aviv, leaving on the beach three hundred Irgun men who began negotiations with one of our company commanders. They argued till dawn, when the three hundred gave themselves up to the Israeli army together with their weapons. My two companies then returned to base. The brief engagement on the Kfar Vitkin shore was over. But the battle did not end there. It shifted to Tel Aviv, with the arrival of the *Altalena*, and became more acute. At Tel Aviv the ship ran aground close to a busy part of the town, just opposite the Ritz Hotel, which had been taken over as the government press centre. It still carried half its cargo of arms – rifles, machine-guns, bombs, explosives, ammunition.

Daybreak lifted the curtain from the vessel, surprising Tel Aviv's early risers, and soon crowds began streaming to the scene. Most of them were curious sight-seers, but there were also members of the Irgun and their supporters who had come to the help of their friends. Deployed on the beach facing the *Altalena* was an Israeli army unit. Fighting soon broke out, with the exchange of fire between the troops and the Irgun men – both those on the ship and their comrades on the shore. This spectacle of Jews fighting Jews was witnessed with interest by United Nations observers and foreign correspondents from the balconies of their nearby hotel, and with anguish and tears by Israeli citizens.

Hours passed, with desultory rifle fire from ship and shore. It was evident that the comparatively small army force were unable to capture the vessel or even gain control of the beach. They needed reinforcements, and they also required some-thing more effective than small arms. A field gun was then brought up. Putting it into action was fraught with danger, because of the explosives aboard the *Alta-lena*. Nevertheless, at 4 p.m. the order was given to fire. The second round scored a direct hit on the ship, and it started to burn. The crew and the Irgun men on board abandoned the vessel, some on rafts, others by swimming, and tried to get beyond the range of danger as quickly as possible. The fire spread to the holds, the ammunition exploded, and the ship went up in flames. Twelve Irgun men and one soldier were killed and scores were wounded on both sides.

Again, the battle ended, but the fraternal hatred grew more intense. Menahem Begin broadcast an impassioned attack on premier Ben-Gurion that night over the Irgun's secret transmitter; and an Irgun broadsheet called Israel's Prime Minister a mad dictator, and his Cabinet a government of criminal tyrants, traitors, and murderers of their brothers.

Ben-Gurion gave his reply at a meeting of Israel's National Council (forerunner of the Knesset) which convened the night following the battle. In his speech, Ben-Gurion said that Israel was now locked in a life-and-death campaign against the Arab armies which had invaded Israel and were still on our soil. Jerusalem was surrounded by the troops and artillery of Jordan's Arab Legion. The road to the Negev was in the hands of the Egyptians. Some Jewish settlements in the north had been captured by the Syrian army. At this moment and in this situation, the presence among us of self-established, independent, armed Jewish bands repre-sented a grave danger to the defence capability of the Jews of Israel. The *Altalena* episode was the most bitter challenge the state had had to meet after the frightful bloody challenge launched against her by the Arab armies.

In the course of his speech, Ben-Gurion used a phrase which became engraved with particular anger in the memory of Irgun men: 'Blessed be the gun that blew up the *Altalena*.' This phrase – converted thereafter into the slogan 'the holy gun', although this term was never uttered by Ben-Gurion – became the symbol of the bitterness and hatred felt by Irgun members towards Ben-Gurion. The *Altalena* battle was brief; but only in 1967, twenty years later, was the breach healed between Ben-Gurion and Begin. The man responsible for this was the President of Egypt, Abdul Nasser, who was about to make war on Israel.

In mid-May 1967 Nasser started to move huge Egyptian forces into Sinai. He followed this up by expelling the United Nations forces stationed along the Israel–Egyptian armistice line and at Sharm e-Sheikh. He replaced them with Egyptian troops, and announced the closure of the straits at the entrance to the Gulf of Eilat, thereby blockading Israel shipping to its Negev port. The Egyptian president knew well that this measure could not possibly be borne by Israel, and that it was really the opening shot of the war.

Despite these aggressive Egyptian moves, the Israeli government did not rush to take military steps. The prime minister at the time was Levi Eshkol, and because of his hesitancy he lost the people's confidence in his capacity for leadership. The heads of the main parliamentary opposition parties, Begin who headed Gahal and Ben-Gurion who was the leader of Rafi, wanted Eshkol replaced. To the astonishment of the members of the Rafi party, Begin and his comrades called on Ben-Gurion at his home, and emerged with an even more astonishing proposal: that a national unity government be established, to be headed by Begin's sworn foe – David Ben-Gurion!

With Ben-Gurion's agreement, Begin went to see Eshkol and told him: 'Mr Prime Minister, I know what harsh things have occurred between you and Mr Ben-Gurion, blighting your relations. But I beg you to recall what happened between him and me! Nevertheless, I am now ready to forget the past so that we may all stand united in face of the enemy.'

Eshkol rejected the proposal, but Begin repeated it to his own party colleagues in parliament. 'We have suggested', he told them, 'that the most determined opponent of our party, Ben-Gurion, be made Prime Minister; but the Alignment of Labour Parties, which had formerly been led by Ben-Gurion, has turned it down. If Eshkol's government were to resign tonight. I would recommend to the President of the State that he call upon Ben-Gurion to form a new government.'

Begin's proposal failed. Eshkol did not resign and Ben-Gurion did not replace him. But the nation became united, and for the first time a government of national unity was established. Three new ministers were added to Eshkol's government, Menahem Begin and Yosef Sapir as Ministers Without Portfolio, and myself as Minister of Defence.

Four days later saw the start of the Six Day War. In the early hours of Monday, 5 June 1967, the Israeli air force attacked Egyptian air force bases, wiped out most of the enemy's warplanes, and thereby decided the course of the war.

WHILE THE *Altalena* incident fired the hatred between the political leaders in 1948, the comradeship among the fighting men grew closer and deeper, and no one bothered about which of the rival underground movements anyone came from, whether Irgun, Lehi or Haganah. The Arab enemy united all of us in the army. The war of life or death, of the survival or destruction of Israel, eliminated the divisions of the past.

When the two companies under Akiva Sa'ar and Uri Bar-On returned to the battalion base following the Kfar Vitkin engagement, Dov's company were called to a special meeting to hear from Brigade Commander Yitzhak Sadeh why they had not been sent to take part in the *Altalena* operation. Yitzhak was frank and straightforward in his talk to these former members of Irgun and Lehi. There was no prevarication. He told Blondie and his men that we had wished to avoid putting them in a fearful dilemma: if they had carried out orders and fought their former comrades, they would never have forgiven themselves; and if they refused to fulfil the commands, we would not forgive them. I do not know whether they agreed with all we said, but that ended the matter. Our real enemies were the Arabs, and the job of our commando battalion was to fight them.

In the course of the battles we came to know one another and there was a special quality to our friendship; but we almost never spoke of the past. Only once did the talk turn to Blondie's activities in the Lehi underground, and even that was neither at his nor my initiative. Our jeep column halted in Tel Aviv one day, and an elderly Jew wearing spectacles and a hat that well-nigh covered his ears came up to me, pointed at Dov, and said: 'That blond head was once worth a lot of money.' I had no idea what he meant, and my blank expression must have shown it, for he added the enlightening information that he had once been a teller in Barclays Bank. I was still at a loss, but when I tried to question him, all he said was: 'Ask the blond; he'll tell you,' and he turned and left.

When I asked Dov later what it was all about, he was not expansive. He simply said that he had held up and robbed Barclays Bank to finance the resistance activities of Lehi, and the British mandatory police had put a high price on his head.

Later in 1948, after the battalion's action in Kharatiya which broke through the Egyptian line and helped open the route to the Negev, I was appointed Commander of Jerusalem. This meant leaving my unit. The company commanders thereupon decided to call on Ben-Gurion and try to persuade him to keep me with the battalion. When they got to his house, Ben-Gurion's wife Paula refused them entry, and there was an argument. Ben-Gurion heard their voices and called out to Paula: 'If they are soldiers, let them in.'

Blond Dov was the chief spokesman. He explained to the Prime Minister and minister of defence the importance of my remaining with this unit. It was a very special formation, he told Ben-Gurion. It was the only commando battalion we had, and it was made up of the most heterogenous hard-to-handle personnel, ranging from former underground fighters of varied beliefs to private farmers, kibbutzniks, and overseas volunteers. He and the others pressed additional reasons upon the Prime Minister. Ben-Gurion heard them out, and then told them that

Action shot in Sinai during the Six Day War

Jerusalem took prioity over the battalion. He would not change his decision. But he was happy to hear that the men of the unit were loath to see me go.

I too left the battalion with regret. Some of the officers were posted with me to Jerusalem. Blond Dov remained with the battalion. We ran across each other from time to time – and then I was called to his funeral. He and his company had been summoned to the support of Shaul Yaffe's armoured battalion which was attacking the Egyptian strongpoints at Auja el-Hafir on the Negev-Sinai border during the fighting in December 1948. Dov's half-track advanced between the Egyptian posts and came under frontal and flank fire. Dov fell with a bullet in his head. His company suffered heavy casualties and was forced to retire. Auja was captured in a renewed attack, and Blond Dov was buried in the temporary military cemetery in the sands of Halutza, south of Beersheba.

Dov and I had fought in the same unit, the 89th Commando Battalion. I had come to it from the ranks of Haganah and he from Lehi. Neither of us denied his past, his convictions, his chosen path, nor his old comrades. But this did not create a barrier between us. To me, Dov was not only one of the most courageous and dedicated fighters of Israel but also a symbol of our nation that was becoming united, determined that not forever would the divisive sword prevail. As the elders had said to David, founder of the kingdom of Israel: 'Behold, we are thy bone and thy flesh.'

20
A united nation

WITH THE REUNION of Judah and northern Israel under the crown of David, the kingdom reached its greatest hour. Internally, the divided nation was now united, consolidated, stable. Externally, the frontiers were widened to give the Israeli kingdom control of the territory from Damascus in the north-east to Eilat in the south, and from the Great Sea – the Mediterranean – to the Desert of Assyria.

David's first action after being anointed king 'over all Israel' was the capture of Jerusalem. It had been in the hands of the Jebusites, cutting off the hill country of Ephraim, to the immediate north, from Judah, to the immediate south. David took the city and fortified it. The land of Israel was now an almost continuous stretch of territory from the settlement region of the tribe of Dan at its northern extremity right down to the southern tribal areas of Judah and Simeon. (A few hostile pockets, however, still remained.) The conquest of Jerusalem also strengthened the link between both banks of the Jordan, for it commanded the main highway, through Jericho, which joined the tribal settlements in Gilead, east of the river, with those on the west bank.

Jerusalem, 'the stronghold of Zion', was given an additional name, 'the city of David'. It was not part of the possession of any of the tribes. It was the royal city of the entire nation of Israel, the city to which the Ark of the Covenant was brought, the city where the king himself lived, and with him the army commanders and the central administration. 'So David dwelt in the fort, and called it the city of David. And David built round about him from Millo and inward. And David went on, and grew great, and the Lord God of hosts was with him.' (2 *Sam.* 5:9, 10.)

The first battles fought by David after establishing himself in Jerusalem were against the determined enemies of Israel, the Philistines. It was they who occupied the hostile pockets, and they now launched two attacks against Jerusalem. They were routed in both. The commanding location of the fortress city on a mountain ridge made it easier for David to thrust back the Philistines who had had to make the climb from the foothills. Furthermore, with the momentum of their success, David's forces advanced northwards and wiped out the Philistine enclaves in the Valleys of Jezreel and Beth-shan and in the Sharon plain. However, David was unable to wrest from the Philistines their main settlement region, the small area in the southern coastal plain running from slightly north of Ashdod southwards to the edge of the desert, just south of Rafah. The Philistines remained the only strangers dwelling within the borders of the Israel kingdom.

After establishing control over the interior of the country, David dealt with his external foes, the surrounding hostile neighbours. He started with Moab, conquered it, and 'the Moabites became David's servants, and brought gifts.' (2 *Sam.* 8:2.) From Moab David turned north to engage the Syrians, and slew 'two and twenty thousand men. Then David put garrisons in Syria of Damascus: and the Syrians became servants to David, and brought gifts. And the Lord preserved David whithersoever he went.' Where he went to next was south, battling the Edomites. He subdued Edom, and there too he 'put garrisons' and exacted tribute.

David's final campaign was against Ammon, east of the Jordan, which had been a constant danger to Israel. Its capital, Rabat Ammon (today's Amman), controlled the 'King's Highway', and the Ammonites were continually harassing the bordering tribal territories of Gad, Reuben and Manasseh. David's war with Ammon lasted two years. The Israeli army under its commander Joab, and his brother Abishai, defeated the forces of the Ammonites and her allies in the first year, but they did not manage to capture the capital. This was accomplished only 'after the year was expired, at the time when kings go forth to battle'. Joab first seized the water sources of the city, and then David, heading a large force, 'went to Rabbah, and fought against it, and took it', gaining mastery over the Ammonites.

David thus ended his military campaigns with his kingdom comprising all the original territories of the tribes of Israel, and also wielding control over the neighbouring lands to the immediate north, east and south which had become his tributaries.

The kingdom of Israel consolidated itself on the highlands: east of the Jordan, it was on the mountains of Gilead; west of the river it was on the Hebron hills, Jerusalem, Shechem and Galilee. The large nations to Israel's north, east and south built their armies round the core of the iron chariot, which was drawn by horses and carried a team of three: a bowman, shield-bearer, and the charioteer. The Israelites of David's time had little use for chariots. Their battles were in the mountains, with their narrow tracks, deep valleys and steep slopes, and they were conducted on foot. The mountains, too, and the fortified cities built on their summit, were David's strongholds. Deserts and seas were the outer circle of defence of his kingdom. Its western border was the coast of the Mediterranean. The rest of its frontier line was a wide arc of desert sweeping round from Sinai in the south-west, which separated Israel from Egypt, through Edom, Moab and Ammon, right up to Syria in the north.

IN OUR OWN DAY, the settlement divisions between Israel and her neighbours are the reverse of what they were in the past. It is the Arabs who now inhabit the highlands, occupying the mountains that rise on both sides of the river Jordan, Gilead on the east bank and the chain on the west bank running from Hebron

The city walls of Jerusalem.

left The Adam bridge, one of the two 'open bridges' on the river Jordan, which link Israel and the West Bank with Jordan and the Arab world

right Allenby bridge, the other open link across the river Jordan. Goods are taken half-way across from one side, to be collected from the other.

through Jerusalem to Shechem. It is the Jews whose most populous settlements are in the coastal region. The biblical 'King's Highway', which at one time served the Israeli kingdom, is today the main arterial route of the kingdom of Jordan, linking Damascus with Amman and continuing southwards to Akaba and Saudi Arabia. The other principal north–south highway of biblical time, the 'Way of the Sea', which once served the great empires, is today's coastal road which passes through the cities of Israel, from Nahariah in the north, through Acre, Haifa, Tel Aviv, Ashdod, Ashkelon and down to Yamit in the south. Just as the Sea Peoples of ancient times who came to Canaan via the Mediterranean settled on the coastal plain and the foothills, so the 'returnees to Zion' of modern times, the Jews who came from Europe, established their first settlements near the sea.

The fords of the Jordan link the people dwelling on both banks, as they did in olden times; but today they may be used only by the Arabs. We call them the 'open bridges', for they are the sole openings in the otherwise sealed borders between Israel and the kingdom of Jordan who, at this time of writing, are not yet at peace with each other. Despite this, there is a free flow across the river in both directions of Arabs from both countries. The Arabs of Shechem cross by the Adam bridge, site of the biblical city of Adam. The Arabs of Hebron and Jerusalem use the Allenby bridge, which carries the road from Jericho to Jordan's capital, Amman. There are many Arab clans who have some members living on the West and others on the East Bank, like the Israelite tribe of Manasseh in biblical times.

All the West Bank Palestinians, like their brothers on the East Bank, are citizens of the kingdom of Jordan. Their representatives from Nablus (Shechem), Hebron, Bethlehem and Jenin sit in Jordan's parliament. Their king is Hussein, and their capital is Amman. This situation is similar in pattern to that of the Jews in the reign of David, when the inhabitants of East Bank Jabesh Gilead, who belonged

to the tribes of Reuben and Gad, were Israelis just like their brothers who dwelt west of the Jordan: David was their king and Jerusalem was their capital.

SINCE THE ESTABLISHMENT of the state of Israel in 1948, Jews have not been allowed to cross the River Jordan eastwards. I have therefore had to acquire from Arab dealers in Jerusalem and Nablus those antiquities in my possession which originated from the East Bank. Among them are basalt figurines and reliefs which come from Irbid and El Hamma in northern Jordan. I also have some crude pottery vessels about six thousand years old, discovered in Chalcolithic tombs at Bab el-Dera, east of the Dead Sea. More recent, dating back to about the tenth century BC, the time of David, are my delicately wrought pitchers and bowls which were found in the mountains of Moab in southern Jordan.

The finest piece of antique sculpture in my Zahala home also comes from Jordan, from the vicinity of Amman. It is an ornate limestone bust of a crowned king, with plaited hair, a curled beard, and pendant earrings. Its special feature is the crown. It is known as a 'wrapped crown', similar to the one worn by Egyptian kings at the time, with an ostrich feather attached to each side. In addition, unlike the Egyptian diadem, this one has flowered reliefs carved in the front part of the rim that rests on the forehead. The flowers in the original crown were no doubt fashioned from precious stones.

When I bought this bust, I realized that I had acquired a rare antiquity. But only later did I learn that it could well symbolize the figure of King David wearing the crown of the king of Ammon!

I was reading through the second volume of *Views of the Biblical World* one evening when, turning a page, I was met by the stare of an ancient king, the very image of the sculpture in my possession. The caption was the biblical quotation from the *Second Book of Samuel* which follows the account of David's victory

Interior of an antiquities shop in Jerusalem, which Dayan often visits.

over the Ammonites. After capturing their capital, Rabat Ammon, David 'brought forth the spoil of the city', and as a mark that Ammon would henceforth be subservient to him, 'he took their king's crown from off his head, the weight whereof was a talent of gold with the precious stones: and it was set on David's head'. (2 *Sam.* 12:30.) The explanatory note to this caption recorded that this sculpture was discovered at archaeological excavations near Amman, bears the likeness of a Semitic personage, and dates back to the opening period of Israelite kingship!

I bought what I now call 'David's crown' from a Jerusalem antiquities dealer named Baidun. How or where he got it I never asked. I follow the principle of my teacher, Professor Givon, who said that whenever one acquires antiquities, one should beware of buying at the same time the tales which the dealers attach to their merchandise. There are four antique stores in the Old City of Jerusalem which I visit regularly, the ones belonging to Abu-Anton, an Assyrian Christian from Bethlehem; Abu-Salah, an Armenian; Abu-Dis; and Baidun.

Trading in antiquities is a singular vocation. An antiquities shop, too, is a world unto its own. The store itself is open to all, but behind and above it are dark attics, hidden recesses and sealed boxes which are revealed only to special visitors. In the dim light, dust-laden pottery vessels acquire a mystical aura. Only when I get home and wash them, scour them, scrape off the accumulations of age-old grime, and remove the modern additions – the repairs, 'improvements' and fakeries – do I reach the truth in all its starkness. Sometimes the only thing to

left The King's Head.

215

do is throw the 'antiquity' into the waste bin. One discovers that the head of a figurine does not belong to the body, and the breasts and nose are made of plaster and glue. I remember acquiring a Hebronite ritual censer, the upper part of which turned out to be a piece of a bowl from ancient Shechem: its base had been sliced off with a steel saw and fitted to the neck of the censer.

Sometimes, however, there are pleasant surprises. I once bought a long, narrow jug for a few cents. After removing the coatings of stone and dust, I found that the vessel had decorative black stripes and small ornamental embossments, typical of Egyptian pottery made more than four thousand years ago. It had been discovered in the Gaza Strip.

Even when I find nothing of interest in the antique stores, I like to wander through the alleys of Jerusalem's Old City bazaar. The stone arches, the worn paving, the darkening shadows, the heady scent of mixed spices, all combine to set the imagination recapturing the patterns and experiences of distant worlds, distant in time yet close to one's heart. The bazaar people around me are Arabs, not Jews, yet this does not in the least disturb me. The young man selling *kak* (ringed cakes sprinkled with sesame seeds), the porter with his donkey laden with sacks of flour, the peasant woman with her elaborately embroidered dress, and even the Arabic tongue heard on all sides, do not give me any feeling of strangeness. On the contrary, not only in their dress but also in their gait and manner of speech, these Arabs – particularly the rural and Bedouin Arabs – seem nearer to the ancient Semitic world than we modern Jews, brought up and educated in the Western culture.

I never pass an Arab ploughman or reaper without greeting him with '*Saha badnu*' ('Health to your body') and hearing his reply, '*Badnu salmo*' ('Peace to your body'). The words are not the same, nor is the language, but the form of expression is similar to the exchange between Boaz and the reapers in his Bethlehem fields. 'The Lord be with you,' said Boaz; 'And they answered him, "The Lord bless thee."' (*Ruth* 2 : 4.) In Jerusalem's Old City, too, when I walk through the lanes and see Arabs sitting at the entrance to their shops drinking coffee, our glances meet. Neither turns his eyes away. We nod to each other. I greet them with the blessing of peace, and they invite me to join them in a coffee. There is no difference between the Arabic *Sala'am alekum* and the Hebrew *Shalom alei-chem* (peace unto you); nor between the Arabic *allah ma'ak* and the Hebrew *Elohim imcha* (the Lord be with you); but the Arabs were not exiled from their land and not cut off from their language, whereas we Jews wandered far and wide, and our style of speech underwent many mutations until we returned to our origins.

The bust of the crowned king of Ammon, the contemporary of King David, rests on a black wooden stand on one of my bookshelves above the volumes of the Bible, the works of Ben-Gurion, and books on the history, geography and archaeology of the land of Israel. That is the appropriate place for this ancient king, for nothing in these books is strange to him – not even in those written three thousand years after his time.

DAVID PASSED ON to his son Solomon a stable kingdom, with an organized central administration, secure borders, commercial ties and diplomatic alliances with its northern neighbours: Hiram, King of Tyre; Toi, King of Hamath; and Talmai, King of Geshur.

With his approaching death, David called Solomon to his bedside and bade him follow this valedictory injunction 'Be thou strong . . . and shew thyself a man; And keep the charge of the Lord thy God, to walk in his ways, to keep his statutes, and his commandments . . . as it is written in the law of Moses,' (1 *Kings* 2 : 2, 3.) When that was over, he mentioned the names of three persons and told his son how they were to be dealt with: one was to be favoured, two were to be killed.

Two of the three were associated with the circumstances of Absalom's revolt. Barzillai had given hospitality to David when he had escaped to Gilead from his son Absalom, and David now charged Solomon to 'shew kindness unto the sons of Barzillai the Gileadite, and let them be of those that eat at thy table: for so they came to me when I fled because of Absalom thy brother'. Shimei, the son of Gera, on the other hand, had joined the rebels and had incited the people against David. David now told Solomon: 'And behold, thou hast with thee Shimei . . . which cursed me with a grievous curse. . . . Now therefore hold him not guiltless: for thou art a wise man, and knowest what thou oughtest to do unto him; but his hoar head bring thou down to the grave with blood.'

However, the main target of David's bitterness whose 'hoar head' Solomon was not to allow to go bloodless was the third man, no less a figure than David's own army commander and nephew, Joab the son of Zeruiah. Joab had fought valiantly for David and had saved his kingdom; yet David harboured a relentless hatred for him – particularly after he had killed the King's beloved though wayward son, Absalom – and even tried to remove him from his post. The 'sons of Zeruiah', Joab and his brothers Asahel and Abishai, were a trial to David. He considered them hard and bloodthirsty men, who preferred the swath of the sword to the path of peace. David had not struck at Joab during his kingship because Joab had the power to sway the tribe of Judah to follow him and abandon the king.

As David grew older, so did his rancour against Joab increase, and when 'the days of David drew nigh that he should die', he bequeathed his prejudice to his son Solomon. 'Moreover thou knowest also what Joab the son of Zeruiah did to me, and what he did to the two captains of the hosts of Israel, unto Abner the son of Ner, and unto Amasa the son of Jether, whom he slew, and shed the blood of war in peace, and put the blood of war upon his girdle that was about his loins, and in his shoes that were on his feet. Do therefore according to thy wisdom, and let not his hoar head go down to the grave in peace.' (1 *Kings* 2 : 5, 6.)

THE ONE NATIONAL LEADER I knew who resembled King David in the strength of his personality was David Ben-Gurion. Towards the end of his life he was sunk in himself, forgetting or forgiving most of his political adversaries who had plagued his later years – when he had left office and broken with his party – and caused him bitter anguish. There was one man, however, whom he neither forgave nor forgot. He was Levi Eshkol, his long-time colleague, who succeeded him as Prime Minister of Israel, and whom Ben-Gurion came to regard as his principal opponent.

When Eshkol died suddenly of a heart attack in 1959, I went to Ben-Gurion to try and persuade him to attend the funeral, or at the very least to visit his bier in the Knesset plaza. He refused. To the many arguments I urged upon him, he gave a short reply: if he did either, it would be hypocrisy. He was sorry to hear of Eshkol's death, but to go to his funeral meant paying respect, albeit last respects, to the deceased, and this he would not do. 'Respect for Eshkol? No.' What he thought about Eshkol never got past his tightly-pursed lips, but his eyes told all. They glowered with the searing pain of an open wound that would never be healed.

SOLOMON RODE ON A MULE to the ceremony at Jerusalem's Gihon spring where he was anointed king. It was his father's mule, the mule of King David, and it was ridden by Solomon at David's express instruction: 'Cause Solomon my son to ride upon mine own mule, and bring him down to Gihon.' (1 *Kings* 1 :33.) This was said to 'Zadok the priest and Nathan the prophet' who were to perform the royal anointing.

David's eldest surviving son, the handsome Adonijah, 'exalted himself, saying,

"I will be king"', though he failed to receive the blessing of his father. He 'prepared him chariots and horsemen' and rode through the streets of Jerusalem on a horse-drawn chariot with 'fifty men to run before him'.

King David had ridden on a mule.

THE HORSE is a noble animal. He holds his head high, his thick mane flutters proudly, he neighs with authority. Mules are graced by none of these qualities. There is nothing majestic about their appearance. But there is none like them for riding in the mountains. Their legs are muscular and wonderfully fashioned, and tipped with hooves that are small but hard as steel. They negotiate steep slopes without faltering, and even when they step on smooth boulders they rarely stumble.

I remember my father's buying a young mule when I was a boy. An Arab dealer with a string of animals had gone from village to village selling them, having started in Damascus. By the time he reached Nahalal he had eight left, and we bought a one-year-old.

We called our mule Eliphalet. He was a sweet animal, with black hide, and hair as smooth as a petal. He was sensitive and scared at first. At the slightest touch he would tremble and his ears would shoot up. The moment of crisis came when Eliphalet was grown and I decided to break him in. I took him out to the fields, leading him with a rope. He had never had a bit in his mouth, and he had no bridle now. I simply bound the rope round his nose, as I had learned from our Arab neighbours. Nor did I put a saddle on his back: neither Eliphalet nor I cared for one. For us, riding was bare-back.

When I mounted him, he was stunned, but only for a moment. He then took appropriate steps to get rid of me. He lowered his head to the ground and broke into a gallop, kicking powerfully with his hind legs from time to time. I was an experienced rider, but it was not long before Eliphalet had gained his objective. We returned home separately, Eliphalet first and I later – much later.

Scratched and bruised after countless falls, I tried again and again to cling to his back, and eventually he got used to me. Thereafter we were inseparable (in both senses) at weekends when I would go riding with my friends, I on Eliphalet, they on horseback. On level ground, they always got the better of me. But as soon as we reached the mountains, none of the horses could match Eliphalet. Light- and sure-footed, he found his way between the terebinth bushes, his hooves keeping to paths that I could not even see were there. This hybrid creature, the mule, had always been the animal of the mountain ridges and passes. The great deserts between Arabia and Egypt were crossed by camel caravans. The coastal plain was the territory of the horse-drawn iron chariot. In our hill country, in Gilead and Galilee, Shechem and Hebron, the kings David and Solomon rode on mules.

DAVID REIGNED forty years, seven in Hebron over Judah, and thirty-three as king in Jerusalem over all Israel. In the first ten years of his Jerusalem rule, he

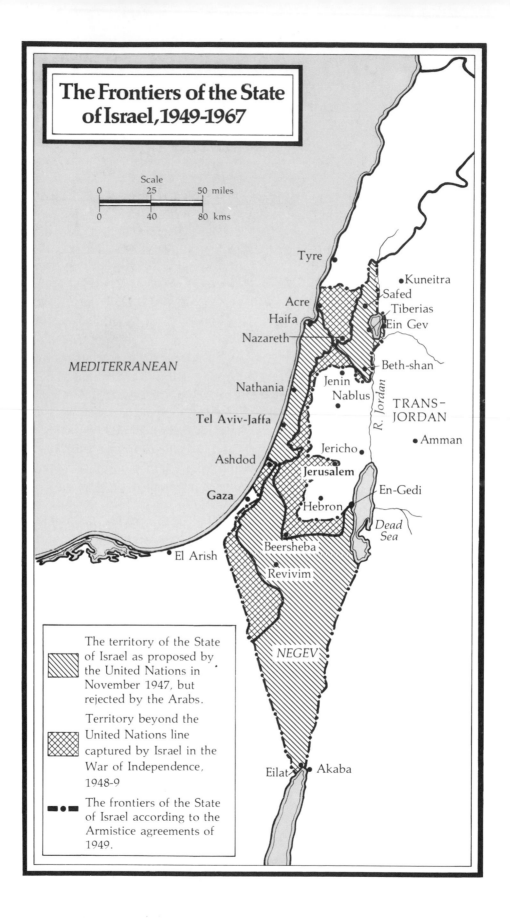

The Frontiers of the State of Israel, 1949-1967

Scale

| 0 | 25 | 50 miles |

| 0 | 40 | 80 kms |

Tyre

•Kuneitra

Acre
Safed
Tiberias

Haifa
Ein Gev

Nazareth

MEDITERRANEAN
Beth-shan

Jenin
Nathania
Nablus

R. Jordan
TRANS-
JORDAN

Tel Aviv-Jaffa

•Amman

Jericho

Ashdod

Jerusalem
En-Gedi

Gaza
Hebron

Dead
Sea

Beersheba

Revivim
El Arish

NEGEV

Eilat• •Akaba

The territory of the State
of Israel as proposed by
the United Nations in
November 1947, but
rejected by the Arabs.

Territory beyond the
United Nations line
captured by Israel in the
War of Independence,
1948-9

The frontiers of the State
of Israel according to the
Armistice agreements of
1949.

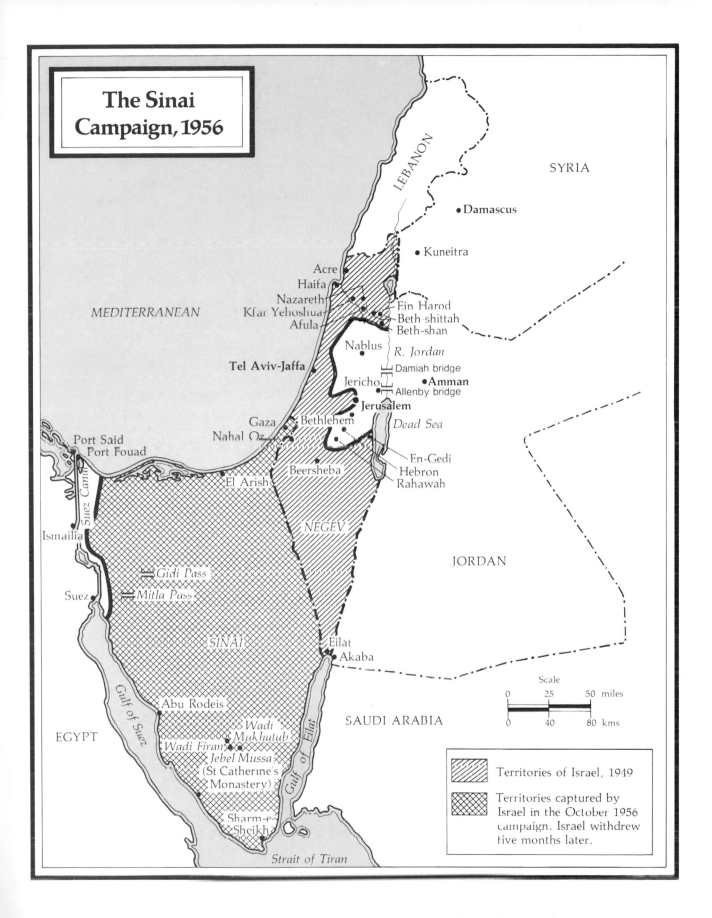

The Sinai Campaign, 1956

SYRIA

•**Damascus**

•Kuneitra

MEDITERRANEAN

Acre
Haifa
Nazareth
Kfar Yehoshua
Afula

•Ein Harod
•Beth-shittah
•Beth-shan

Nablus

R. Jordan

Tel Aviv-Jaffa

Damiah bridge

Jericho
•**Amman**
Allenby bridge

Jerusalem

Gaza
Bethlehem
Nahal Oz

Dead Sea

•En-Gedi
Hebron
Rahawah

Beersheba

El Arish

NEGEV

Port Said
Port Fouad

JORDAN

Ismailia

Suez Canal

Gidi Pass

Mitla Pass

Suez

SINAI

Eilat
Akaba

Scale

0   25   50 miles

0   40   80 kms

Abu Rodeis

SAUDI ARABIA

Wadi
Mukhutub
Wadi Firan
Jebel Mussa
(St Catherine's
Monastery)

EGYPT

Gulf of Suez

Gulf of Eilat

Sharm-e-
Sheikh

Strait of Tiran

Territories of Israel, 1949

Territories captured by
Israel in the October 1956
campaign. Israel withdrew
five months later.

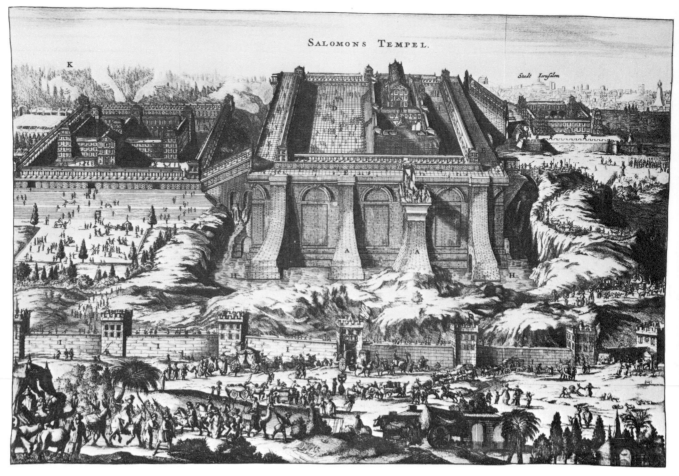

above The Temple of Solomon.
Engraving of a 17th-century
anachronistic model fashioned
by a rabbi of Hamburg.

left The interior of the Temple,
from an 18th-century engraving.

222

Israel Army vehicles and a
patrol boat at Sharm-e-Sheikh,
at the southern tip of Sinai,
after its capture in 1956.

campaigned and conquered and organized the defences of his kingdom. His external foes gave him no trouble after that. The attacks on the tribes of Israel, that were the pattern of the period of the Judges and the reign of Saul, came to an end. None of Israel's neighbours dared to harm the kingdom of David.

Internally, however, within the royal court itself, there was a good deal of strife. Amnon, David's eldest son, seduced his half-sister Tamar and was killed by his brother Absalom. Absalom fled to his maternal grandfather, the king of Geshur, returned after three years, mounted a rebellion against his father David, and was killed by Joab, David's army commander. Sheba, the son of Bichri, also tried to stir up a revolt against David, and failed. He was pursued by Joab, sought refuge with the people of Abel-beth-maachah, was killed by them and his head handed to Joab. The country was also afflicted by natural disaster, by drought and plague. But despite all these trials of man and nature, the political and military greatness of the kingdom of Israel under David was unimpaired, and the borders of the state remained firm and secure.

IN OUR OWN DAY, as in the opening period of David's rule, borders and security have been the central and primary concern of the state of Israel. The first frontier lines were the result of our 1948–9 War of Independence. After the fighting, Israel signed armistice agreements with her neighbours. These agreements fixed the

223

boundaries of Israel along the lines held by the rival Israel and Arab armies at the cease-fire. Thus, the Old City of Jerusalem and the Hebron hills, which had fallen to the Arab forces during the war, remained under Arab control.

The next outbreak was the 1956 Sinai Campaign, which started when Egypt closed the Straits of Tiran and blockaded Israeli shipping through the Gulf of Eilat. It was fought only between Israel and Egypt. Though Israel captured Sharm e-Sheikh which commanded the Straits, Israel's borders remained unchanged. Under pressure from the United States and the Soviet Union, Israel handed the territory controlling the Straits to the United Nations Emergency Forces who were to ensure the passage of Israeli ships without let or hindrance.

Eleven years after the Sinai Campaign came the 1967 Six Day War, initiated by Egypt, who was joined by Syria and Jordan. The cause of this war, too, was

above An Israeli outpost on the river Jordan.

above right One of the Egyptian coastal guns covering the Straits of Tiran which blockaded Israeli shipping in the Gulf of Eilat and were put out of action in the 1956 Sinai Campaign.

Egypt's blockade of Eilat, but this time the results were very different and far-reaching. Israel conquered the whole of the Sinai Peninsula, the West Bank, the Old City of Jerusalem, and the Golan Heights. No armistice agreements were signed at the end of this war, and the frontiers of control between the parties were the cease-fire lines, congruent with the positions of the rival armies at war's end. No negotiations to reach a peace agreement and determine the permanent borders followed the Six Day War, just as there had been none after the Sinai Campaign. The Arabs demanded that Israel withdraw to her previous frontiers. Israel refused to do so without peace treaties.

The next war was launched seven years later, the 1973 Yom Kippur War, when Israel was attacked simultaneously by Egypt and Syria. Jordan did not attack (though her units fought in Golan under Syrian army command), and so there was no change in the Israel–Jordan border. But nor were there significant changes in our frontiers with Egypt and Syria. 'Separation of Forces' agreements were signed after the war whereby Israel retired twenty kilometres from the Suez Canal; but except for this strip she continued to control the whole of Sinai. There were similarly only slight changes in the Israel–Syria border. Thus, for more than ten years now, Israel has the most extensive borders she has ever held in her history.

There is little doubt that these will not be Israel's permanent borders; but it may be that the frontiers will now be delineated within the framework of peace treaties between Israel and her neighbours. Perhaps the Arabs will agree to recognize and reconcile themselves to the existence of Israel in return for an Israeli withdrawal from part of the territories she now holds.

If indeed permanent borders for Israel are to be determined, she will be

confronted with the same problem that faced the kingdom of Israel in David's time: if the frontiers enclose only the territory of Jewish settlement, they will not give her the security she needs. The borders which resulted from the War of Independence gave Israel a narrow waist measuring only ten miles – and this at the most densely populated region of the country, between Tel Aviv and Hadera! Moreover, Israel would have no early-warning observation points against approaching enemy aircraft if she were unable to mount appropriate military installations on the Jerusalem–Nablus hills.

David's kingdom solved this problem by subduing the surrounding hostile neighbours: Edom, Moab, Ammon and Assyria. These lands served as a security belt that encircled the territories of the tribes of Israel. In our time, too, since the Six Day War, Israel has maintained an advanced security belt far from her population centres. The people within this belt are not vassals; the lands are 'occupied territories'. The Yom Kippur War proved the importance of these tracts to the security of Israel. Though the Arab armies succeeded in launching a surprise attack on Israel, no Israel settlement within the country was harmed. The battles took place within the outer security circle – against Egyptian forces in western Sinai and against the Syrian army in the Golan Heights.

The future borders of Israel have been my closest concern since the establishment of the state. What will be the Israel of our own times? From where to where? What portions of our historic land will it contain, and which will be excluded? I had the privilege of playing an active role in the determination of some of the answers.

I took part in the negotiations with King Abdullah of Jordan and his representatives after the War of Independence in 1949. I even signed, in the name of Israel, the map of our armistice agreement with the Hashemite kingdom. After the 1956 Sinai Campaign, when I was Chief of the General Staff, I had a hand in the arrangements that involved us and the Egyptians. In both the wars that followed, the Six Day and the Yom Kippur Wars, I served as Minister of Defence, and was a member of the team that decided in the name of the Israel government on the cease-fire and separation of forces agreements with our neighbours in the east, south and north – Jordan, Egypt, and Syria.

During the planning stage to devise proposals for our borders with the Arab states, I would spend days with our army commanders reconnoitring the fronts, our minds intent on military and political considerations – separation of Arab and Jewish zones, lines of fortifications, observation posts, passable tracks through the desert. But with dusk, in the helicopter on my way home, all these considerations vanished. Beneath me as we flew was a land without division between Arab and Jew; a land strewn with villages and cities, fields and gardens; a land bounded in the east by the River Jordan and in the west by the Great Sea, crowned in the north by the snowy peak of Mount Hermon, sealed in the south by the parched wilderness. One land. The Land of Israel.

The Valley of Jezreel.

Acknowledgments

The majority of the photographs in this book were taken by Gemma Levine. The others were provided and are reproduced by kind permission of the following (numbers refer to page numbers):

Bibliothèque Nationale, Paris 159
Bildarchiv foto Marburg 70
British Museum 76
Camera Press 222–3
Sonia Halliday 54, 174, 200 (top and bottom)
David Harris 56, 62 and 63 (Pappenheim Collection, Jerusalem), 183 (Schocken
   Library)
Keren Hayesod 107
Israeli Embassy, London 41
Israel Museum, Jerusalem 42, 43, 111, 133
Jewish Agency 106
Museo del Prado, Madrid 34
Musées Nationaux (Louvre) (Photo: Snark) 176
NGTV Ltd 184–5
Pierpont Morgan Library, New York 193
Roger-Viollet 64
Ronald Sheridan 207
UPI 78
Weidenfeld and Nicolson archives 123, 140, 143, 222 (top) (Ronald Sheridan)

Extracts from the Authorized Version of the Bible, which is Crown Copyright, are used with permission.

Index

Index